7/02

Avoiding the Scanning Blues

A Desktop Scanning Primer

ISBN 0-13-087322-5

9 780130 873224

90000

Prentice Hall PTR
Upper Saddle River, NJ   07458
www.phptr.com

DEDICATION

To my brother Sid Jr., who has for years given so much love, kindness and support to our family. Our lives and family have been so much richer and better for his love. He deserves the best life has to offer!

Library of Congress Cataloging-in-Publication Data

Tally, Taz.
    Avoiding the scanning blues a complete guide to desktop scanning / Taz Tally.
        p. cm. -- (Avoiding the blues series)
    ISBN 0-13-087322-5
    1. Pictures--Printing--Data processing. 2. Color printing--Data processing. 3. Optical scanners. 4. Desktop publishing. I.
Title: Scanning blues. II. Title. III. Series.

Z257 .T35 2000
686.2`3042--dc21

00-032395

Production Supervisor: Wil Mara
Acquisitions Editor: Tim Moore
Editorial Assistant: Julie Okulicz
Marketing Manager: Bryan Gambrel
Manufacturing Manager: Alexis Heydt
Buyer: Maura Zaldivar
Cover Designer: Anthony Gemmellaro
Color Photography: Gary Adcock
Grayscale Photography: Leslie O'Shaunessy
Artwork: Terry Wessling
Proofreader: Anne Trowbridge
Assistant Proofreader: Jazmine Saige
Content: Taz Tally
Composition: Taz Tally
Composition Assistant: Jazmine Saige

© 2001 Prentice Hall PTR
Prentice-Hall, Inc.
Upper Saddle River, NJ 07458

The publisher offers discounts on this book when ordered in bulk quantities. For more information contact: Corporate Sales
Department, Prentice Hall PTR, One Lake Street, Upper Saddle River, NJ 07458. Phone: 800-382-3419; FAX: 201-236-7141; E-
mail: corpsales@prenhall.com

Printed in the United States of America

10 9 8 7 6 5 4 3 2 1

ISBN 0-13-087322-5

Prentice-Hall International (UK) Limited, *London*
Prentice-Hall of Australia Pty. Limited, *Sydney*
Prentice-Hall Canada Inc., *Toronto*
Prentice-Hall Hispanoamericana, S.A., *Mexico*
Prentice-Hall of India Private Limited, *New Delhi*
Prentice-Hall of Japan, Inc., *Tokyo*
Prentice-Hall Asia Pte. Ltd
Pearson Education Asia Pte. Ltd.,
Editora Prentice-Hall do Brasil, Ltda., *Rio de Janeiro*

Table of Contents

Part I   1

Part II   87

Part III

Index 293

Author bio 299

Color plates 301

Practice images 305

Images to scan Inside back cover

Acknowledgments

APPRECIATIONS

Although it is my name that goes on this book, there are so many people who have contributed to the creation of this scanning book. I want to first thank my editor at Prentice Hall, Tim (the comma man) Moore, for his uncommon support and confidence that he shows in me. Tim's willingness to bend the rules and try new new and different things is a godsend. I never hear him cower behind the "well that's the way we do it here" but rather, I usually hear "good idea, let's see how we can make that happen" or just as often, offering an even better idea. Tim is also a closer; he knows how to get a job done. Without Tim this project would have remained a dream.

I want to also thank Wil Mara, production editor, for his attention to the schedule and helping us get the book done on time. The production staff at Prentice Hall who helped with design and creation of this book should give themselves a pat on the back, as they are so rarely recognized.

I would also like to thank Marie Wesson, the marketing manager at UMAX corporation, whose support of our Taz Tally Seminars and other scanning training venues have provided me with invaluable encouragement and opportunity.

Howie (Zowie) Fenton of GATF deserves a special commendation for all the wonderful, detailed and insightful editing and suggestions, as well as his thoughtful foreword. This book has been greatly improved by his wide-ranging attentions.

Frank Romano should not go unnoticed as he has provided us with valuable reviews. I thank him for his time and attention.

I would like to thank Leslie O'Shaunessy for her grayscale photography, Gary Adcock for his color photography and Terry Wessling for his wonderful line art drawings.

I guess I should thank my rotten brother for being so photogenic and providing us with such a good-looking subject. :-)

There is another person without whom this book would never, ever have been finished. My wonderful Jaz. My partner in work and life. The Jaz, who takes care of so many things, big and little, and makes my life complete. Her copy changes alone have earned her my undying gratitude. To you my love…a huge basket of hugs and kisses! ;-)

Thank you!

The Taz!

Overview

The title of this book, *Avoiding the Scanning Blues,* tells the tale of what this book is about: preventing as many problems as possible when it comes to creating, viewing, and printing images that are created and edited with desktop publishing equipment and software. The keys to good quality images involve using the proper tools and techniques both prior to, during and after an image is scanned.

One of the fundamental tools explored and developed in this book is a technique I call "visualization scanning." This involves previsualizing how a scanner will recreate an image. To effectively use this technique, you must be thoroughly familiar with the images a scanner can create and the building blocks of those scanned images. If you know where you want to take an image, and the steps it takes to get there, you will be able to make the best decision when setting up a scanner for image capture, or deciding how you want to alter an image after it is scanned.

Fundamentals through the details

In this book you will first get a solid grounding in the fundamentals of scanners, scanned images and the techniques of scanning. You will learn about the building blocks of scanned images and the challenges that face us when we want to scan an image. These fundamentals will give you the necessary information to help you understand *why* you perform a technique rather than just teaching you a technique. This critical background information will not only provide you with confidence when you scan, but will also help you troubleshoot problems later on.

After covering all the necessary background information, you will learn all the critical tools and skills to accomplish professional-level scans of your images. You will learn to calibrate your scanner, evaluate and set highlight and shadow points, and properly control image brightness and contrast. You will also learn advanced techniques for applying unsharpmask and avoiding color casts. You will learn how to scan poor quality images and images that have been previously scanned. You will learn to scan all types of media including reflective, positive transparencies and negative transparencies.

This book even covers techniques to use in the post-scan environment in image editing applications such as Adobe Photoshop. Here you will learn how to protect your images during image editing and even improve upon images that were poorly scanned with techniques such as post-scan color correction.

Real-world images for real-world scanning!

Included with this outstanding step-by-step scanning book are real images to be scanned. These sample images include line art, a variety of detail images, images to be corrected, contone photographs, and screened images. So, rather than just learning general principles, you have the opportunity to work with the same real-world images used as examples in this book.

Real-world practice images included in this book

- Actual practice images for scanning
- Black-and-white and colored line art images
- Simple and complex images
- Low-quality images to be corrected
- Grayscale contone photograph
- Color contone photograph
- Screened images
- Practice with the same real-world images used in this book

The truth about desktop scanning

It has been often asserted that good quality images cannot be produced with a desktop scanner. While this was once true, it is no longer. Today's desktop scanning equipment and software rivals the best made. It only falls to us, the operators, to learn how to use these tools to their best advantage. This book is designed to do just that! Enjoy!

Taz Tally

2000

Foreword

Despite significant threats in the past from TV and radio and the future threat from the Internet, print remains the dominant form of communication today. Those who work with print are considered graphic arts professionals, and include artists, designers, typesetters, color separators, prepress professionals, and press people.

Any way you look at it, the graphic arts / printing industry is huge. With about 50,000 plants, the printing industry has more manufacturing sites than any other industry. When you add the related graphic arts sites, the number swells to nearly 75,000.

The printing and graphic arts community employs more people than almost any other single profession. With 1.8 million people employed, the graphic arts industry is the third largest employer. Thirty-six billion dollars is paid annually in wages, and $6 billion in benefits and payroll taxes. In terms of dollar value shipments, the printing industry is in the top 10 with $129 billion.

For Professionals

You may be wondering how this information is relevant to a book about scanning. The answer is two-fold. First, this book is important to the large community of graphic arts professionals who may not have received adequate training as well as professionals who don't understand the "new" way to scan and color correct. The "new" way is to capture and manipulate RGB (red, green, blue) images from flatbed scanners or digital cameras. Second, this book is important to the much larger market of new users with little or no graphic arts experience.

For years, traditional scanner operators learned and mastered scanning in a CMYK (cyan, magenta, yellow, black) workflow. As described in depth in the book, the CMYK workflow refers to the process color model used for four-color printing in which color photographs are broken down into their CMYK components for printing.

Using expensive drum scanners, an original RGB (red, green, blue) image "seen" by a scanner was automatically converted into a CYMK image required for printing. Highly skilled and trained professionals would adjust the knobs and dials on this device to control the illumination of the original and the color conversion from RGB to CMYK.

Due to significant strides in CCD (charge couple device) technology, many professionals are opting to replace their expensive drum scanners with less expensive flatbed scanners that capture RGB data. For many print professionals, the RGB workflow is alien. Often they do not realize that many scanning steps can be done much faster and easier in the RGB mode. As explained in this book, it is very easy to identify and correct color casts by looking at the percentage of RGB colors in neutral colors.

Another reason why this book could be beneficial to professionals is because there is less training available today to those entering the field. Before desktop publishing, training for graphic arts professionals was considered an apprenticeship. Traditionally, these apprenticeship programs were offered by graphic arts unions, and provided one way of becoming skilled at the craft of graphic arts.

Apprenticeship programs emphasize a specific craft, such as camera operator, stripper, lithographic etcher, scanner operator, or pressmen, but the apprentice is introduced to all phases of the operation. However, as the number of unions struggle in our modern workplace, so do the traditional apprentice programs. As a result, the number of apprenticeships available today is significantly diminished.

For Newbees

It was only a decade ago that graphic arts professionals created the majority of printed material. From among the 1.8 million people working in the graphic arts industry, perhaps one in ten, or 180,000, have experience with scanning or color correcting. Let's compare that to the number of people who may buy scanners or digital cameras from their local computer stores.

I would estimate that there are approximately 2 million computers with color monitors that could perform scanning / digital camera capture and retouching functions. This is a huge market that dwarfs the professional market almost ten to one. As the availability of personal computers and desktop publishing software increases, the number of people creating print increases, and the need for good training increases exponentially.

If you fall into this category, you may not have received any formal training on scanning, color correcting, or how to prepare files for printing. For you there are in-depth explanations of how to do things and descriptions of what is going on under the hood while you are performing those steps. There are recommendations on what to look for in a scanner and how to set up and perform your first scans.

Perhaps the most useful information in this book for newbees is the step-by-step exercises that clearly demonstrate how to identify different types of originals, and then scan and retouch them. For you, this book will become an invaluable resource, a book you place with your reference materials that you return to over and over again.

Pebble and stream

Someone once said that a pebble placed in the right spot in a stream could change the direction of that stream. Considering this enormous training challenge; it may be naive to think that any one person can make a difference.

However, for a few select trainers, this is what they believe. These individuals write training books and travel the country, training end-users how to use the latest desktop publishing programs.

Taz Tally is one of these elite trainers. He has spent the last few years traveling from city to city, providing hands-on demonstrations of the best ways to create materials for print.

To say that Taz is energetic is an understatement. He is the Tazmanian devil. At seminars, he is motion personified, alternating between the hands-on computer lessons, running through the audience, and hurling candy at warp speed. His seminars have long been touted as fast-paced, action-packed, and filled, from beginning to end, with incredibly useful information. It is not unusual for people to return to his presentations year after year. These participants will rejoice in the publication of this book and the opportunity to have Taz sit next to you (via this book) as you perform these step-by-step exercises.

If you have ever attended a seminar, you may have recognized the fact that your learning peaks in slightly over an hour. Therefore, the time spent after that does not result in peak learning. As a result, there will be some concepts that are inevitably lost. That is where a book like this one can be useful.

Whether or not you attend a workshop, the ability to work for short periods of time, at your own pace, will increase your learning. Basic learning theory indicates that mastery of a concept occurs when you have time and opportunity to practice that concept a minimum of three times; adult learners generally require up to seven repetitions. This concept is lost in many workplace training programs. A book like this one, filled with concepts and hands-on exercises, is a highly effective, stand-alone training program as well as a perfect complement to hands-on training.

Simple elegance

This book has something for everyone. If you're a beginner, it will allow you to learn the theoretical issues important to scanning as well as go through step-by-step exercises. If you are experienced, it discusses the RGB workflow and contains tips and tricks on how to be more productive with the most popular retouching application Adobe Photoshop.

Regardless of your level of experience, I think you will be struck by the simple elegance of many of Taz's concepts. This book is filled with dozens/hundreds/lots of functional applications.

There is one idea in the book that I find particularly useful in the visualization process. It is an idea that is so simple and elegant you have to wonder why it has not been more widely shared. In brief, the concept is:

¶ Look at your original

¶ Understand the type of original you have

¶ Understand the limits of your scanner

¶ Understand the different scanning and retouching issues

¶ Choose from among the many options that will give you the results you are trying to achieve

This is the second book I have had the privilege to review for Taz, and it is a long overdue companion to his hands-on training. In addition, it is an invaluable resource for those who are not fortunate enough to attend a Taz seminar in person.

As you go through the book, remember you have a little, whirling Tazmanian devil sitting next to you. As you master scanning, may your originals have good highlights and shadows, your contrast be high, and your images properly compensated for dot gain. Enjoy the book.

Howard (Howie) Fenton

Senior Technical Consultant, Digital Technologies
GATF (Graphic Art Technical Foundation)

Meet the bits & bytes Players
Stars of
"As the BYTE Turns"

Danny D'Ziner

Danny is a very bright, creative artist and designer. Although he never intended to, Danny has started working on a computer. Now Danny does nearly all his work on a computer. Danny bought a great system and started to work. All was rosy until Danny started sending out his files to a printer to have them output at high resolution for printing. Danny was used to having everything he handed to the printer work. He was soon to find out that not everything he created on the computer could be output through a high resolution PostScript RIP. Danny had to learn how to avoid the perils and pitfalls of PostScript. He needed help.

Sam E. Sales

Like Danny, Sam E. was educated in the old school. He was used to picking up art boards from his clients and delivering them to scheduling, and then on to prepress. He had been doing most of Danny's printing for several years now, and they had a good relationship with few problems. Sam E. Sales has started having problems with client files, though. He gets more disks, and he has no idea what's on them. Prepress has even sent back some clients' disks with strange instructions about parent EPS files and missing fonts. Sam E. no longer feels comfortable answering client questions or even presenting quotes for these electronic jobs. He might just have to learn about that computer after all.

Pauline E. Prepress

Pauline has been with the same printing company for over ten years. She started out in typesetting and then learned stripping (no, not in a night club) and had become quite proficient at assembling film. Pauline likes technology, so when her printing company started getting computers to do typesetting, she learned to use them. Over time Pauline has graduated from typesetting to page layout and, finally, on to scanning and electronic stripping. Pauline's responsibilities now include pre-

flighting incoming client files. Problems with client files have become the biggest bottleneck in prepress. In fact, the problems have become more numerous and severe as clients send in increasingly complex files and more "finished jobs." Sam E.'s problems were coming to her, and worse, he usually refused to inform his clients about their file preparation problems, so the same mistakes reoccurred. Now, Pauline had a secret crush on one of Sam E.'s clients, Danny D'Ziner, but he is one of the worst offenders! Maybe she could help.

CONVENTIONS USED IN THIS BOOK

Menu choices

The following type of sequence in parentheses indicates a sequence of menu choices in an application (Main Menu – Sub menu – Sub, sub menu, etc.). For instance, this Photoshop sequence: (Image menu – Adjust – Threshold) indicates that first the Image menu is selected, then the Adjust sub menu choice under the Image menu is selected, then the Threshold sub, sub menu choice is selected.

Key words and concepts

The following bold and italics formatting of text will indicate a key word or concept which bears special attention: *edge reproduction.* These key words or concepts will be found in the glossary as well as in the body of the manual.

Part I

Introduction to Scanning

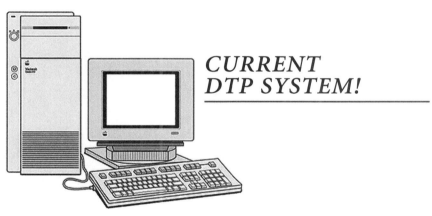

*CURRENT
DTP SYSTEM!*

*THE ORIGINAL
DTP SYSTEM!*

Part I Introduction to Scanning

As the Byte Turns continues…

Will Danny D'Ziner and Pauline E. Prepress meet or will they just scan each other in passing?

I want to jump right in and start scanning! Let's skip all this boring intro stuff!

You and most of the rest of my clients. You want instant high-quality results without having to learn how…And then we get blamed when your image prints poorly.

The secret to good scanning is evaluating your image properly to make the proper scan setup decisions. Image evaluation is not possible without some knowledge of the fundamental challenges. Plus, you must be very familiar with your scanning tools.

CHALLENGES

Mastering scanning involves understanding the nature of the task before you. Scanning is basically a way to reproduce an image so that it can be used for various purposes. Image reproduction involves first and foremost being able to visualize what a scanner will do to your image and what will happen to your image when it is output. Being able to visualize the entire production process is a great aid to making the proper scan setup decisions. Knowing the fundamentally different challenges involved in capturing line art and contone images is critical to making proper scan setup choices. Scanning involves many technical challenges, including paying attention to key variables such as image key, calibration, resolution, highlight and shadow placement, brightness, contrast, sharpness, color cast, and dot gain. Knowing how your image will be used is key to a successful scan. Increasingly, we are wanting to use our images for more than one purpose; that is, we want to multi-purpose our images. Being able to visualize the requirements of each purpose is critical to making proper scan setup decisions, which will lead to the creation of scanned images that will be useful for all of your various imaging needs.

LEARNING THE FUNDAMENTALS

To many, a scanner is a magic, and somewhat intimidating, black box which mysteriously converts line art and contone images into a form that can be used on a computer. This mystery is removed, and our ability to understand and control the scanning process is dramatically improved, when we break our scanned images down into their building block components. Once we understand the basic building block of a scanned image, the pixel, we can learn how to control the nature and content of those building blocks. We can then learn how and when to convert pixel-based images into other useful image types such as vector-based images. Learning key concepts and terms such as bits, bytes, pixels, vectors, and bit depth, and learning to sort out the various resolution terms, are important parts of this discovery process. But rather than just learning terms for the sake of terms, which is deathly boring with no relevance in sight, it is best to learn about these concepts as we learn about the building blocks of our images.

OUTPUT KNOWLEDGE

Most of our scanned images end up eventually being printed. Desktop printing devices are another category of magical black box. We select "Print" from the Print menu, and voilá, a nice printed image emerges from our printer…sometimes! Just as it is important to understand how a scanner converts our images into pixel-based building blocks, it is just as necessary to appreciate and comprehend the printing process. If we understand the basic nature of the spot and dot building blocks out of which our print images are constructed, and basically how our pixel- and vector-based images are rebuilt, we can do a better job of providing the right kinds of pixels to aid this printing process. Matching up our pixels with our spots and dots is the key to high quality and fast printing. Understanding the printing process is crucial to the entire visualization process. If we know all about where we are going, getting there is easier and more reliable. In short, the requirements of our output devices should control the input choices we make when we scan.

SCANNING TOOLS

After we understand how our images are constructed, converted, and finally output, we must master the use of the tools to which we have access to control our scanners. There are basically two categories of tools: hardware and software. The hardware side of the equation is dominated by our scanner, but there are various other tools such as calibration devices which can be added to the mix. And, of course, there are all those output devices, including our monitors. It is a poorly appreciated fact that having high-quality software tools is just as important as having capable hardware components.

A basic tenet of good scanning is that we should perform most of our image correction chores during the scan rather than waiting until after the scan is complete and trying to fix our scanned image in an image editing software. These days, the control of our scanner is accomplished almost entirely through software. To provide us with effective control of our scanners, we need to be able to control crop, size, resolution, highlight and shadow placement, grayscale distribution, and even calibration. Tools such as selection and crop tools, editable histograms, curves, gamma curves, the Info tool, and color cast correction tools will become familiar to you as you learn to control your scanner.

1
Scanning Challenges

As the Byte Turns continues…

Will Danny D'Ziner and Pauline E. Prepress be able to PICT their way through the Perils of PostScript, or will they have one TIFF too many?

*Oh yeah, I know how to scan…
I just click the AUTO button, and
the scanner does the rest.*

*And then we get blamed
when your images do not
print properly!*

*Oh yeah, and then I am expected
to fix those %#@$%^&* images!!
I am good…
but I am not a magician!*

VISUALIZATION

Digital Image Reproduction vs. Alteration

Scanning an image may be done with one of two purposes in mind. You may want to capture and reproduce an image exactly as it is and match it, as closely as possible, to the original. Or, you may want to alter an image from its original form. In either case, it really helps to have an idea of where you are starting from and where you want to go. In this book, we discuss capturing and working with *digital images*, that is, images which can be captured and edited with the aid of a computer. Understanding the basic challenges and building blocks of capturing and altering digital images is the key to capturing and controlling digital images.

Scanners and Scanning

The basic challenge of scanning

The scanning process is a challenge of image reproduction. Our goal is usually to produce a final scanned image with the highest possible quality. The quality of our final images depends upon a number of variables, including the quality of the original image, the capabilities of the scanner and its software, and the skill of the scanner operator. The first variable, original image quality, is an important one. A skilled scanner operator with a high-quality scanner can improve the quality of many images. Image corrections involving problems such as brightness, contrast, and sharpness can be addressed. But, even the highest quality scanners and most highly skilled scanner operators cannot reproduce image details that are not there. The poorer the quality of the original image, the harder we must work to produce a good final image. So, it is always wise to start with a good-quality image if possible.

Once an image is chosen to be captured and reproduced by scanning, a scanner with good capabilities must be used for an image to be captured properly. If all you ever scan is simple black and white line art, a low-cost scanner with limited capabilities may be all you ever need. If your scanning requirements include the need to scan *continuous tone (contone)* images with lots of shadow detail, a much more capable scanner will be needed. Even the most highly skilled scanner operator cannot make up for a poor scanner. On the other hand, the best scanner in the world, in the hands of someone who does not know how to operate it, will rarely produce high-quality results. The information in this scanning book will help you improve your scanning knowledge and skills. This book will also provide you with information on how to evaluate the capabilities of your scanner and the quality of your original images.

New language skills

If you are new to scanning, one of the first hurdles to get over is the terminology of scanning. Terms and concepts such as *input resolution, capture bit depth, dynamic range, unsharp mask, linearization,* and *neutralization* must be learned and understood to fully appreciate and address scanning challenges. This book includes a complete glossary of scanning terms for you to use as a reference..

Thinking of output

One of the keys to good scanning is knowing where you are going with your images before you ever start to scan them. Good scanner operators want to know as much about the future of their scanned images as possible. How an image will be used should affect how it is created or constructed. For instance, an image that is to be printed on an 85-line screen newspaper press will have different characteristics than one that is to be printed at 200 lpi, which in turn will have different characteristics than an image that is to be printed on a large-format inkjet printer or one that is to be used on a Web page or in a presentation.

Following is a list of some of the questions to ask before you scan an image:

• What is the original size of the image to be scanned?
• What will the final size of the image be?
• What is the original color space of the image: B&W, grayscale, or color?
• What will be the final color space(s) for the image: RGB, CIE, CMYK?
• Will the image be printed?
• If an image is to be printed, what kind of printer will be used?
  - Desktop laser
  - Commercial printing press
  - Large-format inkjet printer, etc.
• What screening technology will be used, AM or FM?
• What screen frequency will be used?

Scanning: Digitizing

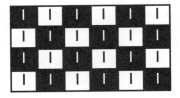

Viewing: Pixels on screen

RIPing: Halftone dots
for printing

▼ *Figure 1.1 The Changed Image*
The process of scanning, viewing, and printing an image
changes it significantly. Here
you see how an original continuous tone image is trans-
formed into 0's and 1's during
the scanning process, then into
grayscale pixels for screen
view, and finally into a pattern
of halftone dots for printing.

• Will this image be used on the Web? In a presentation?

• Is there detail and/or type in the image that needs to be reproduced?

How you will use your images should dictate how you scan them. And, if you intend to multi-purpose an image, that is, use it in several ways, you will want to determine the most demanding use for that image, which is often commercial printing, and use those requirements to guide your scanning choices.

The Production Process

Whenever I am about to scan an image, I try to visualize the production process and steps through which my image will be going. I try to
visualize what will happen to my image at each step of the process. I
try to imagine what each instrument or process will do to my image. I
think about the building blocks of my image and how they will be
altered or changed. This technique of visualization is a valuable tool in
helping us make decisions about how we capture, edit, and reproduce
our images.

Image capture: digitizing

When we capture an image with a scanner or digital camera, or paint
it from scratch in a painting program such as Adobe Photoshop, we
are capturing or building the image from pixels. When we do this, we
are substantially altering the image from its original form. For
instance, if we start with a continuous tone (*contone*) grayscale photograph, this photograph does not have any discernable building
blocks (at least down to the molecular level); it is truly continuous
tone. We see subtle changes in grayscale values as we look across the
image. We do not see discrete building blocks. When we capture this
contone image with a scanner, it is converted into an image that is now
constructed from a pattern of building blocks known as pixels (Fig
1.1). Each pixel has a discrete grayscale value, such as 25% gray. Each
pixel represents a discrete change or jump in grayscale value as we proceed across our previously continuous tone image. This process of
converting our image from continuous tone to a pixel-based image is
called *digitizing*. This digitizing process re-creates our image into a
form which a digital computer can recognize and manipulate. The
process also changes the contrast of the building blocks of our image.
Our image's building blocks change from smooth, gradual changes to
abrupt, discrete changes at the edges of our pixels. This digitizing
process then represents a significant alteration of the image's struc-

TONE REPRODUCTION

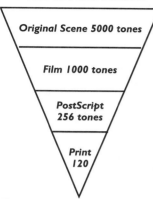

▼ **Figure 1.2 The Tone Pyramid**

Over 90% of the tonal information is lost from an image during its transformation from its original screen to printed piece. Our eyes can recognize approximately 5,000 tonal gradations. High-quality positive photo film captures 20% of the original, while in PostScript we are limited to 256 shades of gray.

ture. In some ways, the digitizing process may lower the quality of our images. But by digitizing our images, we make them infinitely more editable. Once digitized, we can easily alter an image's basic characteristics such as crop, size, brightness, and contrast; we can change images from grayscale to color, or vice versa; and we can create vignettes or silhouettes of our images. Our basic question when we scan an image is what should the size and contents of these pixels that we use to reconstruct or rebuild our images be. Controlling pixel size and content is the key to good scanning.

Image output

When we output our pixel-based images, we change them again. If we output our images to conventional printing presses, our pixel-based images are converted into patterns of dots (Fig 1.1, previous page). This process of converting our images from pixels to dots is called *halftoning.* Once again, we increase the contrast of our building blocks and lower the quality of our images. With halftoning, we end up re-creating our grayscale images out of only black dots on a white page. But, this halftoning process allows us to economically reproduce our image as many times as we want to.

So, in each step of the production process, we change the building blocks of our images, and may even lower the quality of our images (Fig 1.2), but we gain image editing and/or reproduction flexibility and capabilities. Our goal is to minimize image quality loss while gaining the ability to edit and reproduce our images.

Input–output link

When deciding what kind of pixels to create, it is helpful to know how our image will be used. In fact, how we plan to use or reproduce our images should to a large extent control how we capture or scan our images. For instance, if we plan to output our image at 85 lpi on a newspaper press, the scanning setup will be quite different than if we intend to output our image at 200 lpi on a commercial printing press, which will in turn be different than if we plan to use our image on a Web page or in a presentation.

So whenever we scan an image, it is helpful to know how that image will be used. If our image is to be used in several different ways, then we will scan our image for the most demanding use, and create copies fine-tuned for other uses later. I try to visualize what will happen to an image's building blocks with the goal of preserving as much image quality as possible.

GOALS OF SCANNING

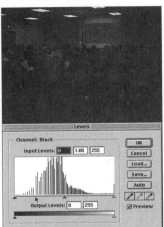

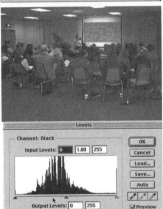

▼ *Figure 1.3 Poor-Quality Scan*
The top image was scanned incorrectly. When it was corrected in Photoshop, the resulting histogram below the image shows many blank areas, which mean missing data. The second image shows the same image corrected during the scan. Note that its histogram (bottom) is higher quality, more complete, with no missing data.

Role of Scanning

Many people regard their scanners merely as image capture devices. Their standard mode of operation is simply to capture an image with their scanner and then perform nearly all of the image correction functions after the scan in an image editing program such as Adobe Photoshop. Back in the early days of desktop publishing when scanners were low-quality and scanner control software was nonexistent, this was a viable approach; in fact, it was the only approach. Today, however, our desktop scanners are far more capable and our software is much more sophisticated. Our approach now should be to perform many of the basic image capture and correction functions during the scan, thereby minimizing the amount of basic image work which needs to be performed after the scan in Photoshop or other image editing software. Adjusting most key image functions, such as calibration, image resolution, highlight and shadow details, brightness, contrast, and in some cases, image sharpening, should be performed during the scan. Performing these fundamental functions during the scanning process will result in higher image quality and faster production times.

This is not to say that we will not use Photoshop or other image editing software to alter or enhance our images. But we do want to clearly separate the functions of basic image capture and correction, which should be scanning functions, from image painting and editing, which are post-scanning functions. Photoshop is NOT a scanning application; it is a painting and image editing application.

In fact, if we perform our scans properly, we will have much higher quality image data with which to work when we set about to adjust, alter, and enhance our images in image editing applications. Poorly scanned images which require substantial post-scan image correction generally result in poor-quality images with precious little image data to edit and/or improve. Fig 1.3 shows the difference between an image that was poorly scanned and corrected in Photoshop (top) vs. an image that was properly corrected during the scan (bottom).

As we say, "The proof is in the pixels." Here we see the image's pixels in histograms. Histograms show the frequency and distribution of grayscale pixels from highlight to shadow. Blank lines in the histogram represent missing data. After post-scan correction, the top, poorly scanned image had many missing data lines and ended up with fewer than 100 shades of gray, while the bottom, scan-corrected image had a nearly complete histogram and therefore a full complement of 256 shades of gray.

A scanner can usually do a better job of basic image correction because it usually has more data to start with. Many of the critical image adjustments that a scanner performs, such as scaling, can often be performed while the image is being captured and the scanner has access to a full, steady stream of image data. Once captured by the scanner, your image editing applications have a much more limited amount of data with which to work because at this point, your image has already been digitized, that is, converted into pixels, so it has a set number of pixels with which to work.

So, our main objective during the scanning process is to capture as much high-quality data as we can. This will result in our capturing images that are more editable and are reproduced with higher quality. As always, we should use the right tool for the job. We use our scanners for image capture and basic correction. We use image editing applications for painting and image editing, not scanning.

Key scan-controlled image variables:

• Calibration (linearization and neutralization)
• Image resolution
• Highlight and shadow
• Tonal control, including overall brightness and contrast
• Image sharpness (sometimes performed in the post scan)

In Chapter 4, to make sure that you have the tools you need to perform a high-quality scan, we will cover the key elements, capabilities, and characteristics to look for in a scanner. In Chapter 2, we will discuss image building blocks and the technique of visualization, two concepts we will use to help us make the proper scan setup decisions which are critical to creating high-quality scanned images.

Some typical image editing chores:

• Image touch-up (such as removing blemishes)
• Combining images (such as montages and collages)
• Creating vignettes, drop shadows, and silhouettes
• Mode changes (such as from color to grayscale)

SCANNING VARIABLES

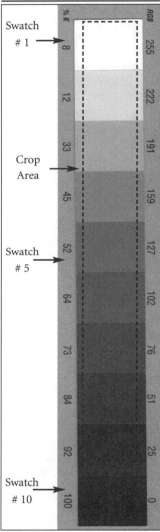

Swatch #1 →

Crop Area →

Swatch #5 →

Swatch #10 →

▼ **Figure 1.4 Calibration Target**
This 10-step grayscale target is used to linearize and neutralize scanners. Chart grayscale values are compared against scanned values. The scanner is then corrected to match the grayscale values of the chart.

Before we can intelligently discuss creating high-quality scans, we need to become familiar with the fundamental concepts, controls, and terminology of scanning.

Calibration

Every image capture device, including scanners, no matter what its cost or capabilities, needs to be calibrated to assure consistent results. Basic calibration involves making sure that a scanner will reproduce grayscale values properly. This means that if a scanner "sees" a 50% grayscale value in an image, it will reproduce that as a 50% pixel. Experience teaches us that nearly all desktop scanners tend to capture images darker than they actually are. It is not uncommon for a scanner to reproduce a 50% original grayscale value as 70%. And, when working in color mode, uncalibrated scanners can add color cast to color images. Each device is different and varies over time with variables such as temperature and bulb age. Calibration helps to standardize the capture response of the scanner, and improve the overall quality of your scanned images. Calibration is initiated by scanning a target that contains swatches with known grayscale values (Fig 1.4). The grayscale values, which the scanner "sees," are then compared with the actual values of the target. The scanner is then adjusted or corrected so that it captures the target values correctly. To assure accurate and consistent scanning of your images, calibration should be performed prior to each scan session. Fig 1.5 shows the different results you can have between a calibrated and an uncalibrated scanner. We will cover how to calibrate your scanner in Part II: Scanning Step by Step. Note: See the back of this book for information on obtaining your own calibration chart.

Optical Resolution

Most scanners provide you with a wide range of resolution choices. For instance, a UMAX PowerLook III, a common desktop scanner, will allow you to scan images from 1ppi to 9600ppi. But within this range, there is a specific resolution known as the optical or hardware resolution of the scanner. This is the resolution at which the scanner actually captures an image without interpolation. *Interpolation* is the generation of new pixels from data which already exists. For instance, the optical resolution of the PowerLook III is 1200ppi. This means

▼ *Figure 1.5 Calibration Results*
On the left is an image scanned on an uncalibrated scanner. On the right is the same image scanned on the same scanner with the same settings, but this time after it has been linearized. Notice how overall image brightness, contrast, and shadow details are improved through calibration.

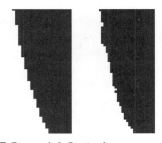

▼ *Figure 1.6 Optical vs. Interpolated Resolution*
On the left is a line art edge captured using the optical resolution of the scanner (600ppi). On the right is the same edge captured using an interpolated resolution (1000ppi). Note the greater "raggedness" of the lower quality, interpolated edge.

that a PowerLook III will capture pixels which are 1/1200" on a side. When the PowerLook III is used at 1200ppi or at some value that is divisible by a whole number of that, such as 600ppi (1/2 of 1200), the PowerLook III will work at its fastest and most accurate. If we scan at a non-optical resolution, such as 500ppi or 1000ppi, the scanner is forced to interpolate, or make up pixels. And if we scan at a resolution higher than 1200ppi, the scanner is forced to interpolate as well. Interpolation leads to less accurate pixel placement and longer scan times, because the scanner must redraw each pixel and replace it after it is initially created and placed. So, it is usually best to scan at the optical resolution or at a value that is divisible by a whole number thereof. For instance, if your scanner has an optical resolution of 1200ppi, scanning at either 1200ppi or 600ppi is acceptable, while scanning at 500 ppi is not because choosing 500ppi will result in interpolation. In Part II: Scanning Step by Step, we will discuss when it would be appropriate to use 1200ppi vs. 600ppi. See Fig 1.6 for a contrast between a line art edge which was captured as an optical edge vs. an interpolated edge. In addition to creating a smoother, pixel-based edge, the smoother optical edge will result in cleaner, less complex vector outlines if we convert our pixel-based images to vector-based images. Please see the step-by-step line art scanning techniques in Parts II and III of this book for more detailed instructions on scanning various types of line art images and their conversion to vectors. Note: You will notice that throughout this discussion, I am using the scan resolution units of ppi rather than dpi. This is because scanners do not create dots, they create pixels. Use of dpi units in scanning is wrong and confusing. In Chapter 3, we will explore and develop this concept of resolution more thoroughly.

Scaling (Resizing)

A topic closely related to image resolution is image scaling or resizing. We often want or need to change the size or scale of an image to suit the design requirements of a document. An original image may be 4" x 5", but we may want to reproduce it at 8" x 10"; this would require that we double both the height and width of the image, or scale it 200%. Scaling can be done at several times, including during the scan, or after the scan in an image editing application such as Photoshop, or even through a page layout program. We should avoid performing final scaling in a page layout application, as these programs have no ability to change the actual pixels in an image. Scaling in a page layout application often leads to lower print quality and significantly longer print times.

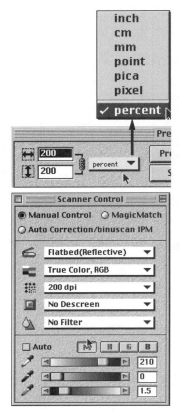

▼ Figure 1.7 Scaling Setup
This scanner's scaling controls are found in the upper left-hand corner of the Preview window (top). Units can be chosen to suit your needs. Assign the final resolution you would like your image to have, here 200ppi (bottom), and the scaling which you would like the scanner to perform, here 200%. The scanner will do the rest. The scan software will direct the scanner to scan at 400ppi, and resize the image 200%. This resizing will lower the image resolution to the requested 200ppi.

The best time to perform the scaling of an image is during the scan. Your scanner has more data to work with, so it does a better job than an image editing program, and it will perform the scaling faster. Scaling is controlled by deciding the final resolution of your image, for example 200ppi, and then assigning a scaling factor, for example, 200%, or a final numeric size. In this example, if we started with a 4" x 5" original image, your scanner would then scan your image at 400ppi and resize your image 200% to 8"x 10", which would then lower the image resolution to your desired resolution of 200ppi. The final result would be a 200ppi 8" x 10" image (Fig 1.7). Since it is generally preferable to perform the scaling of an image during the scan, it is a good idea to have already done some thinking about where and how this scanned image will be used. In the best of all circumstances, you will have the page layout requirements, image size, rotation, and crop defined for your image done prior to completing your scan. If you are unsure of what the final size of your image will be, then scan for the largest size that it might be. Scaling an image down later in an image editing application is generally far less damaging than scaling it up. Resolution and scaling will be discussed more thoroughly in Chapter 3.

Dynamic Range

The measure of a scanner's ability to capture a range of grayscale values is known as its dynamic range. Dynamic range varies on a density or "D" scale from 0 to 4.0, with each integer step being a tenfold (10) increase in grayscale recognition capacity. A density range of 4.0 is the most capable. The lower "D" number is known as the dynamic range minimum, or *Dmin*. The Dmin is a measure of the lightest grayscale values that a scanner can recognize. The higher "D" number is known as the "Dynamic range maximum," or *Dmax*. The Dmax is a measure of the darkest grayscale values a scanner can distinguish. Most scanners perform well in the highlight regions; that is, they have acceptable Dmins. Only the higher quality scanners perform well when it comes to distinguishing shadow detail. Scanners with a high Dmax, >3.0, can see a lot of shadow detail, while those with poor Dmax, <3.0, can see little shadow detail. An example of this difference can be seen in Fig 1.8. A scanner's Dmax is largely determined by the quality of the CCD used in the scanner, so this is not an adjustable feature. However, a properly calibrated scanner allows us to take full advantage of its dynamic range. Increased dynamic range is one of the capabilities you pay for when you purchase a more expensive scanner. Your scanner should have a Dmax of at least 3.0 to be an effective tool for capturing

▼ Figure 1.8 Maximum Density (Dmax)
On the left is an image scanned with a scanner with a Dmax of 2.5. On the right is the same image scanned with the PowerLook III, which has a Dmax, or maximum density, of 3.4. Note the much improved shadow details captured by the PowerLook III.

good shadow details. For the highest quality shadow detail, a Dmax of 3.9-4.0 is required. Just a few years ago, you would have had to pay tens of thousands of dollars to acquire a scanner with a high Dmax and dynamic range. But today you can purchase a scanner with ≥3.0 dynamic range for under $1,000. Be sure to check the Dmax of a scanner before you purchase a new one. The lowest cost scanners still have poor Dmax capabilities, and therefore only slight ability to capture shadow detail. It is important to note if shadow detail is not captured during the scan due to the use of a low Dmax scanner, that detail will not exist in the image and cannot be recovered later on.

Capture Bit Depth

When a scanner captures an image, it converts that image into pixels. The content and arrangement of those pixels determine the basic kind of image which results (black and white, grayscale, RGB color, etc.) The quality of an image, and in particular a grayscale or color image, is partially determined by how much grayscale information is captured within each pixel. The minimum amount of grayscale information that should be captured is 256 shades of gray. To capture 256 shades of gray, 8 bits of information must be captured and stored in each pixel. This is known as the capture bit depth of the scanner, or the number of bits of grayscale information per pixel which a scanner can capture (see Chapter 2 for a detailed description of this concept). It is often useful, to improve image quality and increase our ability to edit images, to have more than 256 shades of gray in an image. To do so requires that we capture more than 256 shades of gray and therefore more than 8 bits per pixel. A scanner that collects 10 bits of grayscale information per pixel will capture 1,024 shades of gray. A 12-bit scanner captures 4,084 shades of gray per pixel, while a 14-bit scanner captures 16,336 shades of gray. The higher the capture bit depth of the scanner, the greater the number of shades of gray that are captured, which in turns leads to higher quality and more editable digital images. Since a scanner actually captures three channels of grayscale pixels when it scans, the total capture bit depth is usually expressed as a multiple of three of the individual pixel capture bit depth. The following list shows the typical scanner bit depth and the number of shades of gray captured:

• 8 bits/pixel x 3 channels = 24-bit scanner = 256 shades of gray

• 10 bits/pixel x 3 channels = 30-bit scanner = 1,024 shades of gray

• 12 bits/pixel x 3 channels = 36-bit scanner = 4,048 shades of gray

• 14 bits/pixel x 3 channels = 42-bit scanner = 16,336 shades of gray

Enhanced capture, and therefore image bit depth, improves image quality by providing more grayscale information with which to work both during the scanning process and in post-scan image editing.

Image Brightness

The overall brightness of an image is determined by several factors, including the overall brightness of the original image, calibration of the scanner, the setting of the highlight and shadow points for the image, as well as any overall brightness adjustment we may make. The general brightness aspect of an image is known as its "key." A *high-key* image is one that has an overall bright nature, such as a brightly lit room with white walls. A *low-key* image is one which has an overall dark nature, such as a late sunset picture. A *mid-key* image is one with average brightness, such as a well-lit portrait of a person's face. The *keyness* of an image must be taken into account when scanning an image. For instance, not all dark, low-key images need to be lightened, and not all high-key images need to be darkened.

▼ *Figure 1.9 Image Brightness and Contrast*
On the left is an image scanned without proper attention to controlling the settings of highlights, shadows, and contrast. On the right, the same image has been re-scanned after setting highlight and shadow points using an editable histogram, and adjusting overall brightness and contrast using a curve adjustment.

We will use a gamma curve tool to calibrate the scanner, an editable histogram to set highlight and shadow points, and a normal curve tool to adjust overall brightness. Perhaps the two most critical data points to set in any image are its highlight and shadow points. Fig 1.9 shows the effect these settings can have on an image. Setting these two points involves identifying the lightest and darkest points in an image which has details, and assigning to these areas specific highlight and shadow grayscale values. The grayscale values we assign will be governed by the devices on which we will output our images. Typical highlight and shadow values for commercial printing are 5% gray for the highlight detail image areas and 95% gray for the shadow detail areas. Newsprint highlight and shadow values are commonly 20% and 80%. Desktop laser printer values generally fall somewhere in between. These values can vary widely for other devices. Whenever possible, the basic image brightness should be controlled during the scan rather than waiting to correct it in the post scan.

Image Contrast

Image contrast is adjusted by controlling the distribution of grayscale values in an image. If grayscale values are concentrated in the highlight and shadow portions of the image, then the image will have high overall contrast. If, on the other hand, an image has much of its grayscale value concentrated in the midtone region of the image, then its overall contrast will be low. Adjusting an image's contrast is a key element in controlling the overall quality of the image. Contrast adjustments should normally be performed after the highlight and shadow points of the image are set. Care should be taken not to alter the highlight and shadow points when contrast is adjusted. The distribution of grayscale values to control the overall contrast of an image, without altering the highlight and shadow points, is accomplished through the adjustment of a curve tool. Fig 1.10 shows the difference between an image that has been captured with poor control over brightness and contrast vs. an image with proper brightness and contrast control. Detailed instructions will be given in Part II: Scanning Step by Step.

Image Sharpness

One of the universal characteristics of all scanners is that they will soften images when they work in anything other than 1-bit mode. For example, a sharply focused portrait will be softened when it is scanned. The reason for this is that scanners sample images rather than copy them, and this sampling produces intermediate grayscale values, which in turn leads to softening of edges. As we will see, this softening can be an advantage when we are scanning detailed line art. With contone images, like portrait photographs, this softening usually needs to be corrected. Softening can be corrected through the application of sharpening controls, and specifically through the use of a tool called unsharp masking. Unsharp masking, while certainly a strange name, is a very powerful tool for helping us combat the softening effects produced by scanning. Unsharp masking allows us to selectively sharpen the higher contrast edges of an image in the reverse manner of how a scanner softens them. See Fig 1.10 for a contrast between a straight scanned image and the same image which has been scanned and sharpened.

▼ Figure 1.10 Image Sharpness
On the left is a portion of an image which has been scanned properly but not sharpened. On the right is the same scanned image, with sharpening applied. Note how the high-contrast portions of the right image, such as the eyes, eyebrows, and hat fabric, are sharper and appear to be in better focus.

When adjusting the sharpness on color images, we need to take special care not to alter the color balance along sharpened edges. Sharpening increases the contrast, that is, the difference in grayscale values between adjacent pixels along high-contrast edges in an image. In an RGB color image, there are three grayscale channels of pixels to which sharpening can be applied (see Chapter 2 for more details on the building blocks of color images). If, as is usually the case, contrast varies for various portions of an image from one channel to the other, unsharp masking may be unevenly applied preferentially to the higher contrast portions of the image on different channels. Since we are unevenly affecting the grayscale value of pixels on different channels, we are altering the grayscale values of the pixels unevenly. Since the grayscale values of the pixels also control the color (RGB) values of the image, this uneven adjustment of grayscale values during sharpening can result in color shifts along high-contrast edges. This color shift can be prevented by restricting the application of sharpening to the luminance values of an image. By applying sharpening only to the luminance values of an RGB image, we can prevent any color shifts from occurring. Procedures for restricting sharpening to the luminance values will be shown in Part II: Scanning Step by Step.

Tonal Regions

The control of tone or grayscale values is the key to capturing and re-creating high-quality images. When describing the various tonal or grayscale regions in an image, we use five terms: *highlight, quartertone, midtone, three-quartertone* and *shadow*. These are general terms that allow us to easily and quickly identify and refer to the five major tonal regions of an image. The *highlight* region generally encompasses the lightest portions of an image, ranging from pure white 100% up to around 10–15% grayscale. The *quartertone* typically centers around

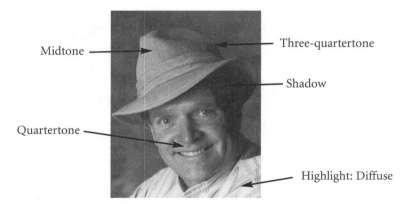

▼ *Figure 1.11 Tonal regions*
Labeled here are the five major tonal regions of a contone image. Notice that the highlight in this image, the white shirt, is a diffuse highlight because it has significant image data in it and it should not print pure white. There is no specular highlight in this image

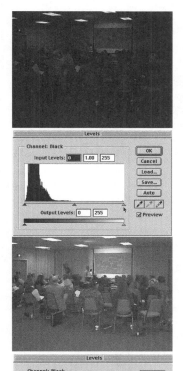

▼ Figure 1.12 Specular Highlight
The top image was scanned
with the specular highlight
area of the image (fluorescent
lights) set, using an Auto button, as printable diffuse highlight. Note the position of the
highlight marker on the far
left-hand end of the histogram.
Notice how dark most of the
image is. The lower image has
the highlight set in the proper
diffuse area of the image. Note
the position of the highlight
marker in the histogram.

the 25% grayscale portion of an image. The *midtone* refers to the middle portion of an image, with a center on 50% grayscale. The *three-
quartertone* is found around 75% grayscale, while the *shadow* generally refers to darker portions of images, typically from 80% to 100%
gray. While there are no hard and fast tonal range definitions, each
term refers to the range of tonal values within 10–15% of the center
value. For instance, the quartertone refers to grayscale values that
roughly range from 10% gray to 35% gray. So, there is some obvious
overlap between the boundaries of the tonal range areas. Controlling
the grayscale values in these five tonal regions is the key to high-quality images.

Highlights

In many images, one of the most important areas of the image to
adjust properly is the highlight region. It is important to note that
there are two types of highlights: ***diffuse highlights*** and ***specular highlights***. Specular highlights are pure white, that is, they have no
grayscale image data and will print without any halftone dots. Pure
white areas with no printed halftone dots look flat. Examples of typical specular highlights include light bulbs and reflections. Diffuse
highlights are the light portions of images that contain grayscale
image data and produce halftone dots when printed. Examples of typical diffuse highlight areas are white shirts and wedding dresses. The
image in Fig 1.11 contains a diffuse highlight, the white shirt, but it
does not contain a specular highlight. We generally focus on reproducing the diffuse highlight areas as these contain the reproducible
image data. We generally do not want our diffuse highlights printing
as specular highlights that are pure white with no image data. If a diffuse highlight area prints as a specular highlight, there will be no highlight detail shown. In the image in Fig 1.11, we want to make sure that
the white shirt prints with at least a little bit of halftone dot information. This is an example of when we want to know the minimum highlight value for our printing device. The minimum highlight value is
the lightest dot that a printing device can print. If this image were to
be printed on a standard commercial printing press with a minimum
highlight value of 5%, then we would set our shirt to print at a highlight value in the range of 5–6%. The shirt would then appear white,
but not flat. If this image were printed on a laser printer, you might
want to set the minimum diffuse highlight to 7–10%. And to print this
image on newsprint, you might want to set the diffuse highlight value
to 15–20%, as any value less than 15% would print as pure, flat white.

Conversely, if a specular, pure white area of an image were assigned a
diffuse highlight value, the rest of the image would tend to print too

dark. Fig 1.12 shows an example where a specular portion of an image, the fluorescent lights, was assigned a diffuse, printable grayscale value. Note how most of the image prints way too dark. This mis-assignment of highlight values is common when automatic buttons are used to adjust the highlight and shadow values in images that contain specular highlight areas. So when we refer to setting the highlight value for an image, we are referring to setting the diffuse highlight. Once we set the diffuse highlight value properly, the specular, pure white highlight will be automatically set to print as pure white. So it is always important to pay close attention to what kind of highlight areas an image contains, and where the highlight marker is set in an image. Remember, it is very important to know the minimum highlight value of your image so that you know what values to assign when setting the image's diffuse highlight. Step-by-step procedures for setting highlight values in images will be covered in Part II of this book.

Shadows

The other key problem area with images can be the shadow region. The term *shadow region* is generally used to refer to those tonal portions of an image that range from the three-quartertone to the deep shadow. We must pay particular attention to these shadow regions with images that have important shadow detail that we want to capture and reproduce. A common tendency is for shadow regions of an image to print too dark and even completely fill in. When this happens, shadow detail is difficult or impossible to reproduce. Just as we need to know the minimum highlight value for an image, we also need to know the maximum shadow dot that can be reproduced on a specific printing device. A typical maximum shadow dot for an offset commercial printing press is 95%. Many laser printers have maximum shadow dot values of 90%, while newsprint shadow values may be as low as 80%. Once we know what the minimum shadow value is, we can make sure that the shadow detail portions of an image are not higher than the maximum value. For example, in Fig 1.11, we would want to make sure that the dark portion of the hat (labeled as the three-quartertone area), which contains important shadow detail, would not print with a higher halftone dot value than 95% maximum, if we were printing on a commercial press. We will control the shadow values of images through a combination of both correct assignment of shadow values and the application of appropriate dot gain correction curves.

Color Control

As we will see in Chapter 2, color images are really constructed out of "sandwiches" of grayscale images. Therefore, the "color" (RGB) values in images are controlled by the grayscale values of the pixels which comprise the "color" layers. So to control the color values in an image, we adjust the grayscale values of its pixels. We rarely know what the color values of all the objects in a color image are supposed to be, even if we have an original photograph. Even if we have the tools to measure the color values of a photograph, it is an expensive and time-consuming process which requires some skill. Therefore, to get our color values correct in an image, we use a technique that involves looking for objects or areas of an image which have color values that are universally recognized or known. The most commonly recognized or known type of area, is the neutral grayscale area. Neutral areas are gray, and therefore have no predominance of one color value over another. Gray defines any area between and including black and white which is neutral, that is, without any color preference value. In fact, in truly neutral gray areas, all the color values will be equal, and therefore appear to have no color value at all. So, the red, green, and blue values of a neutral gray area in a color image will all be equal. Examples of typical neutral areas include white shirts, weathered wood, and white paper.

The key color correction technique we use when capturing color images is called *neutralization*. In neutralization, we measure and then adjust the grayscale (RGB) values of neutral, that is, the gray areas of an image, so that the RGB values are equal. When we correct the RGB grayscale values in neutral (gray) areas of color images, we are also correcting the RGB values in other portions of the color image as well. So, neutralization of color images tends to adjust color values all across a color image. For color correction tips on specific image types, see the step-by-step instructions in Part II of this book.

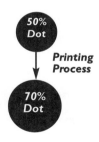

▼ *Figure 1.13 Dot Gain*
During the printing process, the size of halftone dots tends to increase as ink spreads out, causing photographs to darken. Dot gain tends to be greatest in the midtone region, where the percentage of dot gain may be 20% or more.

Dot Gain

The ink on printing presses and toners in laser printers, which we use in the printing process, tend to spread out when they are applied to paper. The halftone dots we use to simulate the appearance of grayscale in a printed image are formed from these inks and toners. We see small halftone dots as light grayscale values, and larger halftone dots as darker grayscale values. The grayscale values of the pixels determine the size of the halftone dots when we print these images. So, a 50% pixel should result in a 50% halftone dot. However, when this spreading ink or toner, which is used to form the halftone dots, is applied to a paper print surface, these halftone dots grow in size (see Fig 1.13). In turn, the larger halftone dots create the impression of darker grayscale values. The net of all this is that our images tend to print darker than they scan if we do not adjust for this growth in dot size or dot gain. And, if we add this dot-gain-related darkening to the darkening that often occurs during the scanning step with a poorly calibrated scanner (discussed earlier), we can end up with some very dark images indeed.

To further complicate the issue, our printing inks and toners react differently on different media. An image printed on coated stock will be much sharper and brighter than an image printed on uncoated stock. Inks applied to uncoated paper are absorbed more and tend to spread out more than inks applied to coated paper. This spreading out of ink and toner is known as *dot gain*. Dot gain can vary from as little as 5% on hard glossy stock to as much as 50% on porous newsprint or laser printer stock. Dot gain tends to be greatest in the midtones of an image and decrease toward the highlight and shadow portions of an image. Dot gain must be compensated for before an image is printed. Dot gain correction can take place during the scan, in the post scan through an image editing application, during gamut conversion for color images, or even during the RIPing process. If you are multi-purposing your images, you will probably want to compensate for dot gain after the scan, as dot gain adjustment will vary from one printing device to another, from one paper to another, and from one screen technology to another. Some non-print uses, such as the Web, do not require dot gain adjustment. But regardless of where dot correction occurs, it usually involves the application of a curve which lightens the image prior to printing.

Scanning for Multiple Purposes

Most scanning used to be done with one primary output device in mind, a commercial CMYK-based printing press. Today we often scan for multiple uses. We may print our images on several different printers, image them to film recorders, and ultimately place them on CDs or Web pages.

Each output device we use has its own *gamut*, or range of reproducible color (see Fig. 1.14). When the gamuts of any two output devices are compared, there may be significant ranges of color which do not match, that is, are not reproducible, on both devices. For instance our RGB-based color monitors usually have different color gamuts than most of our CMYK-based color printers.

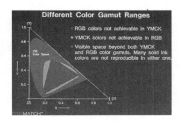

▼ Figure 1.14 Color Gamuts
Color gamut describes the range of color that a particular device can capture or reproduce. This diagram is a two-dimensional slice through three-dimensional color space. Note how much larger the visual gamut of the human eye is (CIE area) than either the RGB (monitor) or CMYK (printer) gamuts. You will also see that there are RGB colors that will not reproduce in CMYK, and vice versa. In this two-dimensional slice, the gamut ranges of RGB and CMYK are of similar extent, but in the entire three-dimensional space, the practical CMYK gamut is much smaller than RGB due to pigment impurities and ink density limitations.

For multi-purposing of images, it is good practice to capture our images into larger, less device-specific color spaces, such as CIE, and then convert our images' colors into smaller, more device-specific color spaces for output on specific devices.

One of the reasons that our various devices have different gamuts is that they operate in different *color spaces.* A color space is a definition of color. For instance, we use a color space known as CIE to define the color range of human vision. Two other common color spaces with which we work are RGB and CMYK. Most RGB color spaces tend to offer a wider range, or gamut, of brighter, more highly saturated colors than do most CMYK color spaces. (See Fig. 1.14.)

Our scanners and monitors, which operate in RGB color space, can typically capture and display more colors than our CMYK color space print devices can reproduce. This means that we can see colors on our monitors that we cannot reproduce on our printing devices. This difference in gamuts between our color monitors and our printing devices often leads to the common lament, "Hey, what I printed doesn't match what I see on my screen."

To add to this basic challenge of accounting for the fundamental differences in color gamuts produced by different color spaces, we find that even devices which have similar color spaces may have significantly different color gamuts. For instance, there is a wide range of color gamuts for color monitors. An 8-bit color monitor has a significantly smaller color gamut than a 24-bit color monitor. And, each CMYK print device has its own color gamut. Inkjet printers typically have different and larger color gamuts than commercial printing presses. And our eyes have a larger color gamut than any of these devices. Further, the gamut of any device can be altered by changing the display substrate or viewing conditions. This device-to-device variation in color is known as *device-specific* color.

This device-specific nature of color creates one of our greatest challenges in electronic publishing: to match as closely as possible the color which we capture with our scanners, see on our monitors, and reproduce with our various other output devices. The greater the number of devices we use to capture, view, and reproduce our images, the greater this "matching" challenge becomes.

This multiple use of images is often referred to as *multi-purposing.* Because of this multi-purposing, it is preferable to create images which are not *device-specific*, so they can be used or modified for use on a variety of different devices. As a result, it is useful to scan for the highest quality, largest gamut, general-purpose use, and then re-purpose the image for other uses. For example, you may want to scan your original images at 200–300ppi as large-gamut RGB- or CIE-based images, and then convert them to other file color modes and/or lower resolutions for other purposes.

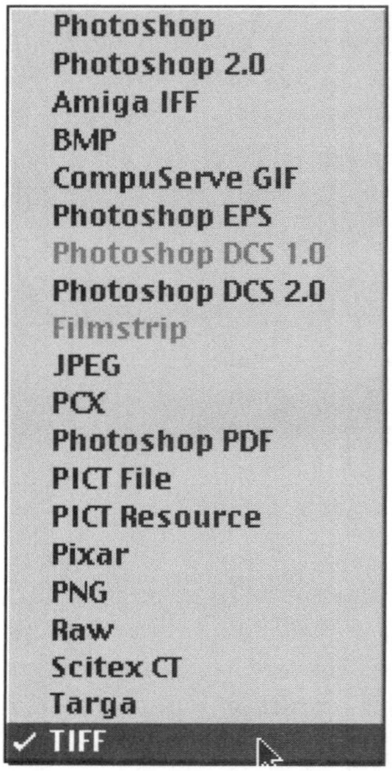

Photoshop
Photoshop 2.0
Amiga IFF
BMP
CompuServe GIF
Photoshop EPS
Photoshop DCS 1.0
Photoshop DCS 2.0
Filmstrip
JPEG
PCX
Photoshop PDF
PICT File
PICT Resource
Pixar
PNG
Raw
Scitex CT
Targa
✓ TIFF

▼ *Figure 1.15 Graphic File Formats*
Shown here is a list of the
graphic file formats in which
an image can be saved.
Although there are only two
basic kinds of images, pixel
and vector, there are numerous different file formats in
which these two image types
can be saved. The file formats
have been devised to suit specific purposes. TIFF and EPS
are formats in which images
should be saved for print,
while GIF and JPEG should be
used for the Internet. The top
two formats, Photoshop and
Photoshop 2.0, are the native
file formats for Photoshop,
which allow you to retain full
editing functions such as layers and transparent back-
grounds.

While all scanners capture "color" in RGB mode, we generally print
color as CMYK images. Many scanners, through software, can convert RGB images to CMYK on-the-fly immediately after the scan.
Whether you capture a color image in RGB mode or have
your scanner convert it to CMYK will depend on how you will
use your image. If you intend to output an image on only one
CMYK print device, then having your scanner convert your
image to CMYK may be a good choice. However, if you intend
to output an image on many devices, you will usually be better served to capture the image into a larger, more device-
independent color space, such as RGB or CIE, and then convert the image to other more device-specific colors such as
CMYK later on.

Let Your Scanner Do the Work

Remember, most of your image correction functions should be performed during the scan rather than waiting until you are working in
the post scan in an image editing application such as Photoshop.
Your scanner has more data to work with and better scans will
result. In particular, proper mode selection, cropping, tone compression (setting highlights and shadows), gray map adjustments
(controlling image brightness and contrast), neutralization (color
images), scaling/resizing (contones), and resolution should be done
during the scan. I often perform unsharp masking and RGB–CMYK
conversion in Photoshop, especially if I intend on multi-purposing
my image and/or performing significant editing or combining of
the image in Photoshop.

File Formats

Pixel-based images created by scanners can be saved in many different file formats. See Fig 1.15 for some examples. It is useful to think
of a file format as a container into which image components, such as
pixels and/or vectors, are stored. The file format we choose for an
image should be determined by how the image will be used. For
example, if we will use our images for printing to a standard
PostScript printer, then a pixel-based TIFF or EPS would be most
appropriate. RIP-specific file formats such as Scitex CT are employed
in some cases when proprietary RIPs are used. If, however, our images
will be used for placement on a Web page, then a GIF, JPEG, PNG, or
SWF file format would be most appropriate. Some file formats such
as PCX, PICT, and WMF tend to be more platform-specific and less

flexible than TIFFs, and are therefore less desirable for use as a standard file format. For most general PostScript printing, we recommend that you initially save your images in the TIFF format. The TIFF format is a flexible, pixel-based file format that is compatible with Mac, Windows, and UNIX systems for print. Always check the specific requirements of your RIP to see if the manufacturer suggests one file format over another. An example would be the use of Scitex CT on a Scitex Pressjet large-format inkjet printer. If you reuse and/or re-create your images for other purposes, you may change the file format of an image. Below are some suggestions for file formats, color spaces, resolutions, and use.

EPS (pixel-based): An alternative to the TIFF format. Some RIPs, workflows, and applications prefer this format for printing pixel-based images. Pixel-based EPSs are typically used in grayscale and CMYK images at 200–300ppi for desktop and commercial printing.

EPS (vector-based): The preferred format for vector-based images to be printed on PostScript printers. This type of image file format is used for grayscale, spot colors, or CMYK for desktop and commercial printing. Pixel-based TIFFs can be converted into vector-based EPSs through applications like Adobe Streamline.

GIF: A pixel-based image format used on the Web. This type of image file format is used for grayscale and index color images (≤ 8 bits), typically at 72ppi.

JPEG: A pixel-based format commonly used on the Web for viewing and image transfer. This type of image file format is used mainly for grayscale and 24-bit RGB images. JPEG can also be used in CMYK format for the storage and printing of high-resolution files, but a JPEG image should be converted into a CMYK, TIFF, or EPS prior to printing.

Scitex CT: A proprietary pixel-based format developed and used by the Scitex Corporation for use with pixel-based printing, for grayscale and CMYK, at 200–300ppi for commercial printing, and 25–100ppi for large-format inkjet printing.

TIFF: A general, pixel-based format used in PostScript printing, for grayscale and CMYK, at 200–300ppi for both desktop and commercial printing, and 25–100ppi for large-format inkjet printing.

File Naming

Place a proper three-character, lowercase format identification extension at the end of your filenames. Examples include: .tif for TIFF files, .eps for EPS files, .gif for GIF files, and .jpg for JPEG files. This three-character extension is not only important for the visual recognition of the file format, but is also necessary for some computers to recognize the file format. Macintoshes do not require a three-character extension because their graphic files have both a resource fork (format information) and a data fork (content information) built into each file. PC/Windows graphic files require a three-character extension because a Windows graphic file only has data fork (content) information. I prefer to use a four-character naming system that contains a logical name, the bit depth of the image, the resolution, and the file format extension. For instance, I might name a 200ppi grayscale photo of an oak tree which I have saved as a TIFF OakGS200.tif. (Note: If I can, I keep the prefix to eight characters or less so that the name will never be truncated by DOS.) This naming scheme helps make it easy for me to recognize the content and characteristics of my graphic files at a glance without opening them.

PAULINE'S SCAN TIPS

Scan Tip # 1-1

The control of tone or grayscale values is the key to capturing and re-creating high-quality images. The most important variables to control are: calibration, resolution, scaling, highlight and shadow values, brightness and contrast, image sharpness, and dot gain.

Scan Tip # 1-2

Dynamic range, Dmax, and capture bit depth are important hardware characteristics of your scanner. They contribute to the quality of the images, and especially shadow detail, which can be captured.

Scan Tip # 1-3

If you intend to multi-purpose your images, create a general, high-quality scan which can then be altered for use on any device. Scan for the highest resolution and largest size use. Apply dot gain after the scan so that printer-specific adjustments can be made.

Scan Tip # 1-4

Save your scanned images in file formats that are appropriate for their final use. Images for use in PostScript printing environments should be saved in either the TIFF or EPS format. Web-specific formats include JPEG and GIF.

PAULINE'S SCAN TIPS

Scan Tip # 1-5

Perform the most fundamental image correction chores such as calibration, setting highlight and shadow points, adjusting overall image brightness and contrast, neutralization (color images), scaling, and resolution during the scan rather than waiting to perform them in the post scan in an image editing application such as Photoshop. Your scanner will do a better job than Photoshop.

Scan Tip # 1-6

When naming your scanned images, always be sure to save your images with the proper three-character, lowercase format extension such as .tif or .eps. This will make your scanned images easier to recognize on all computer platforms.

2

Scanned Image Fundamentals

As the Byte Turns continues…

Will Danny D'Ziner and Pauline E. Prepress be able to master the multiple media monsters or will they be overwhelmed by technical terminology?

Pixels…smixels Don't bother me with technical details. I'm a creative person; I don't need to know technical things.

But you are always complaining that your images don't look the way you want them to!

Many variables affect the printing process. The differences you see boil down to changes in media, image format, and reproduction techniques.

COMPUTERESE DEFINED

Before we go any further, it might be good to review the fundamental terminology. Since this is a chapter on scanned images, let's review the terms we use to describe the contents and size of digital files.

The Basics of Bits and Bytes

Bit (b)
The smallest unit of the digital or binary computer language, restricted to either a 0 or a 1.

Byte (B)
A binary number that defines a computer character such as the number "1" = 8 bits.

Kilobit (Kb)
One thousand (1,000) bits, or 1,000 0's or 1's

Megabit (Mb)
One million (1,000,000) bits = 125,000 bytes (1,000,000 bits ÷ 8 bits/bytes = 125,000 bytes).

Kilobyte (KB)
One thousand (1,000) bytes or characters.

Megabyte (MB)
One million (1,000,000) bytes or characters.

Bit depth
Number of bits per pixel (also known as pixel depth and color depth).

• 1 bit per pixel = B&W (bi-tonal image)

• 8 bits per pixel = 256 shades of grayscale 2^8

• 10 bits per pixel = 1,024 shades of grayscale 2^{10}

• 12 bits per pixel = 4,096 shades of grayscale 2^{12}

• 14 bits per pixel = 16,384 shades of grayscale 2^{14}

▼ *Figure 2.1 Digital Graphic Data*
Graphics are captured, created, stored, and transmitted in the form of 0's and1's. The above example shows how a simple black and white graphic would be constructed out of 0's and1's. This type of graphic would be called a 1-bit graphic because each pixel, or square, is composed of just one bit (0 or 1) of information. More complex graphics will contain multiple bits (8, 24, or 32) per pixel.

IMAGE BUILDING BLOCKS

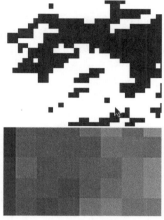

▼ Figure 2.2 Pixel Bricks
Pixels are the basic building blocks of a scanned image. I call them "pixel bricks" because pixel-based images are like brick walls, and the pixels are like the bricks. Scanners convert all images into pixels as they capture an image. Different scan modes will create images with varying numbers of channels (rows) of "pixel bricks" with varying numbers of bits of image data per pixel (bit depth). The top image above shows pixels with a bit depth of 1 bit per pixel. They contain either a 0 for the black pixels or a 1 for the white pixels. This is known as a 1-bit image. The second image above contains pixels with a bit depth of 8 bits per pixel, which provides us with the ability to store up to 256 shades of gray. This is an 8-bit image.

Pixels and Vectors

There are two basic building blocks we use in digital graphic images: pixels and vectors. While these two terms may be a bit foreign to you if you are new to scanning and digital imaging, they are really just new names for old concepts. As the old saying goes, "There is nothing really new under the sun." In the days before digital imaging and desktop publishing, we referred to the two fundamental types of fine arts creation as painting and drawing. We generally used painting to create images with fine details or gradations such as portraits, and drawing for images which were simpler such as logos. And so it is in the digital age. We generally use pixel-based images to create and edit images with fine detail, and are more likely to choose vector-based images when working with simpler line art images such as logos. Scanners convert images into pixels. Pixel-based images can in turn be converted into vectors. (See the pixel-to-vector exercise in Part III: After the Scan.)

Building Blocks of Scanned Images

To obtain a fundamental understanding of scanners and scanned images, it is helpful to know about the basic "building blocks" of scanned images. The most fundamental building block of a digital graphic image is a pixel. The simplest kind of pixel is a square that is assigned a single bit value of one (1) or zero (0). These are known as 1-bit pixels because they are only assigned values of either one or zero. We use these to construct B&W images only. The size of a pixel is determined by the resolution of the file of which it is a part. These 1-bit-per-pixel square building blocks can be assembled, like bricks, to create a wide variety of graphic line art images. Figure 2.1 shows how these simple 1-bit pixels can be assembled to create a black square with a white border. Note how the image is constructed from building blocks which are assigned values of either zero (0) or one (1), the only two values your computer understands.

Scanned images are constructed out of these square building blocks called pixels. To state it another way, scanners convert our images into pixels. Scanners cannot create vectors, although we have the option of converting pixel-based scanned images to vector-based images. A scanned, pixel-based image is like a brick wall, where the square pixels are the bricks. (I like the term "pixel brick.") These "pixel-bricks" contain image information or data. This image information is stored in the form of bits of data. There are only two types of bits: 0's and 1's. The simplest type of pixel, a black or white pixel, will contain only 1 bit of image data. A black pixel may be assigned a bit value of 0, and a white pixel would then be assigned the opposite bit value of 1. More complex images such as grayscale and color images are constructed out of pixels which contain more than one bit of image data per pixel. The number of data bits that a pixel contains is known as its bit depth (Fig 2.2). Note: Sometimes you may see the terms *pixel depth* or *color depth* used to refer to the bit depth of a pixel.

Like a brick wall, our pixel-based images can contain one or more rows of pixel bricks. We call these rows of pixel bricks *channels*. The number of channels (rows of pixel bricks) and the bit depth of the pixels determine the type of image. For instance, a simple black and white line art image will have only one row of pixel bricks, with each pixel containing only 1 bit of image data. We refer to this as a 1-bit image. A grayscale image will also contain only one row, or channel, of pixels, but each pixel will contain at least 8 bits of image data, which will allow that image to store 256 shades of gray (2 x 2 x 2 x 2 x 2 x 2 x 2 x 2 = 256). This is then referred to as an 8-bit image. An RGB (red, green, blue) image contains three rows, or channels, of pixel bricks, each of which contains pixels with 8 bits of image data. The total bit depth of an RGB image is then 24 bits (3 x 8 bits per channel = 24 bits). The other type of image with which we routinely work is a CMYK (cyan, magenta, yellow, black) image. You guessed it, this type of image contains four, 8-bit channels for a total bit depth of 32 bits (4 x 8 bits per pixel = 32 bits). Fig 2.3 shows examples of each type of image.

It is a good idea to keep these basic building block ideas in mind when setting up a scan. When evaluating an original image to be scanned, determine which kind of image you would like the scanner to create, a 1-bit (black & white), an 8-bit (grayscale), a 24-bit (RGB), or a 32-bit (CMYK) image. The scan mode you choose in the scanning software will determine the type of image the scanner will create. If we scan in B&W mode, our scanners create 1-bit images. If we scan in grayscale mode, our scanners create 8-bit grayscale images. If we scan in RGB color mode, our scanners create 24-bit "color" images. And, if we choose a CMYK "color" mode, our scanner actually scans in 24-bit RGB image mode, and the image is converted to a 32-bit CMYK image after the scan, or "on-the-fly" as it is known. Whether you capture a color image in 24-bit RGB

1-Bit Black & White Image

1-bit line art images such as these contain only one layer of pixels with 1 bit of data per pixel. Each pixel is either black (1) or white (0). These are the smallest and simplest types of bitmapped images. File size = 285KB at 300ppi.

8-Bit Grayscale Image

8-bit grayscale images contain only one layer of 8-bit pixels, which has the capacity to store and display 256 shades of gray. Contrast this to the 1 bit per pixel used to create the line art image above. This grayscale file size is eight times (8x) larger than the 1-bit images discussed above. This 8-b/p file is also the basic building block for the RGB and CMYK images shown below. File size = 2.2MB at 300ppi.

24-Bit RGB Color (Screen) Image

24-bit color images contain three layers of 8-bit grayscale pixels, one for each color (RGB). Each color can be shown in 256 shades. Therefore, the total number of colors possible is 256 red x 256 green x 256 blue = 16.7 million colors. This RGB image file size is 24 times larger than the file containing the 1-bit line art image. File size = 6.6MB at 300ppi.

32-Bit CMYK Color (Print) Image

A 32-bit grayscale image contains four layers of 8-bit grayscale pixels, one for each color. Note: A 32-bit CMYK image produces the same number of colors as the 24-bit RGB image above (16.7 million). The fourth black channel (K) is substituted for various portions of the three color channels (CMY). This K channel improves contrast and shadow detail and reduces ink coverage, but does not add any colors. This CMYK image file is used for printing and is 33% larger than the equivalent RGB file, and 32 times larger than a similar 1-bit image file. File size = 8.8MB at 300dpi.

▼ *Figure 2.3 Figure Pixel Depth Of Images*

▼ Digital images are divided into three basic categories: black & white (1-bit), grayscale (8-bit), and color (24 or 32 bits per pixel, depending upon whether they are RGB or CMYK images). File size, storage space, and printing time increase as pixel depth increases.

mode or have your scanner convert it to CMYK on-the-fly will depend upon how you will use your image. If you intend to output an image on only one CMYK print device, then having your scanner convert your images to CMYK may be a good choice. However, if you intend to output an image on many devices, you will usually be better served to capture an image in RGB mode and convert the image to other modes later on.

There's no such thing as a color scanner!

As mentioned before, pixel-based images are composed of square pixels which contain image data in the form of bits. The number of bits of image data controls the number of shades of gray an image can store. A 1-bit image can only store two shades of gray, black and white (bi-tonal). An 8-bit image can store 256 shades of gray. But, regardless of the number of bits which an image contains, all of the bit-based image data is stored as 0's and 1's. This means that there is no real "color" data in any digital image. When we scan in RGB "True Color" or CMYK "True Color," we are not truly capturing a color image at all. All scanners and computers really understand is 0 and 1, black and white. All "color" images are actually created and stored on our computers as black and white images. When we scan in a "color" mode, we are actually capturing three grayscale views of the original color images by viewing the image through red, green, and blue color filters. The color we see on our monitors is the result of the colors generated by the monitor, not by the computer. The color values created by the monitor are controlled by the grayscale values which make up the three RGB channels in the "color" image. To prove this to yourself, open up any RGB image in Photoshop or any other pixel-based image editing software and view each of the red, green, and blue channels separately. You will see that each channel contains only grayscale image data (see Fig 2.4). What this means to us as scanner operators is that whether we are scanning black and white, grayscale, or color images, we must properly control the grayscale values of our pixels if we are to create high-quality final images. The fact that all digital images are composed of grayscale actually makes our job somewhat easier.

Whether we are calibrating, scanning, adjusting highlight and shadow, adjusting brightness and contrast, sharpening, or even color correcting, we are in all cases adjusting the grayscale values of the building block pixels. When we print, we are adjusting the perceived grayscale values of the output image building blocks, dot and spots, to which we apply color on the printing device. If we keep in mind that it all boils down to grayscale, it helps to make the processes of scanning, editing, and printing easier to understand and control.

▼ **Figure 2.4 Figure "Color" Grayscale Channels**
All pixel-based images created by scanners and stored on computers are composed of grayscale pixels. Even "color" images are sandwiches of channels, or layers of grayscale pixels. Above we see the three separate 8-bit grayscale channels (from top to bottom, red, green, and blue) which are the foundation building blocks of RGB "color" images. Each of these channels was created when the scanner viewed the original color photograph through three (RGB) separate filters. Proper capture of both grayscale and color images involves accurate capture and control of the grayscale pixels that compose these images.

RESOLVING RESOLUTION

What is Resolution?

The term **resolution** has its origin in the word "resolve," which means to distinguish or discern. To resolve between two opinions, we take a close look at both opinions to distinguish how they are similar or different. When we look closely at an object, we often see that it is composed of smaller building blocks. The more closely we look, the more we magnify an object or issue, and the more detail we can generally see or resolve. When we look at a house from a half mile away, we see only the entire object, the house. As we move closer, we see that it is composed of walls, a roof, and windows. When we look closely at one of the walls, we see that it may be made up of a repeating pattern of small bricks, separated by mortar between each brick. An even closer look at the mortar reveals that it is composed of grains of sand, and so forth. In each step, we have a more enlarged or magnified view of the house, and we see more detail. By resolving the components of the house, we can understand the composition of the house and how it was constructed. A close look at the brick wall can help us see how it was constructed and have a good idea of how to construct one like it.

A digital image, like a brick wall, is composed of building blocks. Some images, like the brick wall, are composed of a repeating pattern of all the same building blocks. Other images, like the house, are composed of several types of construction components. Similarly, some digital graphic images are simple and composed of one type of building block, while others are more complex and contain several varieties of building materials. Scanned images, like walls, are made up of various-sized building blocks called pixels. The size of a pixel determines the resolution of an image. The smaller the pixel, the higher the resolution, and the finer the detail that can be shown. Some of the lowest resolution images with which we work are constructed out of pixels that are only 1/72 inch on each side. These images are said to have a resolution of 72 pixels per inch (ppi), and are simply referred to as 72ppi images. Image resolutions from 300ppi to 1200ppi are common in electronic publishing. The highest resolution images may have as many as 2400–3600ppi and may be capable of producing very sharp images which resolve very fine detail.

Resolving Resolution Terminology

Image resolution has been and remains a confusing mystery to many. This need not be so. One fundamental problem involves the improper use of terminology. Many people use the term *dpi* (dots per inch) as a unit of measurement when referring to all types of resolution, when *ppi* (pixels per inch) is the more accurate term.

Dots, spots, and pixels

There is much confusion surrounding the meaning and use of these three terms: *dots, spots,* and *pixels.* All three terms, and their respective units of measurement, are used when discussing resolution, and all three are examples of image building blocks. The first step to understanding resolution is to separate *input* (scan or capture) resolution from *output* (print) resolution.

Input resolution

We should use the nature of the building blocks of our images to guide our use of terminology. *Input resolution* is used when discussing image capture, such as with scanners and digital cameras. Here we are working with pixels, not spots or dots (see Fig. 2.5 on page 40). There is not a dot to be seen in any scanned image; there are nothing but pixels for as far as the eye can see! So, when discussing the resolution of pixel-based images, we should always use pixel-based terminology, such as *ppi* (pixels per inch) or "Res" (pixels per mm). The term *ppi* is the most commonly used correct terminology, and will be used here. (Note: Some drum scanners and digital camera softwares use the term *Res*, which equals pixels per mm.) The term *200ppi* refers to 200 pixels per inch. This means that our image is composed of 200 pixels in every inch, horizontally and vertically. This also means that each pixel will be 1/200 inch on a side. Many software programs, including scanning software, will use dpi when referring to their input resolution. This is wrong and confusing, but we know better! The higher the resolution of an image, the smaller and more numerous are the pixels. Smaller pixels generally lead to sharper images. Smaller pixels also lead to larger file sizes and longer printing times. We usually try to strike a balance between resolution and file sizes/printing times. There are diminishing returns when we use too much resolution.

Output resolution

When we reproduce our images by printing them on laser printers or other print devices, the nature of an image's building blocks changes,

CREATING, RIPING AND PRINTING IMAGES

From pixels, to spots and dots, to print

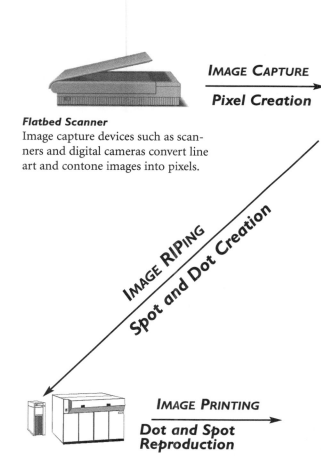

IMAGE CAPTURE

Pixel Creation

Flatbed Scanner
Image capture devices such as scanners and digital cameras convert line art and contone images into pixels.

IMAGE RIPING
Spot and Dot Creation

Scan and Image Edit Machine
The lion's share of image and document capture, creation, editing, printing, and storage and retrieval is controlled at desktop computers like this Macintosh PowerPC. Here the pixels created by a scanner or digital camera can be manipulated. Sometimes the original pixel-based images are converted into vector-based images.

IMAGE PRINTING

Dot and Spot Reproduction

RIPs and Imaging
RIPs (Raster Image Processors) attached to imaging devices such as imagesetters, inkjet printers, and laser printers convert vector- and pixel-based images into patterns of spots and dots.

Four-Color Press
Images, now in the form of spots and dots, print out on this four-color commercial press. The RIP controls the size and placement of the pattern of dots and spots.

▼ Figure 2.5 Scan Resolution
Scanning or input resolution should be controlled through the scanning software. Scan resolutions for line art images are generally higher than for contone images. Line art scan resolutions vary between 500–1200ppi. Contone image scanning resolutions should be controlled by the line screen (lpi) at which the image will ultimately be printed. A formula of 1.5–2.0 x lpi is typically used for scanning grayscale and color contone images. For example, if an image will be printed at 150 lpi, we would scan the image at between 1.5 and 2.0 x 150 = 225–300ppi.

Line art images generally require higher resolution scans because the emphasis in scanning line art images is on edge reproduction. With contone images, the emphasis is on grayscale reproduction, which is less resolution-dependent.

as should our terminology. During the printing process, our pixel-based images are converted into patterns of spots and dots. (This transformation is the job of the RIP. See Chapter 3, "Printing Scanned Images," for more details on this process.) Spots are smaller than dots. Individual spots are used for printing line art and type images, where edge sharpness is at a premium. The term *dpi* here really refers to the spots per inch of the print device. For instance, a 300-"dpi" laser printer is really a 300-spots-per-inch laser printer. This refers to the size of the image spot which is created by the printing device. A 300-"dpi" laser printer creates an image spot which is 1/300 inch in diameter. Most printing companies print with higher resolution printing devices which print in the range of 2400 "dpi," or spots per inch. We will typically scan most line art images in the range of 500–1200ppi, which is higher than what we will typically use for contone images. This is because the emphasis in line art scanning is on edge reproduction, which requires smaller spots.

The larger output dot, also know as the halftone or stochastic dot, is constructed out of groups of spots and is used in the reproduction of contone (8-bit grayscale and 32-bit CMYK color) images. The unit of resolution which printing companies use to describe the number of halftone dots is lpi (lines per inch), or line screen. This pixel-to-dot creation process also occurs at the RIP and will be discussed further in Chapter 4. So, in summary, we capture, create, and view pixels; we print spots and dots.

Resolution vs. file size

Most people think that a 600-dpi laser printer is twice as good as a 300-dpi laser printer. In reality, it is four times better. The reason is that dpi, dots per inch, are not as important as dpi^2, dots per square inch. A 300-dpi laser printer has 90,000 dots per square inch, whereas a 600-dpi laser printer has 360,000 dots per square inch. A 1200-dpi imagesetter must process 1,440,000 dots per square inch (in^2). This accounts for why some documents may print on a laser printer, but not on a high-resolution imagesetter. Therefore, keeping your documents, especially your graphics, as simple and therefore as small as possible, is an important concept to keep in mind. See the Resolution Glossary for a review of the effects of resolution on file size.

Another word used to refer to the concept of resolution is the term *Res* You may hear the terms *Res 12* or *Res 14*. Res is shorthand for pixels per mm. Res 12 is equivalent to 304.8ppi. Conversion from Res to ppi is accomplished by multiplying the Res number, in this

DIGITAL TERMINOLOGY

Digital computer language
- Binary language has only two characters: 0 and 1
- 1 bit = Either a 0 or a 1
- 1 byte = A series of 8 bits, 0's and/or 1's. For instance: 1000001 = 8 bits = 1 byte
- 1-bit graphic = Black & white only
- 8-bit grayscale graphic = 8 bits per pixel = 8 x the file size of a 1-bit image
- 24-bit grayscale graphic = 24 bits per pixel = 24 x the file size of a 1-bit image

File size terminology
- Bit = Either a 1 or a 0
- Byte = 8 bits = 1 character: 1000001 = 1 byte = The character "A"
- Kb = Kilobits = 1000 bits
- KB = Kilobytes = 1000 bytes
- Mb = Megabits = 1,000,000 bits
- MB = Megabytes = 1,000,000 bytes

Scan or input resolution vs. file size
- 300ppi scan captures 300 pixels, vertical and horizontal
- 600ppi scan captures 600 pixels, vertical and horizontal
- 8x10-inch page scanned at 300 pixels (1 bit per pixel) = 7,200,000 bits = 7.2Mb = 900,000 bytes = .9MB
- 8x10-inch page scanned at 600 pixels (1 bit per pixel) = 28,800,000 bits = 28 = 28.8Mb = 3,600,000 bytes = 3.6MB

Output or print resolution
- Spots per inch, also known as dots per inch (dpi) = Smallest building block of print image
  300 spots per inch (dpi) = 300 dpi x 300 dpi (horizontally and vertically)
  600 spots per inch (dpi) = 600 dpi x 600 dpi (horizontally and vertically)
  2400 spots per inch (dpi) = 2400 dpi x 2400 dpi (horizontally and vertically)
- Halftone dots per inch, also known as lines per inch or lpi = Number of halftone dots printed in every inch
  300-dpi Laser printer = 60 lpi
  600-dpi Laser printer = 85 lpi
  2400-dpi Imagesetter = 133–200 lpi
- FM (large-format inkjet) printers ≠ lpi = Random dot patterns whose size depends upon the image size and viewing distance
- Line art and text images are converted into small spots to create sharp edges
- Contone images are converted into halftone (AM) or stochastic (FM) dots to simulate grayscale values
- Halftone and stochastic dots are constructed from patterns of spots

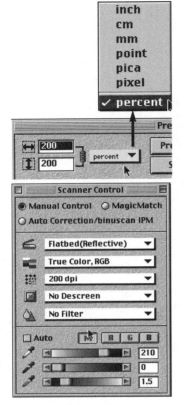

▼ Figure 2.6 Resolution and Scaling Setup

Scaling should be controlled during the scan for contone images. Units can be chosen to suit your needs. Assign the final resolution you would like your image to have, here 200ppi (bottom), and the scaling which you would like the scanner to perform, here 200%, and the scanner will do the rest. Your scan software will direct the scanner to scan at 400ppi, and then resize the image 200%. This resizing will lower the image resolution to the requested 200ppi.

case 12, by 25.4. The term **Res** is most frequently used in some high-quality drum scanners and digital cameras.

Scaling and resolution

All of the above assumes we are not scaling our image after the scan. For complex line art and contone (photographic) images that will remain as pixel-based images after they are scanned, it is best to allow the scanner to perform the scaling. If you scale your images during the scanning process, choose the final resolution you prefer (Fig 2.6). Line art images which will be converted into vectors should generally be scaled after their conversion to vectors. Please see the step-by-step instructions later in this book for specific resolution recommendations for various kinds of images.

Line Art Reproduction

As mentioned above, it is the image spot that is used to reproduce line art images when we print them on our printing devices. The key issue when reproducing line art images is edge reproduction. It is our goal to be able to capture and reproduce the edge of a piece of line art as closely as possible to the original. To do this, we need to pay attention to two variables when we capture line art: 1) We need to choose a fairly high scan resolution, and 2) we need to use the optical resolution of the scanner. Assigning a high scan resolution will result in sharp reproduction of the line art edge with small pixels. Using the optical resolution of the scanner will result in a smooth, consistent line art edge.

Conventional halftone (AM) printers

For simple to fairly complex line art, which we will often convert to vector line art, a scan resolution of 500–600ppi is appropriate. For complex line art, resolutions in the range of 1000–1200ppi are more appropriate. The exact resolution you choose will depend upon the optical resolution of your scanner.

Large-format stochastic (FM) inkjet printers

Large-format FM line art printing devices require far less resolution than for printing most conventional AM line art because most large-format images are viewed from a distance of at least several feet and therefore do not require the edge sharpness of a conventional line art print piece. For most simple, intermediate or complex line art, a full-scale scan resolution of 100–150 ppi is appropriate. Resolutions will vary depending upon the RIPs used by various manufacturers. Many RIPs provide scaling and interpolation capabilities. The key is to test to see what resolutions are required to produce high-quality line art results on your printer. Remember, it is always a good idea to check which file format these print devices prefer. Many of them take TIFFs, but some demand special file formats.

Photographic Reproduction

The second printing output resolution building block is the true dot. There are two kinds of dots. The most common one is known as the halftone (AM) dot. The other kind of dot which is commonly used by large-format inkjet printers is known as the stochastic or FM dot. The terms *AM* and *FM* are used to refer to the techniques used to simulate grayscale values with print. AM refers to Amplitude Modulation, and FM refers to Frequency Modulation. With the AM or halftone dot, printing the size or amplitude of the dot is changed or modulated to effect a visual change in the printed grayscale value. With the FM or stochastic dot, printing the spacing or frequency of the dots is changed or modulated to effect a visual change in the printed grayscale value. See Chapter 3, "Printing Scanned Images," for more detail on this topic.

A halftone dot is much larger than an image spot; in fact, a halftone dot is constructed from a group of image spots. Halftone dots are used in the re-creation of contone images such as grayscale and color photographs. The important output term here is *halftone dots per inch,* more commonly known as *lpi (lines per inch)* or *line screen.* This lpi output resolution is an important number to know, because the output resolution (lpi) of the printing device should control the input resolution (ppi) at which we scan our contone images. The basic, guiding principle here is that we need to make sure that we have enough pixel information in our scanned image to produce a high-quality halftone dot pattern when we print. The basic scan resolution formula we use is 1.5 x lpi. So, if we are printing at 150 lpi, we should scan our image at ~ 225ppi. If you are scanning for the Web, you can scan at 72ppi, the resolution of most monitors, or you can scan for print and then down-sample.

The line screen (lpi) or frequency at which halftones will be printed is: 150-200 lpi is the typical range for commercial offset presses, 60 lpi for 300-dpi laser printers, 85 lpi for 600-dpi laser printers, and 110 lpi for 1200-dpi laser printers. So, applying the above formula would result in the following scan resolutions on these various print devices:

▼ *Figure 2.7 AM vs. FM Printing Dots*
Above are two gradations. The one on the left is generated with conventional AM halftone dots, where the dot size is varied to create the changing tonal values across the gradation. The gradation on the right was produced with FM screening. Note how the dot density, rather than the dot size, increases from top to bottom.

Halftone (AM) conventional screen printers

- 300-dpi (60-lpi) Laser printer: 1.5 x 60 = 90ppi input scan resolution
- 600-dpi (85-lpi) Laser printer: 1.5 x 85 = 128ppi input scan resolution
- 1200-dpi (110-lpi) Laser printer: 1.5 x 85 = 165ppi input scan resolution
- 2400-dpi (150-lpi) Imagesetter: 1.5 x 150 = 225ppi input scan resolution
- 2400-dpi (175-lpi) Imagesetter: 1.5 x 175 = 263ppi input scan resolution
- 2400-dpi (200-lpi) Imagesetter: 1.5 x 200 = 300ppi input scan resolution

Large-format stochastic (FM) inkjet printers

Printing contone (photographic-type) images on large-format stochastic *(FM)* inkjet printers requires significantly less resolution than for *AM* printing of contone images. Fig 2.7 shows a comparison of the two. Whereas most conventional halftone dot printers require 200–300ppi of full-scale resolution to produce a high-quality image, inkjet printers require significantly less than 200ppi. There are three reasons for this. First, the *FM* dot is smaller and requires less data to construct it. Second, most large-format images are viewed from a distance of at least several feet and therefore do not require the image sharpness which a conventional print piece does. And third, FM dots are more randomly placed than *AM* dots and are less likely to create moire patterns with less data. Specific line art resolutions for the various large-format (FM) printers are as follows:

HP and similar desktop large-format inkjet printer: 100–125ppi (after scaling)

Scitex GrandJet printer: 23.125ppi (after scaling)

Scitex Idanit and PressJet printer: 56ppi (after scaling)

The RIPs used by different manufacturers may have various capabilities such as scaling and interpolation. Note how the resolutions for all the above FM printers are significantly lower than the typical commercial print resolutions of 200–300ppi. Required image resolution will vary with the screening technology and intended viewing distance. For instance, large-format printers like the Scitex printers above, which create images that are intended to be viewed from many feet away, produce much larger and more widely spaced dots that require much looser resolution files than standard commercial print material, which is intended to be viewed from a distance of 10"–16". Be sure to become familiar with your RIP's capabilities and the intended use of the images you scan.

Remember that these scan resolutions are for contone images such as photographs, not line art which we discussed earlier. Also remember, it is always a good idea to check which file format these print devices prefer. Many of them take TIFFs, but some demand special file formats.

A Final Resolution

Given the various resolutions and kinds of image components which we need to separate, it is helpful to understand and use the correct terminology. For image capture, viewing, scanning, and monitor viewing, we should speak of resolution in terms or *pixels/in* or *pixels/mm*. For printing to a laser printer or imagesetter, we should use two terms: *dpi* and *lpi*. The building blocks of all images will be dots per inch(dpi)*. When describing the reproduction of contone images, we should use the terms *lines per inch (lpi)* or *halftone dots per inch (hdpi)*, knowing that halftone dots are constructed from grids of image dots or spots.

Note: Some prefer the use of the word *spot* to *dot*. Using the terms *spot* and *spots per inch (spi)* instead of *dot* and *dots-per-inch (dpi)* is desirable for a number of reasons. If we use *spot* instead of *dot*, it makes the difference between spots and halftone dots less ambiguous. However, the term *dpi* is so ingrained in our industry that it might prove more difficult and confusing to try and substitute the word *spot* for *dot* in our lexicon. As an alternative, I suggest that we can accomplish our communication goals if we clearly distinguish between dots per inch (dpi) and halftone dots per inch (hdpi). We will also need to recognize that hdpi and lpi (another ingrained term) are equivalent terms.

Pauline's Scan Tips

Scan Tip # 2-1

All graphic images in a digital file are constructed out of two values: zeros (0's) and ones (1's). The fundamental building block of a graphic image is the pixel, which, in its simplest form, is assigned a single bit value of either a zero (0) or one (1). More complex pixels can be assigned multiple bit-per-pixel values. The bit depth, or number of bits per pixel, of your scanned image will depend upon the scan mode you choose.

Scan Tip # 2-2

There are four basic kinds of digital images: 1-bit (B&W), 8-bit (grayscale), 24-bit (RGB color), and 32-bit (CMYK color). Your scanner can capture 1-bit, 8-bit, and 24-bit images, and it may be able to convert an RGB to CMYK image on-the-fly. The scan mode you choose will depend upon the nature of your starting image and what you want your final image to be.

Scan Tip # 2-3

Contone images, such as photographs, are printed using patterns of dots. There are two types of dot patterns which are used: AM (Amplitude Modulated) and FM (Frequency Modulated) dots. The dot technology used and the resolution required to print these dots vary with the RIP used during the printing process and the intended viewing condition. Be sure you investigate how the image will be printed and used prior to scanning.

3
Printing Scanned Images

As the Byte Turns continues…

Will Danny D'Ziner and Pauline E. Prepress be able to match their pixels and their halftone dots, or will they be RIPped apart?

Why don't the printed versions of my photos look more like the originals?

Let's ask Pauline. She can help explain the details.

Many variables affect the printing process. The differences you see boil down to changes in media, image format, and reproduction techniques.

THE POSTSCRIPT RIP

The Generation of Dots

What is a RIP anyway? The word **RIP** is not really a word at all but an acronym, or shortcut, for raster image processor. Now this sounds like a complex, intimidating term, but in reality, the basic concept of the RIP is quite simple. Let's break the phrase down into its components. First of all, a raster is just a fancy word for *dot*, or line of dots. Image is self-explanatory. A processor is a device that alters the characteristics of something, or changes one thing into another. Now let's read the phrase backward. Processor image raster, or more simply–a RIP processes images into dots.

Every element on a page that is sent to a RIP is converted into dots. That is, all page geometry, text, line art, and contone graphics are converted into dots. This is the sole function of a RIP. While there are certain advantages to working with some graphic images which are constructed out of lines (EPS line art and printer fonts) and others out of dots (contone TIFFs and screen fonts) while we manipulate them on the computer, all of these elements must ultimately be converted into dots when we want to print them.

▼ Figure 3.1 PostScript Laser Printer
Desktop laser printers such as this Apple LaserWriter have a PostScript RIP, or interpreter, built onto an internal board which is built into their cases. The print engine itself would not work without this built-in RIP.
Desktop laser printers have resolutions ranging from 300 dpi to as high as 1200 dpi. Laser printers generally produce lower resolution images than imagesetters and therefore produce far fewer dots which require far less data processing by the RIP.

PostScript printers and RIPs

Nearly all printers which are used in electronic publishing systems work in tandem with a RIP. Page information created on a computer is properly formatted and sent to the RIP. The RIP then rasterizes (makes dots out of) the information, which the printer then images onto a piece of film or paper. The printer itself is merely the dot generation, or imaging, instrument. It is the RIP's job to translate all of the page information coming from the computer, which does all of the heavy work. While there are a wide variety of RIPs and associated printers, the vast majority of printers that are used with current open electronic publishing systems are PostScript printers (see Fig 3.1). This means that these printers are matched with and connected to RIPs which "understand" or can interpret and process PostScript code into patterns of dots. PostScript RIPs are often called PostScript interpreters because they interpret PostScript code into patterns of dots which the printer hardware can work with. Whether you are printing to a 300-dpi laser printer or a 5000-dpi imagesetter, a RIP is used to translate or interpret the information you create on your computer into a pattern of dots which the printer places on a sheet of film or paper.

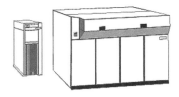

▼ *Figure 3.2 PostScript Imagesetter*

PostScript imagesetters such as this Linotronic 3060 are high-resolution cousins of laser printers. Imagesetters usually have RIPs which are separate from the actual imaging unit. The RIP may be a hardware version with its own RAM, CPU, and storage space, or software which operates on a separate computer station and utilizes the RAM, CPU, and storage capacity of the computer.

Imagesetters range in resolution from 1200 dpi to 6000 dpi. High resolutions require RIPs to generate from 16x to 200x the number of image dots generated by 300-dpi laser printers. This large number of dots means longer and more complex RIPing.

There are two kinds of RIPs: hardware RIPs and software RIPs. Hardware RIPs are really just very specialized computers that have a motherboard just like a desktop computer. Sometimes the RIP motherboard is housed in its own separate unit, as is often the case with imagesetter RIPs (Fig 3.2), or the RIP may be built into the printer box itself, as it usually is in most desktop printers. On a RIP motherboard, the normal CPU chip is replaced by a PostScript processing chip. Hardware RIPs have their own RAM, storage capabilities, and communication ports just like any other desktop computer. And just like desktop computers, there are slow RIPs and fast RIPs, and fast RIPs cost more. Built into the PostScript processing chip is a set of interpretation instructions which are designed to read PostScript instructions sent from an application and/or printer driver and convert that information into sequences of dots, which is the only kind of information that laser printers and imagesetters understand.

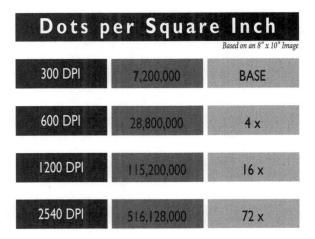

Dots per Square Inch		
		Based on an 8" x 10" Image
300 DPI	7,200,000	BASE
600 DPI	28,800,000	4 x
1200 DPI	115,200,000	16 x
2540 DPI	516,128,000	72 x

▼ *Figure 3.3 File Size vs. Resolution*

This chart shows the dramatic increase in the number of dots which need to be generated to fill a B&W 8" x 10" page as resolution increases. Note that as the linear resolution doubles, the number of dots quadruples. Seventy-two times as many dots need to be generated to fill an 8" x 10" page at 2540 dpi compared with the same page at 72 dpi. (See Chapter 2 for more information on resolution and screening.)

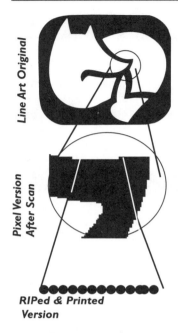

Line Art Original

Pixel Version After Scan

RIPed & Printed Version

▼ *Figure 3.4 Line Art RIPing*
The above sequence shows
how a line art image is captured and converted into dots
by a RIP. An original line art
image (top image) may be
scanned and converted into
pixels (middle image). This
pixelized version is then converted into image spots or dots
by the RIP/printer combination (bottom image). The RIP
determines the placement, and
the resolution of the printer
determines the size of the individual dots or spots. As shown
above, the straight line of
black pixels which compose a
portion of the black background between the nose and
the body of the fox are RIPed
into a series of touching image
spots. Text images are reproduced in a similar fashion.

Software RIPs perform the same function as hardware RIPs; that is,
they convert PostScript information into dots. However, instead of
having a dedicated processor chip, a software RIP operates on a
standard desktop computer. A software RIP uses the computer's
CPU, RAM, and storage for its processing chores. The conversion or
interpretation instructions are contained in the form of software
instead of being hard-wired into a hardware chip. The advantage of
software RIPs is that they are more flexible, easier, and less expensive
to upgrade.

Resolution and RIPing

RIPs, be they hardware or software, that provide PostScript interpretation chores for high-resolution imagesetters are required to generate vastly greater numbers of image dots per unit area than for a laser
printer. Fig 3.3 shows the tremendous increase in dot generation
required at increasingly higher resolutions. These greater processing
(RIPing) requirements of high-resolution printing often result in
increased printing times for many files compared with lower resolution printing of the same file. Many files which print quickly on a 300-
dpi laser may take much longer to print at 2540 dpi or, in some cases,
they may not print at all because there is seventy-two times (72x) as
much information to process. If a file will not print at 300 dpi, don't
expect it to print at 2400 or 3600 dpi; it won't.

Text and line art images

Text and line art images are formed from combinations of continuous
lines with well-defined boundaries or edges, unlike contone images
which are composed of areas that blend into one another with indistinct edges. As a result of this difference, RIPs handle text and line art
images differently than they do contone images. Text and line art
images are reproduced as sequences of touching spots. Refer to our
discussion of halftone dots and image spots later in this chapter and
remember that an image spot is the smallest dot that a printer can create. The crispness or sharpness of line art and text images depends
upon the size and sharpness of the image spots that a printer produces. A 300-dpi laser printer creates image spots or dots which are
$\frac{1}{300}$" across, while a 2400-dpi imagesetter generates image spots or
dots which are $\frac{1}{2400}$" across. Consequently, text and line art images
reproduced with a 2400-dpi imagesetter will be far sharper than those
reproduced with a laser printer. Text and line art images are captured
or created as pixels on your computer and then converted to
sequences of image spots on your printer. The placement of the image
spots is determined by the RIP. Fig. 3.4 shows the processing sequence

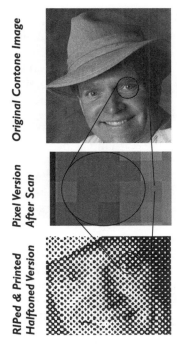

Original Contone Image

Pixel Version After Scan

RIPed & Printed Halftoned Version

▼ *Figure 3.5 Contone RIPing*
In contrast to line art images, which are re-created directly out of individual image spots lined up sequentially, contone images are reproduced through the generation of halftone dots, which are constructed from collections of image spots grouped together to create the halftone dot. The above sequence shows the stages a contone image goes through during the print production process. The original contone image (top) is captured by scanning and converted into pixels (middle). The pixels are then converted into halftone dots by the RIP and printer (bottom). The size and placement of the halftone dots are controlled by the RIP.

a line art image goes through on its way to being printed. Note how the RIPing/printing process converts the pixel-based version of the original line art image into spots.

Digital halftones

As described earlier, halftone dots are used to simulate continuous tone images. The job of the PostScript RIP is to convert the tonal information contained in pixels into halftone dots, which as we know are collections of smaller image dots. Depending upon the resolution of the image, that is, the number of pixels per inch used to create the image, what generally happens is that the tonal values from a group of pixels will be averaged together to create the information that is used to create a single halftone dot. The higher the resolution of the original image, the greater the number of pixels which will be averaged to create a halftone dot. Figure 3.5 shows the sequence a contone image goes through during scanning, RIPing, and printing. Note how the size of the halftone dots varies depending upon the grayscale percentage they are representing, while the spacing of the halftone dots remains the same regardless of the grayscale percentage presented.

> *Many files that RIP fine on a 300-dpi laser will take much longer to RIP at 2400 dpi or in some cases, they may not print at all. If a file will not RIP at 300 dpi, don't expect it to RIP and print at 2400 dpi.*

Unlike line art images where precisely capturing edges is of utmost importance, with contone images, one need only capture areas of tone rather than edges. The proper pixel size of the captured areas, that is, the input or scan resolution, will depend upon the line screen at which the final image will be reproduced. Because RIPs convert areas of tonal information into halftone dots, and higher image resolutions necessarily mean more RIP processing, one needs to be cognizant of the resolution at which contones images are created or captured. This chapter contains a full discussion of the relationship between input and output resolutions in a later section.

PostScript Code

```
0 0 F 4
(I___Copperplate32bc) T F
/I_____CopperplateThirtyTwo
BC 0 T dfnt
0 18 18 f
246 48 135 96 m .55 0 14
149 .5 (PostScript Code)d
end
```

▼ *Figure 3.16 PostScript Code*

This is a small portion of the text formatting information in the PostScript language description of the bordered text box shown above with the words **"PostScript Code"** set in Copperplate 32bc. The entire length of code for an 8.5" x 11" page with just this one bordered text box runs 22 pages.

The RIP as a funnel or filter

To be reproduced or printed on a PostScript device, all elements within a document, text line art, or contone image must be rasterized or RIPed. All the fancy text and graphics which we can create on a computer must be renderable as dots (RIPed). Simple text and graphics are easier to RIP than more complex text and graphics. In fact, there are many types of text and graphic images that are very difficult or impossible to RIP. While the speed and capabilities of PostScript RIPs are always improving, the capabilities of creative software applications and the people who use them seem to be improving faster. It is useful to think of a PostScript RIP as a funnel through which all document information must pass and be converted into dots. Like all funnels, the RIP funnel is a point of restriction; the publishing process slows down, and in some cases, stops here. Whenever we are constructing a document that will be used for print, we should keep this PostScript funnel in mind and remember that whatever we are creating must fit through that funnel. It is a fact of PostScript life that there are many images we can create on a computer and view without problems on a monitor which may not fit through our PostScript RIP. Examples of these items include: very long and complex paths, nested EPS graphics and fonts, multiple font architectures, complex compound graphics with multiple clipping paths, overlapping gradations or multiple masks, and many out-of-gamut colors. We should always try to reduce the size of files and simplify files that we intend to print.

PostScript

PostScript is a page description language, developed by Adobe, which was specifically designed to enhance the creation and integration of complex text and graphics for printing. PostScript is a shorthand language which is used to describe the page geometry as well as the size, shape, placement, and characteristics of text and graphic elements of electronic documents. Although it is unnecessary for you to learn to write PostScript code, it is very helpful to be at least familiar with how PostScript works (see Fig. 3.6). I highly recommend *PostScript: A Visual Approach* by Ross Smith as a good, understandable introduction to PostScript and how it works.

PostScript dictionaries

One key concept to understanding how a PostScript RIP works is understanding some of the basic parts of the RIP. While the entire RIPing process is multi-stepped and complex, there is one concept which I keep in mind when I think about trying to make my files "RIP ready": the PostScript dictionary. A PostScript RIP contains a series of dictionaries, each of which is devoted to processing a certain part of a document. There are font dictionaries, page geometry dictionaries, line art dictionaries, and bitmap art dictionaries. I think of these dictionaries as being storage and processing areas within the RIP. When a PostScript file is received by the RIP, it sends the font portion of the file to the font dictionary, the line art graphics to the line art dictionary, and so forth. The size of the dictionary depends upon how much RAM is assigned to that dictionary. If more information is sent to a dictionary than it can hold, you will receive a PostScript error, the dreaded POSTSCRIPT ERROR: STATUSDICTFUL. This means that the dictionary is too full to receive any more information. This kind of error is common with long, complex outline files such as clipping paths and line art that has been converted to vectors using Streamline. A PostScript RIP must be able to process the entire length of a line art file to continue. If the line art dictionary becomes full prior to completing the processing of an entire line or line segment, a PostScript error will be generated and the RIPing will come to an end; that is, the RIP will "bomb." Dictionary overflow errors can be prevented with line art by decreasing the length of and complexity of line art files. This is why we split paths, increase flatness ratios, and simplify path lengths of line art files (see Part II: Scanning Step by Step and Part III: After the Scan for more complete discussions of line art files and how to treat them). This same attention to reducing size and decreasing complexity of all aspects of a document will help reduce the probability of PostScript errors, particularly when printing to a high-resolution device.

IMAGE REPRODUCTION: SCREENING TECHNOLOGY

Reproducing Images with Dots

Dots

There are four basic kinds of images that need to be reproduced on a printing press: text, line art, tints, and contone images. Most of our current printing technology uses dots to reproduce these images. There are basically three kinds of spots and dots: *laser spots, halftone dots,* and *stochastic dots*. Laser dots, sometimes referred to as laser "spots," are the small, individual dots created by a laser imaging engine such as a laser printer or an imagesetter. The size of the dot produced by a print engine depends upon the resolution of that particular printer. A 300-dpi desktop laser printer creates laser dots that are 1/300" x 1/300" square. A 1200-dpi imagesetter creates laser dots that are 1/1200" x 1/1200" square. Some printers have the ability to create more than one size of laser dot, which allows them to print at more than one resolution. The density of the dot pattern that a laser printer or imagesetter is capable of producing is determined by the resolution of the device. A 300-dpi laser printer can create a pattern of identical dots using 300 dots arranged vertically and horizontally in every square inch (90,000 dpi^2). Any combination of these 90,000 dots can be placed or "turned on" on a page. If all 90,000 dots are placed, a solid 1" black square will result. If none of the 90,000 dots are placed, a solid 1" white square will result. This is how text and line art images are created, by either placing or not placing dots at various places on a page. Halftone and stochastic dots are used to reproduce tints and contones, and are constructed from groups of laser dots.

Reproduction of solid text and line art images, such as the solid "P" shown in Fig 3.7, is fairly straightforward. Solid images can easily be reproduced by merely placing identically sized laser dots end to end and/or side by side in whatever shapes or sequences are required to re-create the image. The size of the dots used is determined by the resolution of the printer. The smaller the dots used to reproduce an image (that is, the higher the resolution of the printer), the finer the detail and the sharper the images that can be reproduced. The solid black "P" shown in Fig 3.7 is a good example of how dots can be arranged to create a text character or line art image. Notice how higher resolutions will create images with sharper edge detail. Colors can be applied to these solid dot patterns if required.

Image Example

Expanded View of Printed Image

Solid Text and Line Art Images

Text and line art images which are solid, that is 100% grayscale or black, can be reproduced by placing solid laser dots end to end with no space in between. Only black and white tones need to be produced. Any solid colors can be assigned to either the black or white area during the printing process. The size of the dots and the stair steps depend upon the resolution of the image. Higher resolution equals smaller dots.

Screened/Tinted Text and Line Art Images

Images such as this 25% grayscale image which are *not* solid images (images of less than 100% gray) require the use of spaced halftone dots. These are collections of dots rather than individual dots that simulate the effect of grayscale images. In a halftoning system, the halftone dots are equally spaced and the size of the dots is modified to simulate various shades of gray.

Gradations / Degradés / Blends

A gradation from one shade of gray to another is the simplest kind of contone image. Images such as this 0–100% grayscale blend, known as a gradation, gray ramp, or degradé, are simulated by generating rows of halftone dots of gradually increasing or decreasing sizes. Blends can be created by forming two overlapping gradations. Often, a different color will be assigned to each gradation.

Contone Images

This is an example of a complex contone. Complex contones have a wide variety of grayscale areas, grading one into another. These complex areas are reproduced using a complex pattern of equidistant halftone dots of various sizes. The sizes vary according to the lightness or darkness of various parts of the image.

▼ *Figure 3.7 Laser Spots and Halftone Dots*

Small, individual dots are all most laser printers and imagesetters have to create images with. Solid areas like the top "P" are fairly easy to construct. A printer lines up laser spots end to end to fill a solid area or create a continuous line. Tones can be reproduced by producing patterns of closely spaced dots, called halftone dots. Traditional halftoning creates patterns of equally spaced dots and varies the size of the dots to produce various shades of gray. Each halftone dot is constructed out of numerous laser spots.

Image reproduction gets a bit more challenging when we try to reproduce a tint or tone (an area filled in with one shade of gray), and particularly when we try to reproduce a conttone image where tonal values vary continuously across the image, such as in a blend from one shade of gray to another, or in a photograph of a person's face.

Why screens?

To fully appreciate the challenge of reproducing a contone image, we must remember that we are restricted to the use of dots when we want to reproduce an image on a printing press. We do not have the luxury of directly creating shades of gray or colors as we can in photography. PostScript laser printers and imagesetters are essentially dot production machines. At any given position on a piece of film or paper, an imagesetter will either place a dot or not place a dot.

Since we cannot directly create tints or shades of gray, we are forced to use patterns of dots called *screens* to *simulate* grayscale values. This simulation takes advantage of the limited ability of the human eye to resolve or distinguish small dots that sit next to each other. Traditionally, we have created dots of various sizes placed closely beside each other to simulate the impression of a grayscale value. These variable-sized dots are called halftone dots. Halftone dots are composite dots constructed out of combinations of laser dots. By using combinations of laser dots to build halftone dots, we can construct halftone dots of various sizes. Unlike laser dots, most halftone dots are separated by space because they are created in a grid pattern known as a halftone grid. Unless the individual halftone dots are large, they do not touch. We generate patterns of halftone dots to simulate the appearance of shades of gray in printed images. Small halftone dots are used to simulate low grayscale, or screen percentages such as 10 or 15%. Large halftone dots create high tonal or screen values. Larger halftone dots require greater numbers of laser dots or spots to construct them. An area filled with halftone dots of all the same size will create a *tint* of one tonal value such as a 25% tint or screen. This area will appear to the human eye as an area filled with 25% gray. An example of a 25% tint and an enlargement of the screen pattern used to create it appears in Fig 3.9. Color can be applied to this area to create a 25% tint of that color. That same area filled with halftone dots of gradually varying sizes creates a graduated screen such as that seen in the third "P" shown in Fig 3.7. A constantly varying pattern of dot sizes will simulate a contone image, that is, one where the grayscale values vary across the image. This is how grayscale photographs (such as the girl's image in Fig 3.10) are reproduced through printing. The gradual change in tonal values across a person's face is constructed from a gradually changing pattern of various-sized halftone dots.

Halftone dots

One additional level of complexity which adds to our resolution confusion is the concept of the halftone dot. Since we cannot produce contone images on a printing press, because we can only produce dots or spots, we are faced with the problem of reproducing these contones. We perform this feat by a process known as halftoning. Halftoning takes advantage of the resolving limitations of the human eye. The concept is basically this: If we place two small dots side by side on a page, up close we can distinguish or resolve those two dots. However, if we begin to move that page farther and farther away, at some distance we will no longer be able to distinguish or resolve those two dots ,and they will appear as one. We essentially trick the eye into seeing only one dot instead of two. Now, if we gradually vary the size of the dots across an area, we will simulate a gradation. It is in this way that we create the impression of tone, using dots.

The technical problem with creating halftone dots is that most laser printers and imagesetters can produce only dots or spots of fixed sizes. The solution is to combine smaller laser spots or dots to create halftone dots of various sizes. A halftone dot is defined by and constructed from a grid of laser spots known as a halftone cell. Any of the cell sites can be filled in with laser spots or left blank. The greater the number of these cell sites that are filled in with laser spots, the larger the halftone dot will be and the darker the shade of gray which will be simulated.

Halftoning: where it occurs

The RIP is the portion of your computer-based publishing system that converts the images you generate on your computer into a form which can be reproduced on a piece of paper or film. To "rasterize" means to create dots, and that is what a RIP does. It generates dots. All elements on your page, text, line art graphics, and contone graphics, must be converted by a RIP into a series of dots to be printed. In a PostScript publishing system, halftoning of contone images occurs at the RIP, not at the design or scanning station. All contone graphic images printed from a computer to a laser printer or imagesetter must be constructed out of a series of dots. For a contone image to be rendered by these printers, the image must first be converted into a special series of dots known as halftone dots or cells. Halftone dots are composed of a series of smaller dots known as image dots. The number of image dots which

OUTPUT RESOLUTION COMPARISON

Resolution is a square function, not a linear one. Therefore, as the line resolution doubles, the amount of data increases by a factor of four (4). For example:

• A 300-dpi laser printer prints 300 dpi x 300 dpi = 90,000 dpi2

• A 600-dpi laser printer prints 600 dpi x 600 dpi = 360,000 dpi2

This means that a 600-dpi laser printer creates four (4) times as much information as a 300-dpi laser printer.

• Calculate how much more information a 2400-dpi imagesetter must process than a 300-dpi laser printer:

A 2400-dpi imagesetter produces _____ dpi^2

This is _____ times as much information as the 300-dpi laser printer.

• Calculate the file size of an 8x10 B&W image scanned at 600 dpi:

bits(b) _____, Megabits (Mb) _____, Bytes(B) _____, Megabytes (MB) _____

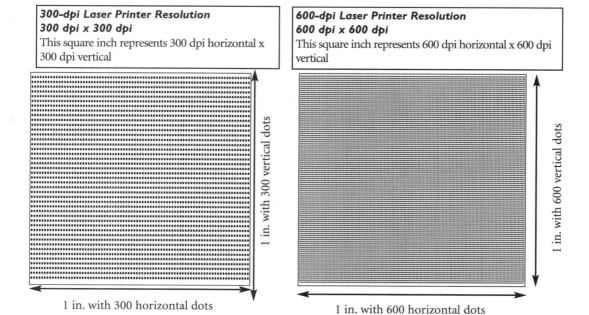

300-dpi Laser Printer Resolution 300 dpi x 300 dpi	600-dpi Laser Printer Resolution 600 dpi x 600 dpi
This square inch represents 300 dpi horizontal x 300 dpi vertical	This square inch represents 600 dpi horizontal x 600 dpi vertical

1 in. with 300 vertical dots

1 in. with 300 horizontal dots

1 in. with 600 vertical dots

1 in. with 600 horizontal dots

▼ *Figure 3.8 Resolution Comparison*

Resolution is a square, not a linear, function. As the linear resolution doubles, the square resolution, and therefore the file size, quadruples. A 300-dpi image is actually a 300 dpi x 300 dpi image with 90,000 dots per square inch. A 600-dpi image is 600 dpi x 600 dpi, or 360,000 dpi^2, or four times the resolution *and file size* of the 300-dpi image.

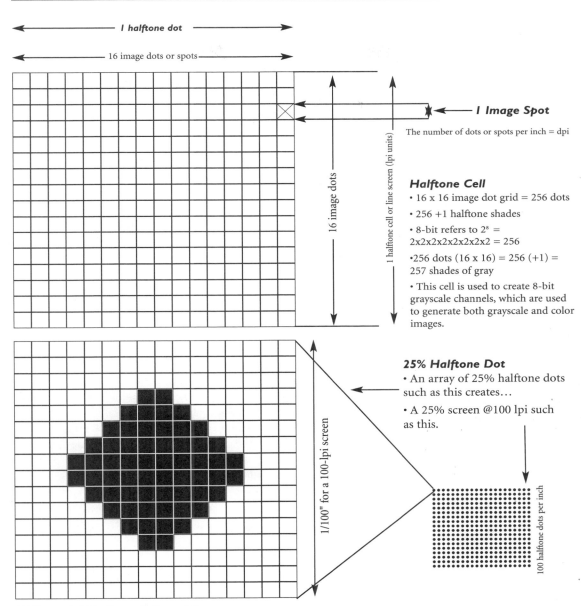

1 halftone dot

16 image dots or spots

1 Image Spot

The number of dots or spots per inch = dpi

16 image dots

1 halftone cell or line screen (lpi units)

Halftone Cell
• 16 x 16 image dot grid = 256 dots

• 256 +1 halftone shades

• 8-bit refers to $2^8 =$ 2x2x2x2x2x2x2x2 = 256

•256 dots (16 x 16) = 256 (+1) = 257 shades of gray

• This cell is used to create 8-bit grayscale channels, which are used to generate both grayscale and color images.

25% Halftone Dot
• An array of 25% halftone dots such as this creates...

• A 25% screen @100 lpi such as this.

1/100" for a 100-lpi screen

100 halftone dots per inch

▼ *Figure 3.9 Halftone Cells and Dots*

Traditional halftone dot patterns are created in set patterns determined by halftone cells. Laser printers and imagesetters use this cell pattern to determine spot placement on film or paper. Collections of image spots are used to create halftone dots. Halftone dots of various sizes simulate various grayscale percentages. Patterns of small and large halftone dots create the impression of light and dark grayscale, respectively. Patterns of variable-sized halftone dots are used to simulate the appearance of continuous tone grayscale.

make up halftone dots determines the number of shades of gray which can be rendered. The number of image dots which are available to construct a halftone cell of a particular size is determined by the dpi of the printer or imagesetter being used. The number of halftone dots per inch determines the resolution or sharpness of the rendered image. Here are some numbers to think about:

The number of halftone dots per inch is equivalent to the line screen of the printed image, that is: lpi = halftone dots per inch (hdpi).

shades of gray = dpi ÷ lpi (hdpi)

Example: (1600 dpi ÷ 100 lpi) = 16-dot cell : 16 x16 = 256 shades of gray

Example: (1200 dpi ÷ 100 lpi) = 12-dot cell: 12x12 = 144 shades of gray

Problem: If you want to reproduce 256 shades of gray at 133 lpi, what minimum dpi will be required on your imagesetter?

dpi vs. lpi vs. shades of gray

The size of a halftone dot is limited by the line screen at which the image is printed. In fact, the side dimensions of the halftone cell are determined by the line screen of the printer. Therefore, lpi (lines per inch) is equivalent to hdpi (halftone dots per inch). Since halftone dots are created by a grid of laser dots or spots which fill in the halftone cell, the relationship of lpi to dpi is set by the grid dimensions of the halftone cell. If a halftone cell is composed of 256 cell sites, the dimensions of the cell will be 16 x 16 (16 x 16 = 256). Note that the number of cell sites in each halftone cell also determines the number of shades of gray that can be reproduced. If the halftone cell is composed of 144 cell sites, then the halftone cell will be composed of a 12 x 12 grid of potential laser spots. Remember that laser spots are the smallest dots that can be created by the printer, and that these laser spots build the halftone dots.

The dpi of the printer required to create any given halftone dot is determined by the line screen (which controls the physical size of the halftone dots) and the number of cell sites required in each cell (which will determine the number of shades of gray that can be reproduced). For example, if we wanted to print a photograph at 100 lpi, which will reproduce 144 shades of gray, we would need to create 100 halftone dots per inch with cell dimensions of 12 x 12 laser spots. This would require an imagesetter that can produce 1200 laser spots per inch (100 halftone dots per inch x 12 laser spots per halftone dot). If we wanted to reproduce this same photograph at 150 lpi, we would need an imagesetter that can produce 1800 dpi (150 lpi x 12 spots per halftone dot = 1800 dpi). Figure 3.9 shows a representation of the

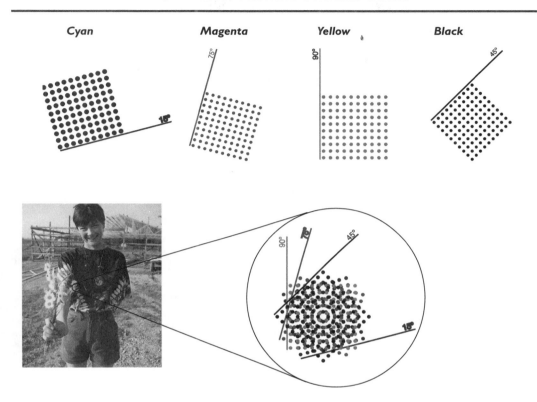

▼ *Figure 3.10 Color Contone Images: Overlapping Four-Color Process Halftone Screens*
Complex color contones, such as this photograph, are reproduced using a complex pattern of four overlapping screens of halftone dots. There is one screen pattern for each process color. Each color is printed at a different angle to avoid the generation of moiré patterns. Colors are separated as much as possible across the available 90°. The three strongest colors–black, cyan, and magenta–are each separated by 30°. The fourth and weakest color, yellow, is separated from two of the other colors, in this case cyan and magenta, by only 15°. When all four color screens are combined, a contone color image simulation is produced. Note the rosette pattern which results when the four screens are in perfect registration.

▼ *Figure 3.11 Moiré Pattern Generation*
When two or more overlapping screens are printed out of registration, repeating geometric patterns known as moiré patterns can result. Printing each screened color at a different and optimum angle helps reduce the occurrence of moiré patterns. It is the repeating pattern of halftone dots which makes conventional screening technology prone to the development of moiré patterns. The use of frequency modulation screening technology, where image dots are more randomly placed, can mitigate this problem of moiré pattern development.

▼ Figure 3.12 Dot Technologies

These are two different dot manipulation methods for generating tonal values from patterns of dots, AM and FM screening. Here we see magnified views of a tint or screen of one tonal value produced by both methods. On the left is a magnified view of the pattern of equally spaced halftone dots which is characteristic of AM screening technology. On the right is a magnified view of a tint generated by randomly spaced dots used in FM screening technology.

relationships between spots, halftone dots, line screen, and shades of gray. Also see Appendix C for more information on the relationship between line screen, spots per inch, and the number of shades of gray which can be reproduced.

Color contones

Meeting the additional challenge of reproducing color as well as tonal variation is accomplished through the use of four overlapping halftone screen patterns. Figure 3.10 shows how a pattern of four overlapping halftone patterns, which have the four process colors, CMYK, applied to them, is used to create a halftone simulation of a continuous tone color image. The enlarged view shows four overlapping patterns of halftone dots, each with a separate process color applied to it. Halftone dots can form various shapes–some are round, others are square, elliptical, or even diamond shaped. The halftone dots shown in Fig 3.12 are round dots.

This process of creating halftone dots was traditionally accomplished by taking a high-contrast photograph of a contone image (another photograph) which was covered with a special photographic screen. The resultant high-contrast image would contain a pattern of dots, called a halftone screen, which had dots varying in size to correspond to the grayscale value of that portion of the underlying image from which that dot was created. In a PostScript-based electronic publishing system, this screening process is performed by the PostScript RIP. Until a digital contone is actually processed by a RIP, the image information retains grayscale values.

Screening angles

Overlapping patterns of halftone dots are usually printed at varying angles from each other. When contone color images are printed with the process colors cyan, magenta, yellow, and black, each color is printed at a different angle to help prevent the pattern of dots from interfering with each other. The conventional angles used for printing the four process colors are: 90° for yellow, 75° for magenta, 45° for black, and 15° for cyan. These angles provide the maximum angular distance between each color, which should minimize the geometric interference between them when they overlap during the printing process. This scheme of separating the angles at which colors are printed helps dramatically, but it is not perfect.

If one or more of the screen patterns is misaligned during the imaging or printing process, the screen patterns can interfere with each other. When this interference pattern occurs, it forms a repeating

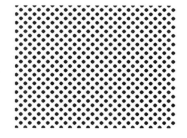

▼ Figure 3.13 Halftone Tint
Above is a magnified view of a tint or screen produced by conventional AM screening technology, which employs equally spaced halftone dots. Note the regularity of the dot pattern. Creation of tonal variations is accomplished by varying dot size. AM screening is prone to the development of moiré patterns due to the regularity of the dot spacing.

▼ Figure 3.14 Stochastic Tint
Above is a magnified view of a tint or screen produced by stochastic or FM screening technology, which employs randomly spaced dots. Note the irregularity of dot patterns. In FM screening technology, dots are randomly placed within an area. Creation of tonal variations are accomplished by varying the density of the dots rather than their sizes. FM screening technology is less prone to moiré creation.

pattern of dot groups called a moiré pattern. Figure 3.11 shows a moiré pattern and how it can be produced by two misaligned screens. Moiré patterns tend to be more obvious in lighter areas of an image such as yellows and tans than in darker areas such as browns and dark greens. This is because the misaligned dots forming the repeating pattern tend to be closer together and in some areas form darker sections of the patterns which will be more obvious when applied to more lightly colored areas. Over the years, there have been numerous attempts to decrease the occurrence of moiré patterns by developing more sophisticated screening algorithms. Screening technologies such as rational and irrational screening, Adobe Accurate Screens, Linotronic HQS, and Agfa's balanced screening technologies use custom screen angles to improve upon the quality of halftoned images and reduce the occurrence and impact of moiré patterns. All these technologies, however, use equally spaced halftone dots. Because of the regularity of their placement, they will always be prone to moiré formation.

Conventional screening

Conventional screening refers to the use of regularly spaced halftone dots. The key term here is "regularly spaced." In conventional screening, we vary the size or amplitude of equally spaced halftone dots to simulate various shades of gray. Technically, this is called amplitude modulation, or AM screening, because we are varying the size or amplitude of the dots to affect our creation of tonal value reproduction. In AM screening technology, the center of each dot is equidistant from all surrounding dots. AM screening works similar to AM radio. With AM radio, we are varying the amplitude or size of the radio wave to change a channel. In the case of AM screening, we are varying the size of the halftone dot to change the simulated tonal value. As mentioned above, this regular spacing of halftone dots has some inherent problems of moiré pattern development, which are difficult to completely overcome. We are not, however, limited to amplitude modulation for accomplishing our tone reproduction.

Stochastic screening

Stochastic screening, also known as FM or frequency modulated screening, uses *irregularly* or *randomly* spaced dot patterns. With FM screening, we vary the *placement* rather than the size of the dots to create tonal variations. Light tonal areas of an image will have widely spaced dots, while darker tonal areas will have more closely spaced dots. One of the several advantages of FM screening is the elimination of moiré patterns created when you have misalignment of two or

▼ Figure 3.15 Gradations
Above are two gradations.
The one on the left is generated with conventional AM
halftone dots, where the dot
size is varied to create the
changing tonal values across
the gradation. The gradation
on the right was produced
with FM screening. Note how
the dot density rather than
the dot size increases from
top to bottom.

more regularly spaced dot patterns. We also find that FM screening
provides smoother gradations from one tonal value to another. FM
screening also requires less image information and therefore lower
resolution images as well as smaller file sizes to produce a quality
equivalent to that of a conventionally halftoned screened image.
Because of these advantages, many of the newer desktop printers use
this new FM screening. I predict that FM or stochastic screening will
largely replace conventional screening as the standard screening
method for the reproduction of tonal values. Figures 3.13 and 3.14
show comparisons of AM and FM screening technologies.

Dot Gain of Screened Images

Any tonal image which is reproduced as a pattern of dots will be
affected by a phenomena known as dot gain. Dot gain is the tendency for dots to grow in size when they are reproduced on a printing
press. Dots of ink grow in size when printed on paper for much the
same reason that a drop of colored water will expand when dripped
onto a paper towel. The printing ink, like the colored water, is
absorbed into the paper and spreads out as it does so. In addition,
since the dots of ink are being pressed onto the page by the press, they
tend to spread out. Some dot gain can occur during the plate making
process, but most of it occurs during the application of the ink onto
the page.

Dot gain values and variables

Dot gain values are expressed in percentages and are usually measured at the 50% dot. The 50% dot is used because 50% is generally
the point of maximum dot gain, with dot gain values generally
decreasing toward the highlight and shadow regions of an image. Dot
gain percentage varies with the kind of paper on which you print.
Coated papers generally exhibit smaller dot gain values than uncoated papers. Coated stock dot gain values will typically vary from 10%
to 20%, while uncoated stocks will exhibit dot gain percentages varying between 20% and 30%. Some newspaper stocks exhibit even higher dot gain values.

Variables which affect dot gain characteristics include: paper stock,
ink characteristics, press setup, screening technology, screen frequency, and paper moisture. Dot gain values often vary with different types
of ink, and may even vary within a set of inks. For example, each of
the four process colors (CMYK) exhibit slightly different dot gain
characteristics. Dot gain tends to be greater with FM screened images

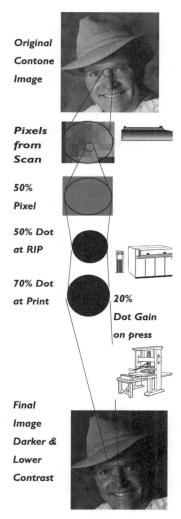

Original Contone Image

Pixels from Scan

50% Pixel

50% Dot at RIP

70% Dot at Print

20% Dot Gain on press

Final Image Darker & Lower Contrast

▼ *Figure 3.16 Effects of Dot Gain*
This sequence shows what happens to contone image data as it is scanned, RIPed, and printed. Dot gain occurs during printing. Here, a 20% dot creates a final image that is darker and lower in contrast than the original.

than with AM screened images due to the larger surface area-to-volume ratio characteristic of the FM screen's smaller dots (Fig. 5.15). With AM screening technologies, higher screen frequencies also tend to create larger dot gain functions than lower screen frequencies, again due to the smaller dots used. Consult your printer to discuss what dot gain characteristics you can expect with the paper stock, screening, and printing setup to be used with your images.

Controlling dot gain

Otherwise high-quality images can be ruined when affected by dot gain. Images which are not dot gain corrected tend to look dark and have lower contrast than they should. Midtones, in particular, tend to look dark due to the high dot gain characteristics at 50%. A 20% dot gain at 50% will push midtone values up around 70%, thereby darkening the entire image. Figure 3.16 shows the progressive changes a contone image experiences as it proceeds through a digital production process, where dot gain occurs, and the effect dot gain can have on an image. If you are creating your own final, high-resolution images, you should always adjust for dot gain to help assure that your images look good when they are reproduced on press.

Grayscale contones

There is no automatic method in Photoshop of applying a dot gain correction to a grayscale contone. There are two easy ways to adjust for dot gain, however. The first method, making a gamma curve adjustment in the Curves dialog box, permanently alters the image. The adjustment is easy. Obtain the 50% dot gain figure from your printing company, open the Curves dialog box, then click on the middle of the gamma curve at the 50% mark and pull it down to the 30% mark. Use the In/Out reading at the bottom of the dialog box to help you place the new point. Figure 3.17 shows how a 20% dot gain adjustment would look in the Curves dialog box. Note how this gamma curve adjustment results in a maximum dot gain compensation at 50% with gradually decreasing values toward the highlight and shadow ends of the curve. The advantage of making a dot gain adjustment with the Curves tool is twofold. First, you see the results of the adjustment on screen, and second, nothing else has to be done to the image for the dot gain adjustment to be applied. The disadvantage of the Curves-adjusted dot gain control is that the change is permanent and specific to that print job. If you use a Curve adjustment to compensate for dot gain, you may want to save a copy of the image before you apply the Curve adjustment. It is also a good idea to label the two images differently so you can easily distinguish between them. I add a

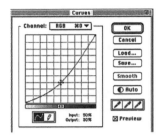

▼ *Figure 3.17 Curves Dialog Box*

Dot gain on a grayscale contone image can be adjusted using the Curves dialog box in Photoshop. Here is a correction for a 20% dot gain at 50%. The midtone point is depressed to 30%. On press, this will return to 50%, rendering the image in its proper tones. The percentage of dot gain adjustment decreases toward the highlight and shadow ends of the tone curve.

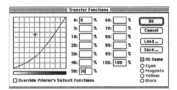

▼ *Figure 3.18 Transfer Functions*

Transfer Functions in Photoshop can help adjust for dot gain on a grayscale contone image. Here is a correction for a 20% dot gain at 50%. The midtone point is again depressed to 30%. On press, this will return to 50%, rendering proper tones. The percentage of dot gain adjustment decreases toward the highlight and shadow ends of the tone curve.

w/C onto my images to indicate they are saved with a Curve correction. For example, an original image may be named Portrait CMYK 200.tif and the Curves adjusted image would be named Portrait w/C CMYK 200.tif.

If you intend to multi-purpose an image (use it for several different purposes), you may want to utilize a second alternative for applying a dot gain correction: Transfer Function. To create a Transfer Function in Photoshop, choose Page Setup from the File menu, then click on the Transfer button in the lower left portion of the dialog box. Tab through the grayscale percentage data areas until you reach the 50% box. Enter the dot gain value, 20%, in the 50% box, and a gamma curve identical to the one you created in the Curves dialog box will be created. Save this Transfer Function. The next step is to save your image as an EPS file along with the transfer curve you just created. You will notice that your image will not be altered on screen. The Transfer Function will be applied only when the image is RIPed. (Refer to Figure 3.18 to see an example of the creation of a Transfer Function curve in Photoshop.)

Again, the advantage of using a Transfer Function is that the curve is applied only when the image is RIPed, and does not alter the original image. Another advantage to using a Transfer Function is that if you have more specific dot gain data which you need to apply to percentages other than 50%, it is easier to create these custom curves as Transfer Functions due to the tab-through nature of the Transfer Function dialog box. If you will be printing your image on several different printing devices, such as a desktop printer for proofing, a banner printer for making a poster, and then finally on an offset press, you can apply a different Transfer Function curve for each printer and never alter the original image.

Color contones

The control for dot gain of a color image can take place as early as during the scan of the image, and this may be desirable if an image is only going to press and will be printed only once on a particular paper stock and on a specific press. However, in the age of multi-purposing of images, it is better to adjust for dot gain later in the production process, either when the image is converted from RGB to CMYK, or through the use of a transfer curve when going to press. Photoshop allows you to adjust for dot gain when you convert an image from RGB mode into CMYK mode. Prior to the mode conversion, you can assign a dot gain value in the Printing Inks Setup dialog box, which will then be applied to the image when it is converted from RGB to CMYK.

With color contones, as with grayscale contones, the advantages of using a transfer curve is that the curve is only applied when the image is RIPed; it does not alter the original image; and custom curves are easier to construct. Images that utilize transfer curves must be saved in EPS format out of Photoshop in a fashion similar to how we saved the grayscale images in the previous section.

A final word about file sizes

There are three variables which affect the file size of an image: the dimension of the image (e.g., 5" x 7", 8" x 10", etc.), the image resolution (e.g., 300 dpi, 600 dpi, etc.), and the pixel depth of the image (e.g., 1, 8, 24, or 32 bits/pixel). An increase in any of these variables will increase the file size of an image and therefore the requirements for processing that image. As an image's file size increases, so does its RAM requirements for opening the image, storage space for storing the image, CPU time for processing the image, and most importantly, the RIP time to print the image. In most cases, the size and pixel depth of an image are determined by the design of the document, and are therefore preset. The one variable that we can control to reduce the overhead which any image imposes without adversely affecting the quality of the image is to keep its resolution as low as possible. Chapter 2 has more information on the relationship between resolution and screening technology.

A final resolution

Given the various resolutions and kinds of image components that we need to separate, it is helpful to understand and use the correct terminology. For image capture and viewing, scanning, digital photography image capture, and monitor viewing, we should speak of resolution in terms or pixels/in or pixels/mm. For printing to a laser printer or imagesetter, we should use two terms: *dpi* and *lpi*. The building blocks of all images will be dots per inch(dpi)*. When describing the reproduction of contone images, we will use the terms *lines per inch (lpi)* or halftone dots per inch (hdpi), knowing that halftone dots are constructed from grids of image dots or spots.

* Note: Some prefer the use of the word *spot* to *dot*. Using the terms *spot* and *spots per inch* (spi) instead of *dot* and *dots per inch* (dpi) is desirable for a number of reasons. If we use *spot* instead of *dot*, it makes the difference between spots and halftone dots less ambiguous. However, the terminology *dpi* is so ingrained in our industry that it might prove more difficult and confusing to try and substitute the word *spot* for *dot* in our lexicon. As an alternative, I suggest that we can

accomplish our communication goals if we clearly distinguish between dots per inch (dpi) and halftone dots per inch (hdpi). We will also need to recognize that *hdpi* and *lpi* (another ingrained term) are equivalent terms.

Note: Remember that the resolution requirements for output depend upon the amount of scaling that needs to be performed, the RIP being used for printing, the screening technology, and the intended viewing distance. Be sure to have a complete understanding of how an image will be used prior to scanning it.

PAULINE'S SCAN TIPS

File Prep Hint # 3-1

If you are ultimately going to print your scanned image it will be processed through a RIP (raster image processor). It is imperative to know the RIP that will be used so that you may choose the proper file format and printer driver for printing your image. The most common type of printer which we use in electronic publishing is a PostScript printer. TIFF and EPS file formats are the two most common formats to use with PostScript RIPs.

File Prep Hint # 3-2

When you print your scanned image, it will be converted into a pattern of spots and dots. There are two basic types of screen technologies: AM and FM, which may be used to reproduce your image. Be sure to properly adjust your images for the output device on that you will print your images. Know the screening technology that will be used to output your images. Different screening technologies require different resolutions. The output resolution at which you print should control the input resolution at which you scan. The objective is to provide enough image resolution to print a high-quality image, but not too much so that the RIPing process is impeded.

File Prep Hint # 3-3

Be sure that dot gain adjustment is applied to your images prior to final output to prevent your images from printing too dark. For color images, dot gain should generally be adjusted during the RGB-to-CMYK conversion. Dot gain adjustment can be applied during the scan. But if you are multi-purposing your images, it is probably best to apply dot gain adjustment after the scan either in an image editing application such as Photoshop or during the RIPing process.

4
Scanning Tools

As the Byte Turns continues…

Will Danny D'Ziner and Pauline E. Prepress be able Resolve their differences, or will they be PICTed apart.

Resolution is KING! Give me the scanner with the highest resolution, and I can scan the world!

Oh Boy! HELP!

Hey! Who put too much testosterone in Danny's breakfast drink??? I'll never be able to print his 10,000ppi scans!!

SCANNING SYSTEM REQUIREMENTS

To effectively engage in scanning as a production process, one must have the proper tools. There are as many different specific scan system requirements as there are people who scan. Some may only scan 10 images per week for the Web, while others may scan 1,000 images per week for offset printing at 200 lpi. But even given this variability, there are some tools which are common to all users, and there are ways of planning and configuring your scanning system for your specific needs. What follows is an overview of some scanning system hardware and software suggestions you may want to consider when designing, upgrading, and/or purchasing a scanning system.

Scanner Choices

In the early days of desktop publishing, there were basically two choices of scanners: excellent and poor. The excellent scanners were represented by Photo Multiplier Tube (PMT) drum scanners, which provided very sophisticated controls, produced the highest quality professional results, worked quickly, handled a wide variety of image sizes, and cost a minimum of $100,000. On the other end were the early-version Charge Couple Device (CCD) flatbed desktop scanners, which had few if any controls, produced poor-quality images, were slow, only handled small images, but were relatively inexpensive ($250–$1,500). Today there is a mind-boggling array of scanners for every need of quality, control, speed, and price.

There are three basic types of graphics scanners available today: PMT drum , CCD multi-purpose flatbed, and CCD dedicated film scanners. Here are some of the characteristics you may want to consider and a review of the capabilities and uses for these various scanners.

▼ Figure 4.1 PMT Drum Scanner
Drum scanners still are the highest quality scanners. These scanners have the highest dynamic range, the best software control, and are also the most expensive. The top end of the CCD scanners are challenging the PMT drum scanners, however, and usually at a significantly lower price.

Photo Multiplier Tube (PMT) drum scanner
The PMT drum scanners (Fig 4.1) traditionally have been, and continue to represent, the highest quality end of the scanning spectrum. Here is a list of the characteristics of a typical PMT drum scanner:

Capture element: PMT (Photo Multiplier Tube)

Software control: Superior

Dynamic range (Dmax): Highest Dmax = 3.9-4.0

Image type: Reflective, transmissive (positive and negative)

Image sizes: Wide range, typically up to 11" x 14"

Optical resolution: High, 4000–8000ppi

Speed: Fast

Cost: $40,000–$100,000

Plus: Excellent quality, very flexible

Minus: Expensive and big

▼ *Figure 4.2 Multi-Purpose*
Multi-purpose CCD flatbed scanners run the gamut from poor to excellent. At the high end of quality, today's CCD scanners rival the capabilities of the PMT drum scanners. When picking a scanner, be sure to look carefully at critical issues such as scan software, Dmax, and optical resolution.

Charge Couple Device (CCD) multi-purpose flatbed scanners

Multi-purpose flatbed CCD (Fig 4.2) scanners are the most common type of scanner available today. There is a wide range of quality, capability, and price in this arena. The high-quality end of the CCD market has scanners that rival the PMT scanners for quality and capabilities.

Capture element: CCD (Charge Couple Device)

Software control: Poor to excellent

Dynamic range (Dmax): Low to excellent Dmax = 2.5–3.9

Image type: Reflective and transmissive (positive and negative)

Image sizes: Wide range, typically up to 11" x 14"

Optical resolution: Low to high, 600–6000ppi

Speed: Slow to fast

Cost: $159–$50,000

Plus: Can be excellent quality, very flexible, affordable

Minus: May be very low quality. Buyer beware: There are lots of poorly performing scanners in this arena. Software quality is uneven, so look carefully. Usually, they are not the best choice for enlarging small transparencies.

Charge Couple Device (CCD) dedicated film scanners

Dedicated CCD film scanners (Fig 4.3) are designed specifically for scanning film. There are no glass-image boundaries to interfere with the light path. These scanners have a fairly wide range of quality, although most tend to be at least good if not excellent.

Capture element: CCD (Charge Couple Device)

Software control: Poor to excellent

Dynamic range (Dmax): Intermediate to excellent Dmax = 3.0-3.6

▼ Figure 4.3 CCD Dedicated Film Scanner
Dedicated film scanners often give you superior results for the money when scanning transparencies, but they lack the flexibility of the more versatile multi-purpose flatbed scanners.

Image type: Transmissive only (positive and negative)

Image sizes: Wide range, typically up to 11" x 14"

Optical resolution: Moderate to high, 1200–8000ppi

Speed: Typical, moderate to fast

Cost: $1,200–$10,000

Plus: Can be of excellent quality, and affordable

Minus: Not very flexible; dedicated to film work. Software quality is again uneven in this category, so look carefully. Usually, a good choice for scanning and enlarging (depending upon the optical resolution) small transparencies.

Things to Look for in a Scanner

Software is # 1 issue

Software should provide flexible and easy-to-use tools for:

Color space conversion choices (RGB, Lab, CMYK); cropping; preview with rapid magnification; histogram/levels control for tone compression; intensitometer and RGB channels control for scanner neutralization/color cast correction; curve control for image neutralization/color cast correction and image lightness and contrast adjustment; unsharp masking tool with control of Amount, Radius, and Threshold for controlling image sharpness/focus; descreening (should have lpi-specific settings); rotation, gang and batch scanning, the ability to create, save, and load settings such as curves and color cast correction values; and support of ICC calibration profiles.

Hardware issues and recommendations

1) Dynamic range (Dmax): Minimum Dmax value = 3.2

2) Pixel depth: Minimum of 12 bits/pixel, 36 bits/image

3) Speed: 1 pass

4) Optical resolution: At least 1200ppi; 4000–8000ppi if you intend to significantly enlarge images

Automated scanning functions

• Saving/loading capabilities for specific scan settings

- Gang scanning: Scanning two or more photos with the same settings
- Batch scanning: Scanning two or more images with separate settings
- Automatic color space conversions to CIELab and CMYK for either flexible or device-specific scanning
- Ability to apply ICC color profiles

SYSTEM/STATION RECOMMENDATIONS

CPU
Macintosh: Power Macintosh 200 MHz or higher

Windows: Pentium II (or higher)-compatible CPU, Pentium with MMX preferred, 200 MHz or higher

Memory
64MB bare minimum, 128MB or more preferred

RAM requirement formula: Scan file size x 3 + 50MB

Example for 70MB scan files: 60MB x 3 = 50MB = 260MB

Video display
Macintosh: Color monitor with 24-bit (millions of colors) video

Windows: VGA minimum, 800 x 600, Super VGA preferred (high color, 16-bit or higher)

CD-ROM drive
Usually required for installation

Hard drive space
1GB minimum, 5GB+ preferred

Hard drive space formula: OS + applications + active file size x 3

Example OS (100MB) + applications (1GB) + active files (3GB) x 3 = 12.3GB

Operating system
Macintosh: System 8.0 or later

Windows: Windows 95, 98, or NT 4.0 or later

Interface
Macintosh: Plug-in or Twain

Windows: Twain

SOFTWARE OVERVIEW

One of the most important aspects of your scanning system is the software that controls your scanner. This software allows you to take advantage of the scanner's features and capabilities. Using flexible, sophisticated scanning software is key to creating high-quality scanned images. This section contains an overview of some of the fundamental scanning software controls you should have. See Fig 4.4 for an example of some of these controls.

▼ *Figure 4.4 Scanner Control Software*

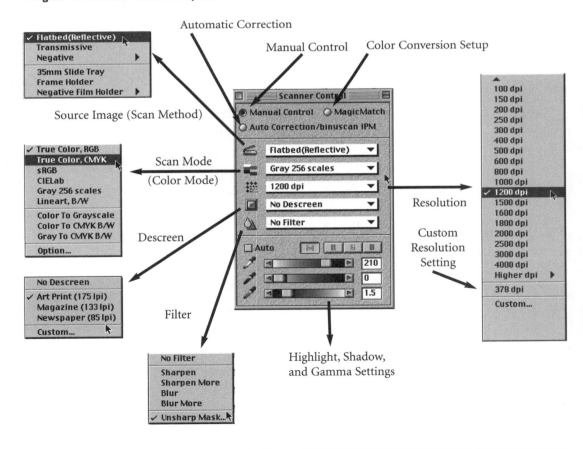

▼ Figure 4.5 Acquire Menu
Scanners can be acquired though plug-ins or Twains.

Plug-in and Twain

It is important first to point out that while many people scan *through* Photoshop or other image editing software, it is not the image editing software, but the scanner driver software, that controls the scanner. Scanning software can be loaded, launched, and used as a stand-alone piece of software, or used as a plug-in (Mac) or Twain (Mac and Windows) to your image editing software. The advantage of using your scanning software as a plug-in or Twain module through Photoshop or other image editing applications is that once you complete the scanning process with your scanning software, your image will automatically be opened in your image editing application for viewing or editing. In either case, the scanning software has the same capabilities. Plug-in and/or Twain access to the scanner through Photoshop is usually made through the File – Import menu and sub menu in Photoshop (see Fig 4.5).

Fundamental Scanning Controls Needed

Scanner mode control

Good-quality scanning software will provide you with the ability to both control your image manually and take advantage of various automated scan functions (see Fig 4.4).

Mode method selection

You should have the ability to select various scan and conversion modes. Typical scan modes include B&W, grayscale, and RGB color. Typical conversion modes should include conversion to CMYK and CIELab (see Fig 4.4). If you intend to use the conversion mode capabilities of your scanner, be sure that the scanning software supports the use of ICC color profiles (more on ICC color profiles and color space conversion in Chapter 11).

Scaling control

Particularly for contone images, you need to be able to control the scaling of an image during the scan (see Fig 4.6).

Resolution control

Resolution control is critical and should be performed during the scan. Scanning and scaling controls should be linked so that if you designate a scaling percentage, the scanning software will

▼ *Figure 4.6 Image Preview Window*

Scaling Controls

Selection Frame

Multiple Selection Frame

Selection Rotation

View Zoom

View Move

Highlight Eye Dropper

Shadow Eye Dropper

Flip/Rotate Controls

Invert

Image Enhancement

Preview, Scan, Proof, and Quit Buttons

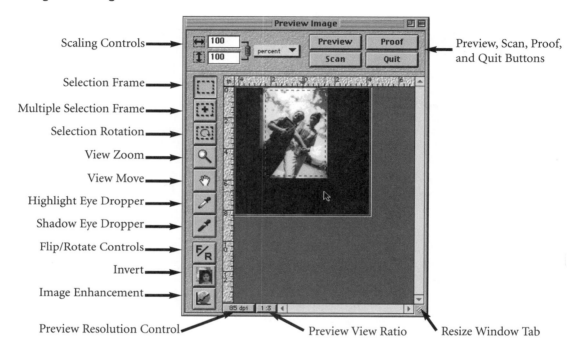

Preview Resolution Control

Preview View Ratio

Resize Window Tab

▼ *Figure 4.7 Image Info Tool*

automatically adjust for the proper resolution, and vice versa (see Fig 4.4)

Image correction tools

Fundamental image correction tools such as descreening (used when scanning previously screened or printed images) and unsharp mask (used to correct the softening which occurs during the scanning process) are two key image correction features you should look for (see Fig 4.4).

Multi-scan frame selection

Control over your preview selection frames is very useful. You should be able to make new selection frames, delete, duplicate, rename, and get completely separate scan setup information on any selection.

Image information tool

The image Info tool (Fig 4.7) allows you to obtain numeric information about the grayscale values of various portions of an image. This is one of the key tools we use when measuring and adjusting highlights, shadows, linearization, and neutralization. The Info window seen in Fig 4.7 displays a variety of handy information about the image in the preview window. It displays the RGB grayscale values of the portion of the image directly beneath the cursor. It also shows the x/y coordinates of the cursor on the preview image, the scaling which has been set to take place during the final scan, any rotation which has been assigned, and at the bottom, the size of the final scan and the amount of space available on the target storage drive. The image Info tool is often used in conjunction with other tools.

Preview window and controls

Good-quality scanning software will provide you with a high-quality preview as well as flexibility in manipulating that preview. The resolution-adjustable preview window seen in Fig 4.6 is where a scalable and movable preview of an image appears after a preview scan is completed. This preview image should be used to set up critical scanning functions for the second/final scan, which is done after you complete your preview scan, including: image selection, scaling, rotation, setting highlight and shadow points, flip/rotation, positive/negative control, image brightness and contrast, and color correction.

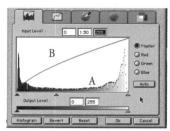

Editable Histogram and
Gamma Curve

C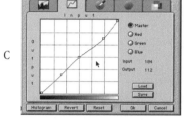

Curve Tool

D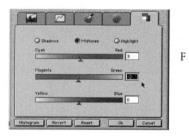

HSL Eye Dropper Tool

E

HSL Adjustment Tool

F

Color Cast Adjustment Tool

▼ *Figure 4.8 Image Enhancement Tool Windows*

Duplicate
Save
Get Info
Delete

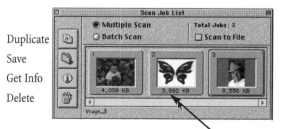

G

▼ *Figure 4.9 Scan Job List Window*

File Size of image

Interactive Help menu

A good Help menu will provide you with basic information about how to use specific features of your scanner and software.

Keyboard shortcut control

One key to working quickly with any tool, including your scanning software, is the ability to quickly access and control your scanner through the keyboard. Important keyboard control functions should include: zooming and panning, tools access, palette access, and access to and through dialog boxes such as those used to set resolution and scaling.

Editable histogram (A)

An editable histogram is a key tool for evaluating and adjusting grayscale values in an image. The histogram shows a graphical display of the frequency and distribution of any selection's grayscale data. Highlight data is on the right end of the chart; shadow data is on the left. All the data in between these two endpoints are represented by the peaks and valleys seen in the graph. The editable histogram seen in Fig 4.8 gives us the the ability to adjust both input and output highlight and shadow values.

Gamma Curve (B)

The *Gamma Curve* tool can be used to adjust your scanner's overall response to the capture of grayscale, and can therefore be used to calibrate your scanner. Seen in Fig 4.8, the Gamma Curve tool is contained within the editable histogram window.

Curve tool (C)

The *Curve tool* (Fig 4.8) is commonly used to control overall distribution of grayscale within an image, and can therefore be used to adjust image brightness and contrast. The Curve tool controls the relationship of grayscale input values to grayscale output values. Input values are along the horizontal axis, while output values are along the vertical axis. The Curve tool can also be used to make adjustments to specific portions of images, and to make color adjustments to images.

HSL tool (D)

The *HSL Eye Dropper tool* allows you to capture hue, saturation, and lightness (HSL) data from images (see Fig 4.8).

HSL Adjustment tool (E)

The *HSL Adjustment tool* allows you to make whole image color cast adjustments (see Fig 4.8).

Color cast adjustment tool (F)

Use the *Color Cast Adjustment tool* to help remove color cast when calibrating your scanner. The RGB values can be adjusted in various portions of the grayscale spectrum (see Fig 4.8).

Scan Job List window (G)

The *Scan Job List* window (Fig 4.9) is used to display a thumbnail view of the selected images to be scanned. Any rotation applied should be shown in these thumbnail images. This is also usually the window in which you can set up multiple scans. Multiple scans allow you to save time by scanning more than one image or view during any particular scanning event. If you prefer, your scanning software can scan your images to disk rather than having them open after the scan (see the *Scan to File* Check box in Fig 4.9).

The Best Quality Images

We strongly recommend that you take the time to thoroughly review your scanning software manual to gain a full understanding of your scanner's and software's capabilities and procedures. Remember that the best quality images are obtained by performing most of the image correction functions during the scan rather than waiting to perform those functions in Photoshop after the scan.

PAULINE'S SCAN TIPS

Scan Tip # 4-1

If you intend to only scan line art, then a relatively low-quality scanner will probably suit your needs. But if you need to capture contone images, then a more capable scanner will be required.

Scan Tip # 4-2

Dynamic range and capture bit depth are important hardware characteristics of your scanner which contribute to the quality of the images captured. You will need a Dmax of at least 3.2 to capture good shadow detail. A minimum of 12 bits/pixel (36 bits/image) is recommended for capture bit depth.

Scan Tip # 4-3

Dedicated film scanners tend to produce better results for film scanning than multi-purpose flatbed scanners. Flatbed scanners tend to produce better results on larger format ($\geq$ 21/4" x 21/4") film than they do on 35mm films.

Scan Tip # 4-4

High-quality software is a must if you intend to create high-quality scanned images. The best hardware scanner in the world is of limited use if you do not have good-quality software to control it. You should have the following minimum tool capabilities: crop, scale, preview scan and good preview view, resolution, mode selection, Info tool, Gamma Curve tool, editable histogram, Curve tool, and color cast correction. Other desirable tools include: multi-image scan, descreen, unsharp mask, gamut conversion, and save and load settings.

PART I REVIEW

Visualize the Scan

When choosing a scan mode, try to visualize how the scanner will "see" or capture the image. Imagine the building blocks that will be used by the various scan modes to re-create your image. The scan and print production processes tend to lower the quality of images. Our goal is to minimize image quality degradation while maximizing our editing and output flexibility. Visualization will help you choose the proper scan mode with which to capture an image.

Match your Scanner to your Needs

Good software is the key to controlling your scanner. Dynamic range, specifically your scanner's Dmax, is a key hardware characteristic to look for. The Dmax of the scanner, which should be ≥3.2, will determine how much shadow detail it can capture. Other hardware characteristics to look for include high optical resolution (for scaling) and a high capture bit depth (12 bits/pixel minimum).

Let your Scanner do the Work

Calibration: Makes sure your scanner is linear and neutral before beginning your scan. Scan a multi-step grayscale target with a known grayscale value and correct the scanner to match the target.

Mode selection: Controls basic type of image created: B&W (1-bit), grayscale (8-bit), color (24-bit), etc.

Crop & size: Determines physical size and boundaries of an image.

Tone compression: Controls placement of highlight and shadow points. I like to use a histogram to set highlight and shadow because I can see where the data begins and ends. Remember, avoid using specular highlights, or pure white regions of the image which have no grayscale value.

Gray map adjustment: Controls overall image brightness and contrast. I use curve controls here, rather than overall brightness and contrast controls, to protect the highlight and shadow point assignments made in the previous tone compression step.

Color cast removal: Removes unwanted color cast, through neutralization, from the scanner and/or image. I use separate color cast correction tools to adjust for the scanner and image. I scan a grayscale target to neutralize my scanner. I then look for neutral areas in my images to neutralize, or color correct, my images. My favorite tool for color correction is the Curve tool, which I adjust with the guidance of a densitometer.

Sharpening: Returns or improves sharpness or focus of an image. Some starting values for scanning a portrait at 200ppi: Amount = 100–150, Radius = 1, Threshold = 6–8.

Resolution: Determines the number of pixels per inch (ppi) at which the scanned image will be captured. Your image's resolution should be determined by its use. If you multi-purpose your image, scan for the purpose that requires the highest resolution. This is often print. A good resolution rule of thumb to follow for standard halftone (AM screen) printing is: 1.3 x lpi x scaling factor. For FM screening, since there is no line screen in FM printing, scan at a resolution that will provide you with 125ppi after your image is scaled to full size. Images which are scanned and used at 100% have a scaling factor of one. Images whose dimensions will be doubled have a scaling factor of 2.0, etc. It is best for contone images (photographs) to allow the scanner to perform the scaling, as it will generally do a better job than Photoshop.

Scanning for Output

Match input to output resolution

When scanning contone images, your output resolution in lpi should control the input resolution at which you scan.

Optical vs. interpolated

For consistent line art edges, scan at whole number multiples or divisions of the optical resolution of your scanner. For example, if the optical resolution is 1200 x 1200, scan at 300, 600, 1200, or 2400.

Multi-purposed images

If you intend to multi-purpose your images, scan your images into a larger, less device-specific color space, then copy and convert your images for other uses. Choose your scan resolution and image size based upon your largest format and highest resolution requirements.

Part II

Scanning
Step by Step

*CURRENT
DTP SYSTEM!*

*THE ORIGINAL
DTP SYSTEM!*

Step-By-Step Introduction

As the Byte Turns continues…

Will Danny D'Ziner and Pauline E. Prepress be able to visualize the future of their images, or be forced to pass on their scans?

This whole production process seems so complicated. Why can't I just scan my image quickly and be done with it?

Scanning used to be a craft, which people took years to learn how to do properly. Now everyone wants an automatic quick-scan, and they expect the same results as before… NOT!

The most successful scanner operators always consider how an image will be used before they scan it. Previsualizing the production process is an enormous benefit!

SCANNING FOR USE

Before You Scan

Before you ever place an image in or on your scanner, you should ask yourself a few questions. First and foremost you want to ask, "How will this image be used?" The answer to this question may have a significant impact on how you scan your images. For instance, if an image will be used strictly for commercial printing, you may decide to have the scanner perform nearly all the image correction and preparation functions, such as RGB to CMYK conversion, dot gain adjustment, and complete unsharp masking. While an image that will be multipurposed, and on which we intend to perform significant image editing in Photoshop, will probably be left in RGB mode. Wait until you finish your image editing before applying the unsharp mask and dot gain adjustments in this case.

The more we know about how an image will be used, the better the decisions we can make concerning our scanner setup and when various functions such as resizing, color conversion, dot gain adjustment, and unsharp masking will be performed.

Following is a list of some of the key questions to ask and associated issues raised about an image:

1) What is the basic nature of the image?

- Simple-intermediate line art

- Complex line art

- Grayscale (contone) image

- Color (contone) image

Key issues: Scan mode, scan resolution, pixel-to-vector conversion decision, and when scaling will take place

2) If an image is line art, what is the quality of its edge?

Key issues: Scan mode, scan resolution, and post-scan image editing techniques applied

3) Is the image original art or a printed piece?

Key issues: If the image is printed, it may need descreening

4) What is the original size and final size of the image?

Key issues: Scaling during the scan and scan resolution

5) If this image is to be printed, what is the line screen at which this

image will be printed?

Key issues: Scan resolution and sharpening settings

6) Is the image reflective or transparent media?

Key issues: Scan mode

7) If the image is transparent:

- Is it positive or negative?
- If the image is a negative, what is the film emulsion type?

Key issues: Scan mode and film emulsion adjustment selected

8) Will this image be resized after scanning? If so, how much?

Key issues: Scan resolution and how much sharpening will be applied

9) Will this image be used for multiple purposes? If so, which ones?

Key issues: Scan mode, scan resolution, color space conversion that will be required either during or after the scan, when and how much sharpening will be applied

VISUALIZE THE PROCESS

When I pick up an image to scan, I try to visualize the entire production process through which that image will be sent. This is why I ask all of the above questions. Three specific examples will serve to illustrate why this question and answer process is so important.

Example 1: Simple line art that will need to be scaled and edited, maybe many times, after the scan.

If I know that the simple piece of line art I am about to scan is to be scaled and edited after I scan the image, I am sure to make the following scan and edit decisions:

- I decide this image should be converted into vectors, rather than remain as pixels, to take advantage of vector scalability and editability.
- I will scan at the *optical resolution* of the scanner to prevent interpolation of my image's edges and assure a clean, consistent edge for conversion to a vector-based image.
- I will scan my image at 100% to eliminate any edge degradation due to interpolation during scanner-based scaling.
- I will wait until after my image is converted into vectors to scale and edit my image.

Example 2: Grayscale photo which will be printed on both a laser printer and an imagesetter.

If I know that a grayscale contone image is to be output on two or more devices:

- I will find out the largest size at which the image will be reproduced, and the line screen of the highest quality output device on which my image will be printed, in this case, the imagesetter, and use that device to determine the resolution and scaling settings for the scan.
- I will not perform dot gain correction during the scan, as this should be adjusted differently for both the laser printer and the imagesetter. This adjustment can either be made during the post scan in Photoshop or during the RIPing process.
- I will perform minimal or no sharpening during the scan, but will wait to make this adjustment on copies of the original scanned image after scaling. Plus I may want to vary the sharpening separately for the laser printer and imagesetter.
- I will save the original, device-independent grayscale image scan as an archive image for later reuse.

Example 3: Color contone image which will be multi-purposed and may be edited and/or combined with other images after the scan.

If I know that a color contone image is to be used or output on several devices and is likely to be significantly edited:

- I will capture and save the image into a large color space such as RGB or CIELab. I will not have the scanner perform the RGB to CMYK conversion. This will preserve the most color saturation and allow for a smaller file size.
- I will not perform dot gain correction during the scan as this should be adjusted for the various output devices and papers on which my image will be printed.
- I will perform minimal or no unsharp masking during the scan so that I will have the greatest variety of grayscale values to work with during the image editing process. Plus I may want to vary the sharpening for specific output devices.
- I will find out the largest size and highest quality output device on which my image will be printed and use that device to determine the resolution and scaling settings for the scan.
- I will save the original, device-independent image scan as an archive image for later reuse.

The more I know about how an image will be used, the better scan setup and post-scan image handling and editing decisions I can make.

5
Line Art Step By Step

As the Byte Turns continues…

Will Danny D'Ziner and Pauline E. Prepress be able to Line up their images on their scanner properly, or will they get to EDGY for success?

Line art scanning is easy! Just click the line art button and GO! … Right??

Let's ask Pauline. She'll explain the details. Don't we all wish it were that simple!

Your line art edges are rough, and the vector images you create from your pixel-based line art are way too complicated!

LINE ART SCANNING

▼ Figure 5.1 Pixel vs. Vector Art
On the left is a typical pixel-based edge. The individual building block pixels can be easily seen on this angled edge. On the right is the same edge constructed from a vector. Note that the vector edge does not show the typical visual stair stepping associated with the pixel-based edge. The vector edge is not only sharper and cleaner than the pixel-based edge, but it can be scaled and rotated without loss of edge quality. It is often a good idea to convert simple and intermediate detailed pixel-based line art into vector-based images, especially if they will be scaled and/or rotated.
One of the keys to creating smooth-edged vector line art from pixel-based images is to scan at the optical resolution of your scanner. Detailed line art should remain as pixels.

What is Line Art?

Line art images are characterized by solid areas with edges. Typical examples of line art images include logos, pen and pencil drawings, and other solid, hard-edged objects. Type characters which you want to capture and edit as graphics may be considered to be, and treated as, line art. Basic digital line art images are composed of pixels with only two shades of gray (black or white) assigned to them. It is the change from black to white pixels which defines the edge and therefore the shape of line art images.

Line Art Challenges

When we are challenged with capturing and reproducing line art images, our main focus should be on the *edge* of the line art. It is the edge of a piece of line art that determines the nature and quality of a line art image. Often our emphasis is on *edge reproduction*. When we want to faithfully reproduce a line art image so that our version is as close as possible to the original, our focus is on edge reproduction. In other circumstances, we may want to alter a piece of line art from its original form with the intent of improving and/or just changing the line art. In either case, whether we are reproducing or altering a piece of line art, we will focus on the line art's edge. When scanning line art, we nearly always use the optical resolution of our scanner when capturing the line art image. Using the optical resolution of the scanner is a key factor in accurate edge reproduction. Even if we want to alter our line art edge, we usually want to start with an accurate reproduction of the original edge.

Pixels vs. vectors

One of the decisions we should make early when capturing line art is whether we want our line art images to end up as pixel-based images or as vector-based images. All of our scanned images will be initially created as pixel-based images, as this is the only form in which scanners capture images. Some line art images will work best when they are converted into vector-based images using a pixel-to-vector conversion program such as Adobe's Streamline or similar software.

Vector-based images have the advantage of sharper, cleaner edges and smaller file sizes compared to pixel-based images. In addition, vector-based line art images can be scaled, rotated, and skewed without compromising any edge quality. Plus, vector-based images can take advantage of the high resolutions of high-quality printing devices such as imagesetters. Pixel-based images have specific resolutions, such as 600ppi, and therefore print with the same edge sharpness at 600 dpi as they do at 2400 dpi. A vector-based image by contrast has no set resolution; in fact, a vector-based image is resolution-independent. The resolution of a vector-based image is not determined until it is output. Therefore, a vector-based edge output at 2400 dpi will look much sharper than one output at 300 dpi.

The primary advantage of pixel-based images is their ability to display details. So, the primary characteristic we will use to determine whether an image will be ultimately re-created as a pixel- or vector-based image is the detail in the original image. Simple line art images will often be converted into vectors to take advantage of the enhanced editing features of vectors, while high-detail images need to be captured and maintained as pixel-based images. See Fig 5.1 for a comparison of a pixel and a vector image.

Resolution requirements for line art images

Resolution requirements for line art images are generally higher than those required for contone (photographic) scanning. Line art scanning resolution ranges from 500–600ppi (for simple line art which will be converted into vectors) to 1000–1200ppi (for detailed line art which will remain as pixels). In either case, and particularly for the simple line art which will be converted into vectors, it is important to scan at the optical (sometimes called the *hardware*) resolution of the scanner or some whole number division thereof. For instance, using a scanner with an optical resolution of 1200ppi, scan at 600ppi (1/2 of the 1200ppi) for simple line art images which will be converted into vectors, and at 1200ppi for more complex line art images which will remain as pixels. Scanning at the optical resolution of the scanner results in cleaner, smoother edges which are easier to convert into high-quality vector art. In addition, scanners operate faster when they are used at their optical resolutions. All line art scan resolutions recommended in the following step-by-step tutorials are based upon an optical resolution of 1200ppi.

Following are step-by-step procedures for the capture of various kinds of line art.

Low Detail Line Art Techniques

▼ *Figure 5.2 Simple Low-Detail Line Art*

Simple line art, like this butterfly, has large areas with few details. Scanning at the optical resolution of the scanner is the key to edge consistency and clean conversion to vector line art. A scan resolution range of 500–600ppi is generally sufficient for simple line art which will be converted into vectors. If you intend to leave your line art image a pixel-based image, then scanning at a higher variation of the optical resolution of your scanner (1000–1200ppi) is recommended.

Find this image to scan in the "Practice Images" section on page 306 in the back of this book.

Simple black and white line art issues

For simple, low-detail line art, including images such as the one in Fig 5.2, our emphasis, as previously mentioned, is on *edge reproduction.* The key to good edge reproduction with low-detail line art is to scan at the optical resolution of your scanner.

Step-by-step: low-detail line art

1) First, clean your scanner bed and your image. (See the section "Scanning Environment" at the end of this chapter for more information on setting up your scanning environment.)

2) Place your simple line art image squarely on the scan bed. If you have line art with straight horizontal and/or vertical edges, it is very important that these straight edges be placed parallel to the edges of the scan bed and the scan direction. Any straight edges which are not parallel to the edges of the scan bed will be reproduced with obvious stair steps along the edges. (Note: The simple line art image in Fig 5.2 is available as a printed practice image in the section labeled "Practice Images" at the back of this book.)

3) Set scan mode to 1-bit (B&W). 1-bit mode should capture sufficient image data if you start with a well-defined, high-quality edge, and your intention is merely to reproduce the edge. If your edge quality is poor or is high-detail, see the sections on high-detail line art and low-edge quality line art.

4) Set scaling to 100%. Any necessary scaling will be done after conversion to vector line art. Scanning at 100% will provide the most accurate and consistent, and therefore smoothest, edge, which is important for conversion to vector line art with clean, smooth edges. Scaling prior to conversion to a vector will result in a roughening of the edge and lower-vector edge quality.

5) Perform a preview scan at low resolution (50–72ppi) to create a preview of the image(s) on the scan bed.

6) Crop the portion of the image you want to scan.

7) Set the final scan resolution.

7a) If you intend to convert your line art image into vectors, use a lower resolution for the final scan. Set the scanner resolution at 500-700ppi, or one-half or one-quarter of your scanner's optical resolution if its optical resolution is ≥ 1000ppi. (For instance, a UMAX PowerLook III has an optical or hardware resolution of

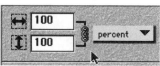

Scale percentage

Preview Resolution

▼ **Figure 5.3 Scan Setup for Simple Line Art**
Setup for vector conversion:
Mode = B&W (1-bit)
Resolution = 600ppi (for vector conversion)
Scaling = 100% (only)
Preview = 72ppi

Setup for pixel-based only:
Mode = B&W (1-bit)
Resolution = 1200ppi
Scaling = 100%
Preview = 72ppi
Remember, the actual scan resolution number will be determined by the optical resolution of your scanner. The above setup is for a scanner with an optical resolution of 1200ppi.

1200 by 2400ppi, so you would set the resolution at 600ppi.) If the optical resolution of your scanner is 1000ppi, you would choose 500ppi instead of 600ppi.

7b) If you intend to convert your line art image to remain as a pixel-based image, use a higher resolution for the final scan. Set the scanner resolution at 1000–1200ppi, depending upon your scanner's optical resolution. (For instance, a UMAX PowerLook III has an optical or hardware resolution of 1200 by 2400ppi, so you would set the resolution at 1200ppi.) If the optical resolution of your scanner is 1000ppi (or some multiple of 1000), you would choose 1000ppi instead of 1200ppi.

8) If your scanning software is set so that your image will be saved to disk instead of opened in an editing application such as Photoshop, set the image to be saved as a pixel-based TIFF. A TIFF (.tif) is a pixel-based file format which works equally well on both Mac and Windows platforms.

9) Scan the image at this higher (600ppi, in this case) resolution for the second and final scan.

10) If your image has not been scanned to disk, but rather opens in an image editing application like Photoshop, name the image Bfly GS_600.tif, and save the image as a TIFF.

11) Post-scan image conversion and editing.

11a) To edit your pixel-based image, open your image in a pixel-based image editing application such as Photoshop to modify your line art image.

11b) To convert your pixel-based line art image to a vector-based image, open the image in a pixel-to-vector conversion application such as Adobe Streamline*. This conversion allows for geometric manipulation such as scaling and rotation without degradation of edge quality, with easier editing of color assignments, and with dramatic file size reductions. See Fig 5.3 for setup examples.

12) Save the vector graphic in Adobe Illustrator EPS format.

13) You may now open your newly created vector-based image in your choice of drawing applications (Macromedia Freehand, Adobe Illustrator, or Corel Draw) to edit this image (assign colors, scale, rotate, etc.).

14) See Part III: After the Scan for more information on converting and editing low-detail, pixel-based line art images.

*Adobe Streamline is a dedicated pixel-to-vector conversion program available from Adobe in both Mac and Windows versions. And your scanner software plug-in or Twain will work fine in Streamline, so you

▼ Figure 5.4 Intermediate- and High-Detail Line Art Image

More detailed line art images like these butterflies often have thinner lines and/or smaller detail points than simple line art images (contrast these images with the simple line art image in Fig 5.2). Again, scanning at the optical resolution of the scanner is the key to edge consistency and accurate detail capture and reproduction. Two key scan variables are altered for the capture of detailed line art. For detailed line art, it is usual to scan at a higher optical resolution setting (1000–1200ppi), and at an increased capture bit depth (8 bits or higher).

Find this image to scan in the "Practice Images" section on page 306 in the back of this book.

can scan directly into Streamline! Scanning directly into Streamline allows you to bypass your pixel-based image editing application, thereby saving you production time.

Intermediate- to High-Detail Line Art

Intermediate- to high-detail line art issues

More complex line art, such as the intermediate-detail butterfly in Fig 5.4, often has thinner lines and more detail than simple line art. Most complex line art, like the high-detail butterfly in Fig 5.4, will have even more detail. This kind of detail can be difficult for a scanner to capture at a low resolution and/or if the detailed areas are close together. This added detail and fineness of line usually require a bit more resolution and greater pixel depth to capture the image accurately.

To make sure you can capture all the details possible, and to give you the ability to control the details after the scan, you should scan at a high resolution (1000–1200ppi) and capture the image in 8-bit (or higher) grayscale mode. The grayscale version of the line art image can then be controlled and edited after the scan in a pixel-based image editing application such as Photoshop.

(Note: The intermediate and detailed line art images in Fig 5.4 are available as printed practice images in the section labeled "Practice Images" at the back of this book.)

Step-by-step: intermediate to high-detail line art

1) First, clean your scanner bed and your image. (See the section "Scanning Environment" on page 168 for more information on setting up your scanning environment.)

2) Place your detailed line art image squarely on the scan bed. If you have line art with straight horizontal and/or vertical edges, it is very important that these straight edges be placed parallel to the edges of the scan bed and the scan direction. Any straight edges which are not parallel to the edges of the scan bed will be reproduced with obvious stair steps along the edges.

3) Set scan mode to 8-bit (grayscale). This additional bit depth will create a more editable edge when we open up our image in an image editing application such as Photoshop.

4) Set scaling to whatever percentage you would like (200% here). Scaling of pixel-based images is best accomplished during the scanning

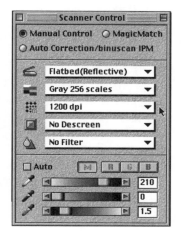

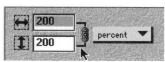

Scale Percentage

Preview Resolution 72 dpi

▼ **Figure 5.5 Scan Setup for Detailed Line Art**
Setup for pixel-based only:
Mode = Grayscale (8-bit)
Resolution = 1200ppi
Scaling = 200% (to suit)
Preview = 72ppi
Remember, the actual scan resolution number will be determined by the optical resolution of your scanner. The above setup is for a scanner with an optical resolution of 1200ppi.

process. Scan-based scaling usually results in higher quality edges.

5) Perform a preview scan at low resolution (50–72ppi) to create a preview of the image(s) on the scan bed.

6) Crop the portion of the image you want to scan.

7) Set the final scan resolution: Detailed line art images are rarely converted to vectors. To do so generally results in the loss of image detail and the creation of very complex paths which are difficult to edit and print. So, we intend our detailed line art images to remain as pixel-based images. We therefore will want to use a higher resolution than we did for our simple line art scan for our final scan. Set scanner resolution at 1000–1200ppi, depending upon your scanner's optical resolution. (For instance, a UMAX PowerLook III has an optical or hardware resolution of 1200 x 2400ppi, so you would set the resolution at 1200ppi.) If the optical resolution of your scanner is 1000ppi (or some multiple of 1000), you would choose 1000ppi instead of 1200ppi.

8) If your scanning software is set so that your image will be saved to disk instead of opened in an editing application such as Photoshop, set the image to be saved as a pixel-based TIFF. A TIFF (.tif) is a pixel-based file format which works equally well on both Mac and Windows platforms.

9) Scan the image at this higher (1200ppi, in this case) resolution for the second and final scan. See Fig 5.5 for some setup examples.

10) If your image has not been scanned to disk, but rather opens in an image editing application like Photoshop, name the image Bfly_Detail_GS_1200.tif, and save the image as a TIFF.

11) Post-scan image conversion and editing: To edit your pixel-based image, open the image in a pixel-based image editing application such as Photoshop to modify it.

12) See Part III: After the Scan for more information on editing high-detail pixel-based line art images.

▼ Figure 5.6 Low Edge Quality Line Art

Low edge quality line art has poorly defined edges. The key to being able to control images like these is to scan in 8-bit or higher mode, allowing the use of unsharp masking and thresholding to help define the details of the edges.

To obtain the sharpest quality line art edge, you will want to be sure to convert your finished images to 1-bit prior to printing.

If you intend to color your line art image, or you would like to print the image with soft edges, you can leave the image in 8-bit (or higher) mode to keep line art edges soft and editable. Find this image to scan in the "Practice Images" section on pg 307 in the back of this book.

Low-edge-quality line art issues

The term low-edge-quality line art is not a comment on the artistic quality, but rather a description of the technical quality of the edge of the line art. A low-quality edge is one which is poorly defined. While poor edge quality often occurs in poor-quality images such as faxed or copied images, it can also occur in some high-quality images such as the soft edges of the pencil drawing seen in Fig 5.6. Most poor edge quality images will remain as pixel-based graphics for editing, although sometimes, when properly scanned and edited, edge quality and consistency increases to the point where these images can be converted to vectors if that is desirable.

Step-by-step: Low-edge-quality line art

1) First, clean your scanner bed and your image. (See the section "Scanning Environment" on page 168 for more information on setting up your scanning environment.)

2) Place your detailed line art image squarely on the scan bed. If you have line art with straight horizontal and/or vertical edges, it is very important that these straight edges be placed parallel to the edges of the scan bed and the scan direction. Any straight edges which are not parallel to the edges of the scan bed will be reproduced with obvious stair steps along the edges.

(Note: The line art image in Fig 5.6 is available as a printed practice image in the section labeled "Practice Images" at the back of this book.)

3) Set scan mode to 8-bit or higher (grayscale). This additional bit depth will create a more editable edge when we open up our image in an image editing application such as Photoshop.

4) Set scaling to whatever percentage you would like (200% here). Scaling of pixel-based images is best accomplished during the scanning process. Scan-based scaling usually results in higher quality edges.

5) Perform a preview scan at low resolution (50–72ppi) to create a preview of the image(s) on the scan bed.

6) Crop the portion of the image you want to scan.

7) Set the final scan resolution:

Low-edge-quality line art images are rarely converted to vectors. To do so generally results in the loss of image detail and the creation of very complex paths which are difficult to edit and print. So, we intend our low-edge-quality line art images to remain as pixel-based images. We

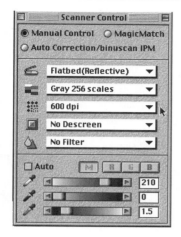

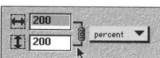

Scale Percentage

Preview Resolution

▼ Figure 5.7 Scan Setup for Low-Edge-Quality Line Art
Setup for pixel-based only:
Mode = Grayscale (8-bit)
Resolution = 600ppi
Scaling = 200% (to suit)
Preview = 72ppi
Remember, the actual scan resolution number will be determined by the optical resolution of your scanner. The above setup is for a scanner with an optical resolution of 1200ppi.

therefore will want to use a higher resolution than we did for our simple line art scan for our final scan. Set scanner resolution at 500–600ppi, depending upon your scanner's optical resolution. (For instance, a UMAX PowerLook III has an optical or hardware resolution of 1200 x 2400ppi, so you would set the resolution at 600ppi.) If the optical resolution of your scanner is 1000ppi (or some multiple of 1000), you would choose 500ppi instead of 600ppi.

Note: If your low-detail image has a large amount of recognizable detail, you may want to set the scan resolution in the 1000–1200ppi range to be sure to capture all the detail present. Through experience you will gain the judgement you need to decide whether you should choose the moderate (500–600ppi) or high-resolution (1000–1200ppi) values.

8) If your scanning software is set so that your image will be saved to disk instead of opened in an editing application such as Photoshop, set the image to be saved as a pixel-based TIFF. A TIFF (.tif) is a pixel-based file format which works equally well on both Mac and Windows platforms.

9) Scan the image at this moderate (600ppi, in this case) resolution for the second and final scan. See Fig 5.7 for sample setup values.

10) If your image has not been scanned to disk, but rather opens in an image editing application like Photoshop, name the image TheTaz_GS600.tif and save the image as a TIFF.

11) Post-scan image conversion and editing: To edit your pixel-based image, open the image in a pixel-based image editing application such as Photoshop to modify it.

12) See Part III: After the Scan for more information on editing poor-edge-quality pixel-based line art images.

▼ Figure 5.8 Colored Line Art
The key to setting up a scan for capturing colored line art is to visualize the image as the scanner will see it, as a black and white or grayscale image. Easily separated colored line art images may be scanned successfully in B&W (1-bit) mode. Sometimes, applying a threshold adjustment during the scan may help the scanner separate colored image components from a background. More complex colored line art images generally need to be scanned in 24-bit (RGB) or higher mode to allow for the creation of color channels which can be used to select and separate the various colored portions of the images.
Note: To see a colored version of this image, refer to the scan samples page in the back of this book.
Find this image to scan in the "Practice Images" section in the back of this book.

Color line art image issues

Once you have mastered the line art techniques, you will be ready to tackle colored line art images. Color images are seen by the scanner as black and white in 1-bit mode and as grayscale in any other mode. The basic goal for capturing either simple or complex colored line art is to be able to separate out the various colored portions of the image into elements that can be combined and/or edited individually later in a painting or drawing program.

For colored line art where the various colored segments are already separated from each other and the background, such as solid, colored type on a white background, you can scan in 1-bit (black and white) mode. The various text character segments can then be either colored in a painting program, or converted to vectors and edited in a drawing application. Sometimes the adjustment of the black and white threshold in 1-bit mode can help in the separation of colored line art images from their background.

For complex and/or overlapping colored line art images, or colored line art images on dark backgrounds, scanning in 24-bit (RGB) mode will generally be required. Scanning in 24-bit (RGB) mode will create three different grayscale versions of your image. Various portions of the colored line art will be most visible on different channels.

The object of our scanning exercise should be to capture our colored line art so that the various colored portions of our image can be separated and easily selected and edited. In some cases, if our line art is simple, we may want to convert our colored line art images into vectors, like we did in the previous simple line art scan exercise, prior to final editing including scaling and colorizing. More detailed line art we may want to leave and edit as pixels. In either case, the key is to separate the color image components as much as possible during the scan. The following exercise will demonstrate the use of various scan modes on a color image.

Step-by-step: colored line art

B&W (1-bit) mode with no threshold adjustment

1) First, clean your scanner bed and your image. (See the section "Scanning Environment" on page 168 for more information on setting up your scanning environment.)

2) Place your colored line art image (the multi-colored Apple logo with a black background) squarely on the scan bed. If you have line art with straight horizontal and/or vertical edges, it is very important

Scale Percentage

Preview Resolution 72 dpi

▼ *Figure 5.9 B&W Scan Setup for Colored Line Art*
Setup for pixel-based only:
Mode = B&W (1-bit)
Resolution = 600ppi
Scaling = 100%
Preview = 72ppi

▼ *Figure 5.10 B&W (1-bit scan) No Threshold*
A straight B&W (1-bit) scan of a colored line art image without any threshold adjustment may result in a totally black image as seen here. This is because the scanner sees the colored line art as well as the dark background as black .

that these straight edges be placed parallel to the edges of the scan bed and the scan direction. Any straight edges which are not parallel to the edges of the scan bed will be reproduced with obvious stair steps along the edges.

(Note: The simple line art image in Fig 5.8 is available as a printed practice image in the appendix labeled "Practice Images" at the back of this book.)

3) Set scan mode to 1-bit (B&W). 1-bit mode may capture sufficient image data if you start with a well-defined, high-quality dark colored edge on a light background, and your intention is to merely reproduce the edge. If your edge quality is poor or is high-detail, see sections on high-detail line art and low-edge-quality line art issues in this chapter.

4) Set scaling to 100%. Any necessary scaling will be done after conversion to vector line art. Scanning at 100% will provide the most accurate and consistent, and therefore smoothest, edge, which is important for conversion to vector line art with clean, smooth edges. Scaling prior to conversion to a vector will result in a roughening of the edge and lower vector edge quality.

5) Perform a preview scan at low resolution (50–72ppi) to create a preview of the image(s) on the scan bed. See Fig. 5.9 for sample setups.

Note: If the colored portions of the image are similar in grayscale value to the background color, as they are here, the scanner may not be able to distinguish the colored line art portions of the image from the background and the entire image will appear black as in Fig. 5.10. In order to continue with our image capture, we must adjust our scanner to help it distinguish the colored text characters from their black background.

B&W (1-bit) mode with B&W threshold adjustment

To help the scanner distinguish the colored line art text characters from the black background of this image, we will adjust the threshold value. Fig 5.10 shows an image with no threshold adjustment. The threshold value controls which portions of an image will be converted to black pixels and which ones to white pixels. The normal threshold value is 50% gray, which results in any image areas with grayscale values greater than 50% gray being converted to black pixels during the scan, while image areas with grayscale values less than 50% are converted to white pixels. The key here is again to visualize your image as your scanner will "see" the image. In this multi-coloredApple logo image with the black background, the colored text

Scale Percentage

Preview
Resolution 72 dpi

▼ *Figure 5.11 B&W Scan*
Setup for Colored Line Art
Setup for pixel-based only:
Mode = B&W (1-bit)
Resolution = 600ppi
Scaling = 100%
Preview = 72ppi
Threshold = 89

▼ *Figure 5.12 B&W (1-bit*
scan) With Threshold
A B&W (1-bit) scan of a colored line art image with a
threshold adjustment may
result in a clear separation of
the line art, or in a partial separation of the line art as seen
here.

characters are clearly distinguishable to our eyes because our eyes see
in color. To the scanner, which only sees in black and white, when we
set it to capture in 1-bit mode, all the colored portions of the image
are seen as dark grayscale values and are therefore captured as black
pixels. However, if we adjust the black/white threshold value so that
darker grayscale values will be converted into white pixels, this should
help the scanner "see" and separate the colored text characters from
their black background.

6) Adjust the threshold control to move the black/white threshold
point far enough into the black until the text characters begin to
be separated from the background. Continue moving the threshold value until you achieve maximum separation of the line art
text characters from the black background. The further you move
the threshold, the more separation you should achieve; but if you
move the threshold too far, the black background itself will begin
to turn white. Once the background begins to turns white, the
separation between the text characters and the background will
begin to degrade. So, move the threshold until you achieve maximum separation (here, +89), but not so far that the background
begins to turn.

Note: Each colored line art image will be different. Some will require
only minor adjustments in the threshold value until the text characters
are clearly separated from their backgrounds. Once again, the key to
understanding this process and knowing how much you will need to
adjust a threshold is being able to visualize the colored line art as
grayscale values, just like your scanner does.

6) Crop the portion of the image you want to scan.

7) Set the final scan resolution: Use 500–600ppi for low-detail-edge
images which you intend to convert into vectors. Use 1000–
1200ppi for high-detail-edge images and/or images which you
intend to keep as pixel-based. See the more detailed discussions in
the earlier sections for more information. We will use 600ppi in
this Apple logo example since these text characters have low-detail
edges. Again the key is to use the optical resolution of your scanner to achieve the best possible edge quality.

8) If your scanning software is set so that your image will be saved to
disk instead of opened in an editing application such as
Photoshop, set the image to be saved as a pixel-based TIFF. A TIFF
(.tif) is a pixel-based file format which works equally well on both
Mac and Windows platforms.

9) Scan the colored line art image with the threshold set (Fig 5.11).

10) You will notice that more of the colored line art image is visible, but

Scale Percentage

Preview Resolution

▼ *Figure 5.13 RGB Scan Setup for Colored Line Art*
Setup for pixel-based only:
Mode = RGB (24-bit)
Resolution = 600ppi
Scaling = 100%
Preview = 72ppi
Threshold = 89

Red Channel

Green Channel

Blue Channel

▼ *Figure 5.14 Colored, Separated Line Art*
The three R, G, and B versions of the above colored word. Note how various text characters are more easily recognized, on the different channels.

not all of the colored characters are readily distinguishable (Fig 5.12). The second "P" and the "L" are not well-defined. Therefore, we must make further adjustments to our scanner if we are to achieve good separation of all of our colored text characters during the scan.

Note: For many colored line art images, and particularly those colored line art images on lighter backgrounds, this threshold adjustment may be all that is required. We have chosen a particularly difficult image to separate in this case, so that you can be prepared for the worst.

RGB (24-bit) mode scan

Since even an extreme threshold adjustment in B&W (1-bit) mode was not enough to have the scanner separate the colored portions of this Apple logo format's dark background, we will need to scan in a mode which allows us more variation in the grayscale values of our text characters.

11) Set the scan mode to RGB (24-bit+) mode. The entire Apple logo with all the characters should be clearly visible in the low-resolution preview window.

12) Adjust the crop of the image if you need to.

13) If your scanning software is set so that your image will be saved to disk instead of opened in an editing application such as Photoshop, set the image to be saved as a pixel-based TIFF. A TIFF (.tif) is a pixel-based file format which works equally well on both Mac and Windows platforms.

12) Scan the image at a high resolution in RGB mode (see Fig 5.13).

Note: This will result in the creation of three 8-bit grayscale images of the Apple logo (see Fig 5.14).

13) If your image has not been scanned to disk, but rather opens in an image editing application like Photoshop, name the image AppleLogo_RGB_600.tif, and save the image as a TIFF.

14) Open this image in Photoshop or similar image editing software. You will see when you view the three RGB channels individually that various characters are more visible on each channel. See Part III: After the Scan for more information on separating and editing these colored pixel-based line art images.,

Note: With some experience, you will not need to go through all this experimentation to decide the scan mode and adjustments you need to set to capture a colored line art image. You will be able to evaluate an image by previsualizing what the scanner will be able to "see" in various scan modes.

PAULINE'S SCAN TIPS

Scan Tip # 5-1

The key issue when scanning line art is edge reproduction. Our goal is to reproduce as smooth and consistent an edge as possible.

Scan Tip # 5-2

All line art should be scanned at the optical resolution of your scanner to prevent interpolation, and therefore roughening of the line art edge. Full number division of the optical resolution, such as 1/2 the optical resolution, is acceptable as well.

Scan Tip # 5-3

Simple- to intermediate-detail line art can be scanned in 1-bit (B&W) mode, and at a resolution of 500-600ppi (depending upon the optical resolution of your scanner). Edge consistency is far more important than pixel size when capturing and reproducing low-detail line art edges.

Scan Tip # 5-4

Simple- to intermediate-detail line art images can be effectively converted into vectors to take advantage of the scalability, skewability, editability, and reduced file size of vector-based images. Scanning at the optical resolution of your scanner and controlling your vectorization program are keys to simple, smooth vector edge conversions.

PAULINE'S SCAN TIPS

Scan Tip # 5-5

Detailed black and white line art should be scanned in 8-bit+ (grayscale) mode and at a resolution in the range of 1000-1200ppi (depending upon the optical resolution of your scanner). The grayscale scan will provide you with the ability to precisely control the density of the detail in a post-scan image editing application such as Photoshop.

Scan Tip # 5-6

Be sure to convert all grayscale versions of line art images to 1-bit B&W if you want the line art edges to print crisply.

Scan Tip # 5-7

Scan colored line art in 24bit (RGB) mode. This produces three grayscale versions of your images with varying contrast, which can be used to separate the various colored line art areas after the scan.

Scan Tip # 5-8

Always work on a copy of your image, never the original. Keep the original as an untouched archive image to which you can return later. This is particularly important with detailed and/or colored line art images scanned in 8-bit grayscale and/or 24-bit color mode.

6

Step-By-Step Grayscale Photos

As the Byte Turns continues…

Will Danny D'Ziner and Pauline E. Prepress be able to capture the subtle grays of life, or will they be forced to see only in black and white?

Hey…How come my grayscale photos print so dark? What are you doing to them???

Let's ask Pauline. She can help explain the details.

Three variables are making your images print too dark. Your scanner is not calibrated, you set your highlights and shadows incorrectly, and you never compensate for dot gain…
Besides that, your images are just fine!

GRAYSCALE PHOTO (CONTONE) SCANNING

What Is a Grayscale Contone?

The term *contone* is short for continuous tone image. A contone image is one which is characterized by gradually changing grayscale values throughout the image. Photographs of people and landscapes are examples of common contone images. Grayscale contone images contain grayscale values only; that is, there are no color attributes to be found in grayscale contone images. Digital grayscale contone images are composed of pixels with various grayscale values assigned to them. It is changes in the grayscale values of these pixels that define the composition and detail of a grayscale contone image.

Grayscale Contone Challenges

When we are challenged with capturing and reproducing grayscale contone images, our main focus should be on **grayscale reproduction.** It is the grayscale values of an image that determine the composition and quality of a grayscale contone image. When we want to faithfully reproduce a grayscale contone image so that our version is as close as possible to the original, our focus is on grayscale reproduction. In other circumstances, we may want to alter a contone image from its original form with the intent of improving and/or just changing the image. In either case, whether we are reproducing or altering a grayscale contone image, we will focus on the grayscale values of the image.

One of the most common problems we see with scanned images is that they tend to reproduce too dark. But whether our images are too light, or too dark, or the contrast is poor, control of our images always boils down to control of our images' grayscale values. There are three primary factors to which we need to pay the most attention if we want to control our grayscale values: 1) scanner **calibration**, 2) setting of **highlight** and **shadow** values, and 3) controlling the distribution of grayscale data to control **contrast**.

Pixels vs. vectors

One of the decisions we should make early when capturing any image digitally is whether we want our images to end up as pixel-based images or as vector-based images. All of our scanned images will be initially created as pixel-based images, as this is the only form in which scanners capture images. Some of the simple line art images we created and discussed in the previous chapter were good candidates to be converted into vector-based images.

The primary advantage of pixel-based images is their ability to display detail. So, the primary characteristic we will use to determine whether an image will be ultimately re-created as a pixel- or vector-based image is the detail in the original image. Simple line art images will often be converted into vectors to take advantage of the enhanced editing features of vectors, while high-detail images need to be captured and maintained as pixel-based images. Grayscale contone images, which by their very nature contain a great deal of detail, will be captured as, and remain as, pixel-based images.

Resolution for scanning grayscale contone images

Resolution requirements for grayscale contone images are generally lower than those required for line art scanning. While line art scanning resolution ranges from 500–1200ppi, grayscale contone scan resolutions are usually significantly less than this, generally in the range of 200–400ppi (unless scaling is performed during the scan). Input or scan resolutions for grayscale contone images should be controlled by the output resolution at which we will print or otherwise reproduce our image and how much scaling will take place during the scan. For printing, this output resolution is typically defined as the number of halftone dots per inch, also known as line screen, or lpi (lines per inch). A good, general formula to use is: 1.5 x lpi x scaling factor. For instance, if we intend to print our image at 150 lpi and scale our image 200%, our input scan resolution should be 1.5 x 150 lpi x 2 =450ppi.

As with capturing line art, when scanning grayscale contone images, it is usually a good idea to use the optical resolution of our scanners. Using the optical resolution of the scanner is a key factor in accurate grayscale reproduction. Using the optical resolution of your scanner will also reduce the *interpolated*-related softening of the image which occurs as a result of scanning, and will noticeably decrease scan times. (See Chapter 1 for an in-depth discussion of optical resolution.)

All contone scan resolutions recommended in the following step-by-step tutorials are based upon an output print resolution of 150 lpi and an input scan optical resolution of 1200ppi. Therefore, we would round the 450ppi resolution above to 400ppi, which equals 1200ppi÷3.

GRAYSCALE CONTONE SCANNING

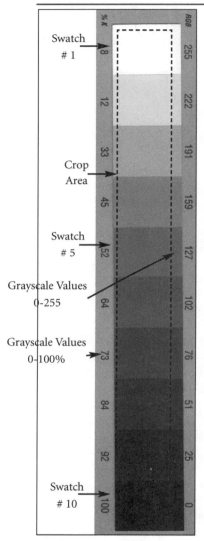

▼ Figure 6.1 Calibration Target
Use this 10-step grayscale target which comes with your scan software manual to linearize your scanner. Note that the RGB values are conveniently listed on the right side. The dashed line is the crop/selection area to be chosen.

Calibration of your Scanner

Scanner calibration issues

When challenged with capturing and reproducing grayscale contone images, our main focus needs to be *grayscale reproduction*. *Linearization* calibration and setting proper *highlight* and *shadow* points are key factors in accurate grayscale value reproduction.

Nearly all scanners tend to capture images darker than they really are, and particularly in the midtone and shadow portions of an image. The solution to this is to perform a calibration of your scanner.

Calibrating your scanner is the first key step to creating of good-quality scanned contone images like photographs. Without calibration, you may not receive consistent results from your scanner. The most fundamental calibration procedure for grayscale images is called *linearization*. When we linearize a scanner, we make sure that the scanner will capture grayscale values accurately. For instance, if an image has a 30% grayscale area, the scanner will create a 30% pixel and not a 40% pixel when it reproduces that area. If the image has 73% gray, the scanner will capture 73% and not 82% or some other grayscale value. A linear scanner will accurately reproduce grayscale values.

Tools required for calibration

To perform a calibration of your scanner, you will need the following hardware and software tools:

1) Scanner

2) Scanning software with the following tools:

• Editable histogram or some other tool to set highlight and shadow

• Gamma curve adjustment tool

• Info tool to measure grayscale values

3) Multi-step grayscale target

4) Data sheet containing grayscale values of the chart

Note: The grayscale calibration target used in this book was developed by the author specifically for desktop reflective scanners. It is a 10-step

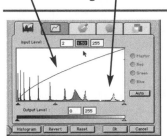

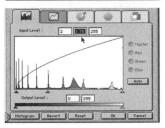

▼ *Figure 6.2 Gamma Curve Linearization*

Seen here is a scanner's editable histogram and gamma curve. The top box shows the default settings; the bottom dialog box shows the calibrated settings. Compare the top and bottom boxes for: 1) positions of the highlight and shadow pointers; 2) shapes and positions of the gamma curves; and 3) the position of the midpoint and midpoint numbers (1.5 and 1.75). The calibrated settings are obtained by setting the shadow pointer (far left) and highlight pointer (far right) so that the first (white) and last (black) grayscale swatches measure 255 and 0, respectively. Then, the position of the midtone number is adjusted so that the fifth grayscale swatch measures 127 when measured with the scanner's intensitometer. The midtone gamma curve number will generally be between 1.9 and 2.0 after the adjustment.

target with the grayscale values printed on the target. See the back of this book for ordering information.

Step-by-step: linearization for grayscale

Simple, step-by-step linearization calibration for grayscale images:

1) Clean your scanner bed and place your 10-step calibration target and your first images squarely side-by-side on the scanner bed.

2) Under the Settings menu, set the Preview size to Max. area. Then, preview the target in 8-bit mode (256 grayscale values).

3) Select the 10-step grayscale portion of the target, including the pure white and pure black end swatches. (Be careful to just select the grayscale portion of the target (Fig 6.1.)

4) Select/crop the editable histogram within the Enhancement tools.

5) Adjustment: Click the Auto button to move the highlight and shadow pointers so that they are at the beginning and end of the data peaks. This can be confirmed by measuring the grayscale values of the pure white (255) and pure black (0) swatches.

6) Zoom in a bit on the middle portion of the grayscale target so that you have a good view of the middle swatches. Use Swatch #5 (127) to start (counting down from the white swatch).

7) With the built-in Info tool, measure the grayscale value of Swatch #5. Swatch #5 will probably register a grayscale value lower (darker) than its actual value of 127.

8) To make a quick overall correction of your scanner's response to grayscale values, adjust the midpoint of the gamma curve (Fig 6.2) by changing the value in the middle box of the histogram tool, until the Info tool measures the #5 target swatch at ~127 (see Fig. 6.3). The default gamma value in the scan software is 1.5 on a Mac and 1.0 on a Windows system. Adjust the gamma curve midtone value up until the #5 grayscale swatch is 127. Perform this change incrementally, 0.1 per change, and watch how the intensitometer readings gradually increase. You may have to jiggle the intensitometer slightly (move the cursor) after each adjustment to make sure the software registers the change in grayscale value. A typical adjusted midpoint in the gamma curves may be 1.9–2.0. Note how the curve arches up and the entire image lightens when you make this adjustment. Don't worry if the intensitometer doesn't read exactly 127, or if the value varies slightly (by one or two points), as you move the intensitometer around the swatch.

9) Save the corrected scanner settings as default settings so that they will

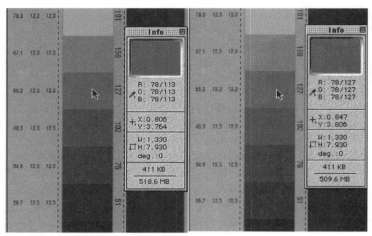

▼ *Figure 6.3 Info Tool*
This scanner's Info tool is used to measure grayscale values on targets and images. Note the starting (113) and ending (127) values before and after gamma curve adjustment.

automatically be applied to each image scanned. Under the Settings menu, set the scan software Preferences to Keep current parameter settings. The gamma curve should not be touched again while adjusting individual images, or it will destroy the calibration adjustment just performed.

10) For best results, linearization calibration should be performed at the beginning of each scan session.

Note: Protect your targets. When not in use, we recommend that you keep your targets in moisture-proof, light-tight containers. Constant exposure to light and humidity will progressively degrade the target, which will then no longer be consistent with its published data values. These targets should be replaced every two years if they are well-protected, and every year if they are not.

This simple linearization adjustment provides you with an easy way to make noticeable improvements in the overall quality and consistency of your scanned images, without drowning you in technical details, long procedures, or costly purchases. Remember that once you have set the gamma curve midpoint, do not adjust it when you are scanning individual images, or you will destroy the calibration setup. Any tool which is used for calibration should not be used for any other purpose.

Measuring grayscale values

There are numerous ways to measure grayscale values with different scales and units of measurement. The two most common systems of grayscale measurement found within desktop scanning and image editing software are: 1) the percent grayscale system which offers a 100 units of measurement scale (0–100%); and 2) the 8-bit grayscale system, which offers a 256 units of measurement scale (0–255).

In a 0-100 percent scale system, 0% is 0 percent gray, or pure white, while 100% is 100 percent gray, or pure black.

▼ *Figure 6.4 Grayscale Photo*

In the 0-255 scale system, 0 is pure black and 255 is pure white.

Scanners often will use the 0–255 grayscale measurement system. Image editing applications such as Photoshop will often employ the percent scale when measuring grayscale values in grayscale images.

Grayscale Image Scanning

Step-by-step: grayscale photo scanning

Linearize your scanner, as described above, at the beginning of each scan session. Clean your scanner bed and place your grayscale image (Fig 6.4) squarely on the scan bed.

Note: Find this photograph to scan in the pocket in the back of this book.

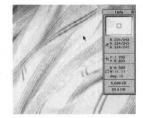

1) Set your basic control to Manual.

2) Set scan mode to 8-bit+ (grayscale) in the scanner control palette.

3) Make sure there is not an "X" in the box before "Auto" in the bottom half of the scanner control window.

4) Preview at low resolution (72ppi). Set the preview resolution in the bottom left side of the Preview window.

5) Crop the portion of the image you want to scan using the *Selection Frame tool*. Please crop the image accurately so the corrections you apply are to the image data, not the surrounding data.

6) Activate the editable histogram in the Enhancement tools.

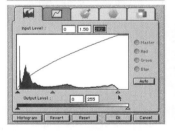

▼ *Figure 6.5 Tone Compression*

Use the editable histogram at the left above (Image Enhancement tool) to set highlight and shadow points. The highlight and shadow pointer triangles should be placed near the beginning and end of the image data in the histogram as shown above. For even better results, fine-tune the placement of these highlight and shadow point slider triangles by using the Info tool, at the right above, along with the editable histogram. Set the highlight point in the histogram so that the diffuse highlight area (shirt) in the image reads ~ 242 (5% gray) in the Info tool, so that a minimum dot will print in the highlight area. Set the shadow point so that the shadow area (hat) reads ~12–24 (90–95% gray) for standard commercial printing.

7) To adjust the highlight values on a Macintosh, arrange your Info tool (see Fig. 6.3) and editable histogram so that they and the white shirt area are all visible. Raise or lower the highlight value by moving the highlight at the right end of the histogram until the RGB values in the right-hand side of the Info tool measure about 242 when placed over the left-hand side of the shirt (see Fig 6.5). On a Windows system, you will need to make a histogram tool adjust-

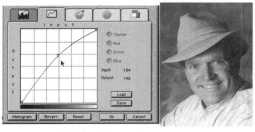

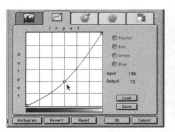

▼ *Figure 6.6 Curve Tool: Lighten*
Curve tools are used to adjust image brightness and contrast. Here we are lightening the entire image. Contrast with image in Fig 6.7.

▼ *Figure 6.7 Curve Tool: Darken*
Curve tools are used to adjust image brightness and contrast. Here we are darkening the entire image. Contrast with image in Fig 6.6.

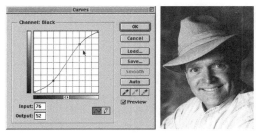

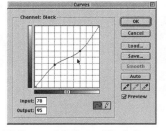

▼ *Figure 6.8 Curve Tool: Increase Contrast*
Curve tools can also be used to adjust image contrast. Here we are increasing contrast across the entire image. Contrast with original image in Fig 6.9.

▼ *Figure 6.9 Curve Tool: Decrease Contrast*
Here we are decreasing contrast across the entire image by flattening the curve in the midtones. Contrast with original image in Fig 6.8.

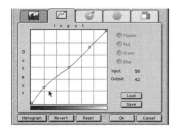

▼ *Figure 6.10 Curve Tool: Selective Lightening*
Curve tools can also be used to adjust specific portions of images. Here we are lightening just the midtone to shadow area of the image.

ment as described above and then click "OK." Re-measure the image area. If another adjustment is needed, re-open the histogram tool and move the curve again.

8) If a diffuse highlight (light detail area like a white shirt) is available in the image area, measure this highlight area with the Info tool. Next, adjust the position of the highlight slider in the editable histogram to be sure that the highlight values do not exceed the highlight reproducibility limit of your printing device. Minimum highlight values vary on different devices. A typical highlight value to set for a standard commercial press is 5% gray (242 in the Info tool). For a standard desktop laser printer, a minimum highlight value of 10% is typical. And for newsprint, the minimum highlight value may be as high as 20%. If you are printing in-house and are unsure of your printer's highlight values, please check with the manufacturer, or you can determine it yourself by experimentation.

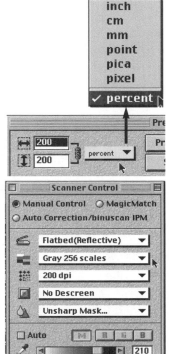

▼ Figure 6.11 Resolution and Scaling Setup

This scanner's scaling controls are found in the upper left-hand corner of the Preview window (top). Units can be chosen to suit your needs. Assign the final resolution you would like your image to have, here 200ppi (bottom), and the scaling which you would like the scanner to perform, here 200%, and the scanner will do the rest. The scan software will direct the scanner to scan at 400ppi and resize the image 200%. This resizing will lower the image resolution to the requested 200ppi.

9) If the highlight value is too high or light (≤5% or ≥242), move the highlight tab to the right until the intensitometer measurements in the diffuse highlight area are ~242. This will prevent your images from "blowing out" in the highlight areas. If the highlight values are too dark (≥5% ≤242), move the highlight slider to the left until the highlight areas measure ~242.

10) Shadow point adjustments can be similarly made. Here we will adjust the left (shadow) slider until the shadow area measures ~95%, or 12 in the Info tool. Output levels, which are set with the twin slider bar at the bottom of the editable histogram tool, can be used to set maximum shadow values and minimum highlight values to specific values. For instance, if you didn't want any highlight value to go below 5% (242) gray or any shadow value to go above 95% (18) gray, then the highlight and shadow slider values in the Output Levels dialog box can be set at these values. Then, no matter what values the scanner may capture, the final image will have maximum and minimum grayscale values of 95% and 5%, respectively.

11) Use the Curve tool to adjust the overall brightness and contrast of an image. To lighten or darken: Move the midpoint of the curve up or down (see Figs. 6.6 and 6.7). To adjust the contrast, flatten the curve where you want grayscale values to be concentrated. Flatten the curve near the highlight and shadow ends to increase overall image contrast (see Fig 6.8). Flatten the curve in the midtone area to lower overall image contrast (see Fig 6.9). Specific sections of the grayscale spectrum of an image, such as the shadow areas, can be lightened or darkened by raising or lowering specific sections of the curve (see Fig 6.10).

12) Set the resolution to 200–300ppi, depending upon the line screen at which you intend to print. See the sections on contone scanning resolutions in Chapters 2 and 3 for more information on setting scanning resolutions for contone images (see Fig. 6.11).

13) Set the scaling percentage to match your output needs using the Scaling tools in the upper left-hand corner of the image's Preview window. Be sure that horizontal and vertical scaling are the same so that you do not apply any distortion to your image. You should have the scanner perform the scaling whenever possible, rather than performing this scaling in the post scan in Photoshop or other pixel-based imaging software. Your scanner will perform the scaling faster and do a better job (see Fig. 6.11).

Note: Your scanning resolution will automatically increase to accommodate any scaling percentage you assign. For example, if you assign the scanner to perform 200% scaling, then the resolution of the scan-

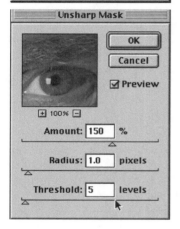

▼ *Figure 6.12 Image Sharpness*
On the left is a portion of an image which has been scanned properly but not sharpened. On the right is the same scanned image, with sharpening applied. Note how the high-contrast portions of the right image, such as the eyes, eyebrows, and hat fabric are sharper and are in better focus. This sharpening can be applied either during the scan (top) or in the post scan in Photoshop (middle). Note that the Threshold value is set at 5 to protect the facial skin areas from too much sharpening.

ner will automatically increase 200%. This increase in scanning resolution will not appear in your scanner control window, however; it occurs automatically in the background. The resolution you set in the scanner control window will determine the final resolution of your image at the end of the scan. For more information on the relationship between scanning resolution and scaling, see the sections on resolution and scaling in Chapter 2 of this book ("Scanned Image Fundamentals"), and in the "Photographic Reproduction" section near the end of Chapter 2. Remember that the resolution requirements for output depend upon the amount of scaling which needs to be performed, the RIP being used for printing, the screening technology, and the intended viewing distance. See Chapter 2 for more discussion on AM and FM screening technologies and variations in resolution.

14) Double-click the thumbnail image in the Scan Job List window to set the image to be saved as a pixel-based TIFF. A TIFF (.tif) is a pixel-based file format which works equally well on both Mac and Windows platforms.

15) Sharpening is the final step in capturing and correcting an image. All scanners soften images during the scanning process. To improve image sharpness, we use a tool called *unsharp mask*. This sharpening can be applied during the scan or, if you prefer, you may use the Unsharp Mask tool in Photoshop to apply unsharp mask and improve image focus.

16a) To apply unsharp mask during the scan with the scan software, click the Filter menu in the Scan Control palette. Select Unsharp mask at the bottom of the menu. Try the Medium and High choices (see Fig 6.12) and see which one gives you the best results for your images.

16b) For a bit more control over your unsharp masking, you can apply unsharp mask through Photoshop after you have scanned your image. Here are some starting values for a 200ppi grayscale portrait image opened in Photoshop: unsharp mask Amount = 100–150, Radius = 1–2, Threshold = 3–6 (see Fig 6.12). You may go as high as 200% in some cases, but it will vary with each image. For the best results, if you have the time, you may want to apply the unsharp mask filter 50% at a time. Unsharp masking may be performed during the scanning process. If you know that you will be combining this image with another and/or performing significant image editing, it is generally best to wait until these chores are finished before applying unsharp mask.

Note: Be cautious with your application of unsharp mask. If too much unsharp mask is applied, white haloes, sometimes called blooming, can form along high-contrast edges where pixels have been pushed too far apart in their grayscale values. For images with typical desktop resolutions of 200–300ppi, unsharp mask values above 200% and a pixel radius above 2.0 can be dangerous. Remember, you can always add more unsharp mask, but you can't effectively remove it once it has been applied and saved.

17) Scan the image at this higher resolution and with the proper scaling set for the second and final scan.

18) Name and save the image as Portrait_GS_200.tif.

19) Your scanned image can now be opened and edited in any pixel-based image editing software such as Photoshop. If you have used the plug-in or Twain module to activate your scanner through your image editing software, your image may already be open and available for editing.

Poor quality image note:

Setting highlight and shadow points properly using editable histograms is a first step to helping improve poor-quality images. Significant adjustments of an image's brightness and contrast, using a curve tool, may be required to correct images that have initial lightness and contrast problems. Some images require mostly global changes, others may need only specific area adjustments, such as lightening of shadow regions, while some others will require both. Nearly all scanned images require the use of unsharp masking to improve their sharpness or focus.

PAULINE'S SCAN TIPS

Scan Tip # 6-1

Grayscale photos should be scanned in 8-bit (or higher) mode to capture grayscale values.

Scan Tip # 6-2

Most scanners capture images darker than they really are. So, prior to scanning a grayscale photo image, you should calibrate your scanner. You need to have a grayscale chart which has known grayscale values. The purpose of this exercise is to linearize your scanner. See the back of this book for information on where to obtain a 10-step grayscale calibration chart made specifically for desktop scanners.

Scan Tip # 6-3

Setting highlight and shadow points are two critical adjustments to make when setting up a scan. Use your histogram to place your highlight and shadow points as it will allow you to see the distribution of grayscale data in your image.

Scan Tip # 6-4

Be sure to clearly distinguish between any specular highlights that your image may contain, as well as the diffuse highlights which contain the critical highlight image data. The diffuse highlights should be located in the lightest portions of the image which still have detail.

PAULINE'S SCAN TIPS

Scan Tip # 6-5

Use a curve tool, rather than linear sliders, to adjust image brightness and contrast. Using a curve tool tends to maintain a higher percentage of image grayscale data, and allows you to protect the highlight and shadow values you may have set.

Scan Tip # 6-6

Determine the maximum print/reproduction size of the final image you may need before you scan, and allow your scanner to perform the scaling duties. This will save you time and result in higher quality images compared to performing these chores in an image editing application after the scan.

Scan Tip # 6-7

When determining the input resolution at which you will scan grayscale photos, use a formula of 1.5 x lpi at which the image will be printed. Remember that this image should not be scaled up after the scan as there will not be enough pixel data to support the printing.

Scan Tip # 6-8

During the scanning sampling process, your scanner will soften your image. To return an image to its original sharpness/focus, apply unsharp mask to your image. This can be performed during the scan if you do not intend to edit your image. If post-scan image editing is in order, perform the unsharp mask after the scan and image editing processes have been completed. For portrait images in particular, be sure to utilize a threshold value (3–5) to prevent over-sharpening of smooth, low-contrast portions of your image.

7

Color Contones Step By Step

As the Byte Turns continues…

Will Danny D'Ziner and Pauline E. Prepress be able color their images of each other properly?

*Yuck!
Where did those weird colors come from? The white shirt looks blue! What happened?…it looked fine on the screen.*

We tried to tell you about using your monitor…

*Well…
Neither your scanner nor your monitor is linear or neutral. You need to calibrate both and perform color correction by the numbers, and NOT based upon your screen view.*

COLOR PHOTO (CONTONE) SCANNING

What Is a Color Contone?

The term *contone* is short for continuous tone image. A contone image is one which is characterized by gradually changing grayscale and/or color values throughout the image. Photographs of people and landscapes are examples of common contone images.

Contrary to popular perception, there is no color captured by our scanners or manipulated on our computers. Our scanners and computers are digital devices and therefore only really understand two values, black and white. Therefore, digital color contone images are composed of a sandwich of three channels, or levels, of pixels with various grayscale values assigned to them. The grayscale pixels control color attributes such as hue, saturation, and tonal value. It is changes in the grayscale values of these pixels which define the composition, detail, and color of a color contone image.

Color Contone Challenges

Since it is the underlying grayscale values that control the composition, quality, and color values in a digital color contone image when we are capturing and reproducing color contone images, our main focus should be on accurate reproduction of *grayscale*. When we want to faithfully reproduce a color contone image so that our scanned version is as close as possible to the original, our focus is on grayscale reproduction. In other circumstances, we may want to alter a contone image from its original form with the intent of improving and/or just changing the image. In either case, whether we are reproducing or altering a color contone image, we will focus on the grayscale values of the image.

Two of the most common problems we see with scanned color contone images are, like with grayscale images, they tend to reproduce too dark, and color images often have unbalanced color, which leads to obvious color casts in images. But whether our images are too light or too dark, or the contrast is poor, or the color balance is wrong, control of our images always boils down to control of our images' grayscale values. There are four primary factors to which we need to pay the most attention if we want to control our color values: 1) scanner *calibration (linearization* and *neutralization)*, 2) setting of *highlight* and *shadow* values, 3) controlling the distribution of grayscale data to control *contrast*, and 4) neutralization of images to remove image color cast.

Pixels vs. vectors

All of our scanned images will be initially created as pixel-based images, as this is the only form in which scanners capture images. Some of the simple line art images we created and discussed in the chapter on line art scanning were good candidates to be converted into vector-based images.

The primary advantage of pixel-based images is their ability to display details. Color contone images, like their grayscale contone cousins, by their very nature contain a great deal of detail, and will be captured as, and remain as, pixel-based images.

Resolution for scanning color contone images

Resolution requirements for grayscale contone images are generally lower than those required for line art scanning. While line art scanning resolution ranges are from 500–1200ppi, grayscale contone scan resolutions are usually significantly less than this, generally in the range of 200–400ppi (unless scaling is performed during the scan). Input or scan resolutions for grayscale contone images should be controlled by the output resolution at which we print or otherwise reproduce our images and how much scaling will take place during the scan. For printing, output resolution is typically defined as the number of halftone dots per inch, also known as line screen, or lpi (lines per inch). A good general formula to use is 1.3 x lpi x scaling factor. For instance, if we intend to print our image at 150 lpi and scale our image 200%, our input scan resolution should be 1.3 x 150 lpi x 2 =390ppi.

As with capturing line art, when scanning grayscale contone images, it is usually a good idea to use the optical resolution of our scanners. Using the optical resolution of the scanner is a key factor in accurate grayscale reproduction. Using the optical resolution of your scanner will also reduce the *interpolated*-related softening of the image which occurs as a result of scanning, and will noticeably decrease scan times. (See Chapter 1 for an in-depth discussion of optical resolution.)

All contone scan resolutions recommended in the following step-by-step tutorials are based upon an output print resolution of 150 lpi and an input scan optical resolution of 1200ppi. Therefore, we would round the 390ppi resolution above to 400ppi, which equals 1200ppi÷3.

COLOR CONTONE SCANNING (REFLECTIVE)

Gamma Curve

Editable Histogram

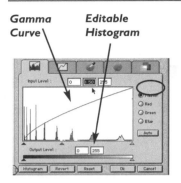

▼ *Figure 7.1 Gamma Curve Linearization*

Here is a scanner's editable histogram and gamma curve. The top box shows the default settings. The bottom box shows the calibrated settings. Compare the top and bottom boxes for: 1) the shapes and positions of the gamma curves, and 2) the position of the midpoint and the midpoint numbers. Note that the calibrated curve has a higher midtone value (1.95 vs. 1.5) and a higher arched curve than the uncalibrated curve, resulting in brighter images with better shadow detail. Note that the calibration is performed with the Master channel selected.

When we are challenged with capturing and reproducing color contone images, our main focus, as with grayscale contone images, needs to be grayscale reproduction. *Linearization* and *neutralization* calibration and setting proper highlight and shadow points are key factors in helping us reproduce grayscale, and therefore color values, accurately. In this section, we will discuss reflective images, which are created on opaque surfaces such as paper, and are captured by light, which is reflected off that opaque surface.

Calibration of your Scanner

Linearization and neutralization for color scanning

Calibrating your scanner is the first key step to the creation of good-quality, scanned contone color images like photographs. Without calibration, you may not receive consistent results from your scanner. There are two related fundamental calibration procedures for color images, *linearization* and *neutralization*. This calibration will help us control the brightness and contrast, and remove any unwanted color cast from our color images.

There are two kinds of color cast: scanner and image. Scanner color cast may be created when a scanner shows unequal sensitivity to red, green, or blue light. Image color cast can be created in many ways, including lighting conditions, film emulsion bias, or exposure problems. These two sources of calibration should be isolated and treated separately. The following is used for the isolation and removal of instrument (scanner) color cast. Any color cast remaining after the scanner color cast has been removed will belong to the image. Clean your scanner bed and place images squarely on the scan bed.

We will perform a linearization similar to the one described for grayscale contone calibration, with the only difference being scanning in 24-bit RGB mode.

Step-by-step: simple linearization calibration for color images

1) Under the Settings menu, set the Preview size to Max. area. Then preview the target in 24-bit RGB mode.

Before Calibration   Linearized   Neutralized

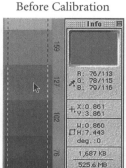 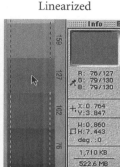 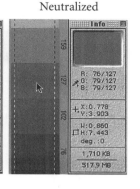

▼ *Figure 7.2 Info Tool*

This scanner's Info tool is used to measure grayscale values on targets and images. The starting RGB values are 113, 115, and 116, before any calibration is performed. After initial linearization, the RGB values are 127, 130, and 130. After final color cast removal and neutralization with the color cast adjustment tool (Fig 7.3), the values are all equal (RGB = 127, 127, and 127). The scanner is now linear and neutral.

2) Select the 10-step grayscale portion of the target, including the pure white and pure black end swatches. (Be careful to select only the grayscale portion of the target.)

3) Select the editable histogram within the manual tools. Be sure the Master channel is selected (see Fig 7.1).

4) Click the Auto button to move the highlight and shadow pointers so that they are at the beginning and the end of the data peaks. You can confirm this by measuring the grayscale values of the pure white (255) and pure black (0) swatches.

5) Zoom in on the middle portion of the grayscale target so that you have a good view of the middle swatches. Start with Swatch #5, counting down from the white swatch.

6) Now with the Info tool (Fig 7.2), measure the grayscale value of the #5 target swatch. Swatch # 5 may register a grayscale value in the 115 range. Its grayscale value should be at 127 (seen at the right of the target).

7) To make a quick overall correction of your scanner's response to grayscale values, adjust the midpoint of the gamma curve by changing the value in the middle box of the histogram tool until at least one of the RGB values in the Info tool measures ~127 for the #5 target swatch. The default gamma value in the scan software is 1.5 on a Mac and 1.0 on a Windows system. Adjust the gamma curve midtone value up until the #5 grayscale swatch is 127. Perform this change incrementally, 0.1 per change, and watch how the intensitometer readings gradually increase. You may have to jiggle the intensitometer slightly (move the cursor) after each adjustment to make sure the software registers the change in grayscale value. A typical adjusted mid-point in the gamma curves may be 1.7–2.0. Note how the curve arches up and the entire image lightens when you make this adjustment. Don't worry if the intensitometer doesn't read exactly 127, or if the value varies slightly (by one or two points), as you move the

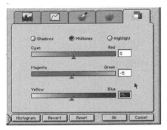

▼ *Figure 7.3 Color Adjustment Tool for Neutralization*

A color cast adjustment tool, such as this one in the Enhancement tools, allows you to adjust the red, green and blue response of the scanner separately in the highlight, midtone, and shadow regions. These numbers are adjusted so that the scanner will capture neutral grayscale areas with equal RGB values when measured with the scanner's intensitometer.

Here, the green and blue values are adjusted down -5 so that they match the red value. See the change in the Info palette from the linearized to neutralized portions in Fig 7.2 to see the results of these adjustments.

intensitometer around the swatch. Remember that a one-unit movement only represents a 0.4% change.

Neutralization for color images

1) Once the overall gamma curve has been set as described above, you may notice that the RGB values are not equal. This means that the scanner is not neutral; that is, it will create a color cast in any image it captures. The greater the disparity in the RGB values, the greater will be the color cast imposed by the scanner.

2) We want to adjust the RGB values so they are all equal when measuring the grayscale portions of the target with the intensitometer. To accomplish this, we will use the color cast correction tool in the manual controls.

3) Activate the color cast adjustment tool (see Fig 7.3). Select the midtone button. Adjust the midtone red, green, and blue values up and down until all three values are equal to 127.

4) Save the corrected scanner settings as default settings so that they will automatically be applied to each image scanned. Under the Settings menu, set the the scan software Preferences to Keep current parameter settings. This color cast adjustment tool should not be used again while adjusting individual images or else it will destroy the calibration we just performed. We will use other tools to adjust the color in individual images.

5) For best results, linearization and neutralization calibration should be performed at the beginning of each scan session.

Note: Protect your targets. When not in use, keep your targets in moisture-proof, light-tight containers. Constant exposure to light and humidity will progressively degrade the target, which will then no longer be consistent with its published data sheet values.

These affordable, simple linearization and neutralization adjustments are intended to provide you with an easy way to make noticeable improvements in the overall quality and consistency of your scanned images without drowning you in technical details, long procedures, or costly purchases. More detailed fine-tuning adjustments can be accomplished by measuring, comparing, and adjusting additional grayscale swatches in other sections of the grayscale spectrum or through the purchase and use of color management software.

Linearize and neutralize your scanner, as described above, at the beginning of each scan session.

Some calibration tips

1) Use only targets that have known grayscale and/or RGB values associated with them such as the target shown in this book.

2) When linearizing and neutralizing a scanner, measure and correct at least three swatches of the grayscale spectrum, preferably near the highlight, midtone, and shadow regions of the spectrum.

3) Use a separate tool for calibration (linearization–gamma curve, neutralization–color cast adjustment tool) which you do not adjust after you linearize and/or neutralize the scanner. This way, you will only need to calibrate the scanner once for the entire scan session. Any other adjustments that need to be made on an image should be performed with a different tool, such as editable histograms and curves.

4) To save time on color contone scans, a combined linearization/neutralization calibration can be performed at the beginning of each scan session. Note: As mentioned above, you should use separate tools for calibration of the scanner and then use other tools to adjust individual images.

5) It is usually better to linearize and neutralize a scanner than to wait to make these corrections in the post scan in Photoshop.

6) Calibration settings can be saved either as default settings, so that they will automatically be applied to each image scanned, or as separate data files, which can be loaded and used whenever you choose.

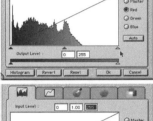

▼ *Figure 7.4 Original Color Photo*
Numbered squares are referenced in the text.

Color Image Scanning

Step-by-step: color contone photo scan

Clean your scanner bed and complete the linearization and neutralization described above using the calibration target provided. Place your first color contone image squarely on the scan bed. Note: Find this photograph to scan in the pocket in the back of this book.

Note: Find this photograph to scan in the pocket in the back of this book.

Note : Always flatten and stabilize all reflective images and take particular care of transparent film images.

1) Set the basic scanner control to Manual.

2) Set the scan mode to 24-bit+ (RGB color). Note that RGB and CIELab conversion modes are only available with some scanning software. See Chapter 11 for more information on color management.

3) Make sure to disable any auto scanning tools and settings.

4) Preview the scan at a low resolution (72ppi). Set this in the bottom left corner of the Preview Image window.

5) Crop the portion of the image you want to scan using the Selection Frame tool in the Preview Image window. Please crop the image accurately so that the corrections you apply are on the image data, not the surrounding data.

6) Activate the editable histogram from the Image Enhancement tool window. Select the Red channel.

7) To approximately set the highlight and shadow points of your image, move the highlight and shadow tabs (the left and right tabs below the histogram) so that the two pointers are at the beginning and the end of the image

Before Correction

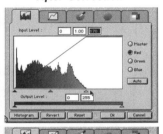

After Correction

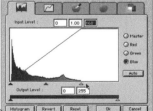

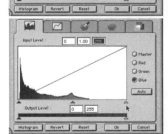

▼ *Figure 7.5 Setting Tone Compression*
Setting highlight and shadow points should be performed on individual channels, as shown above, rather than on the Master channel. As a starting point, set the highlight and shadow points visually by placing the highlight and shadow pointers at the beginning and the end of the image data in the histogram. These highlight and shadow points can be fine-tuned using the Info palette either here in the histogram or later with the curve tool. (See page 302 for color version.)

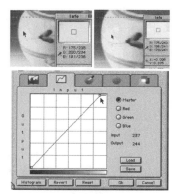

▼ *Figure 7.6 Highlight Adjustment*
Here we are raising the high-light value using the curve on the Master channel. This will raise all three (RGB) values simultaneously. Adjust the position of the highlight end of the curve until all the right side RGB values of the Info tool ~242 (right). (See page 302 for color version.)

data as seen in the histogram. IMPORTANT: In images that have neutral white highlights, perform this tone compression (setting highlight and shadow points) separately on each channel (Red, Green, and Blue), rather than on the Master channel. For images with strong color casts, such as sunset pictures, it is usually best to use the Master channel, to maintain the color cast and to set the highlight and shadow points. Avoid the use of any Auto button in either case (Fig 7.5). We will fine-tune these values during the neu-tralization in the next scan step.

Image neutralization: color cast removal

8) We will neutralize this image by measuring and adjusting two areas of the image: the white milk in the top of the pitcher (location ③, Fig7.4), and the white tile in the lower left-hand corner (location ⑥, Fig7.4). Neutralization of the image, to remove unwanted color cast, and fine-tuning of the highlight and shadow values can now be per-formed. Identify one or more areas of the image which should be neu-tral (an area such as a white highlight is often appropriate for both neutralization and fine-tuning highlight values). There are several neutral areas in this photo which can be used for color cast determi-nation and adjustment. We will measure several neutral areas, including the milk in the pitcher, the rim of the white ceramic bowl, the white plastic cover of the Kitchen Whiz computer, and a couple of areas in the white tiles.

We will use the curve tool to make adjustments to the color values which the scanner will record. In some cases, such as when we fine-tune the overall highlight value, we will adjust the curve on the Master channel, which will adjust the red, green, and blue values simultane-ously (Fig 7.6). When we are removing color cast, we will adjust curves for individual RGB channels. Making curve tool adjustments involves click-ing at various places on the curve and then moving the curve up or down to either increase or decrease the value of the selected color in a specific portion of the tonal range, such as the quarter-tone or midtone of the image.

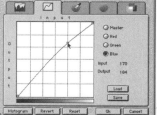

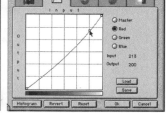

▼ *Figure 7.7 Neutralization of Quartertone*
Here we are raising the highlight value using the curve on the Master channel. This will raise all three (RGB) values simulta-neously. Adjust the position of the highlight end of the curve until the right side RGB values of the Info tool ~242. (See page 303 for color version)

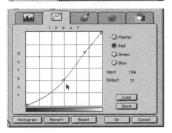

▼ *Figure 7.8 Midtone Neutralization*
Here we are measuring and adjusting a neutral area in the midtone region of the image. In the top, uncorrected image, the histogram shows a high red value of 144 compared with 124 for the green and blue values. To correct this excess of red, we activate the red curve and lower the curve in the midtone until the red value ~124. The second, corrected image shows all three R,G, and B values = 124.(See page 303 for color version.)

Neutralizing and fine-tuning highlight values:

8a) There are two highlights in this image: a specular highlight, which is a white image area which has no detail, and a diffuse highlight, which is a white image area with some detail. The specular highlight area is the bright white area of the white tiles on the left side of the image (see location ⊏1⊐, Fig 7.4). The diffuse highlight area is the white area on the left side rim of the white ceramic bowl (see location ⊏2⊐, Fig 7.4). When adjusting the RGB values in a white diffuse highlight area of an image, we adjust the diffuse highlight values so that they are appropriate values for printing that highlight. As mentioned in the grayscale section, a typical highlight for a commercial press as well as many desktop printers is 5% (0–100) or 242 (0–255). So, a typical RGB measurement for a white highlight in a color image would be 242, 242, 242 or 5,5,5 (depending on the grayscale measurement units used by your scanner). If you are printing in-house and are unsure of your printer's highlight values, please check with the manufacturer, or you can determine them yourself by experimentation.

8b) Quartertone neutralization: With the Info tool, measure the RGB values of the milk in the pitcher. The Info tool will show the following unequal RGB values: R=223, G=209, B=189 (Fig 7.7, upper left). Note that your values may vary slightly. The overall presence of this red color cast can be confirmed by measuring other neutral areas such as locations ⊏4⊐, ⊏5⊐, and ⊏6⊐. To correct this imbalance, activate the Curve tool (Enhancement tools). We will lower the red values and raise the blue values until all three equal ~209, or whatever your green value is. Activate the Red channel. Now, drag the upper end of the red curve down until the red value in the milk equals 209. Now, activate the blue curve. Drag the upper end of the blue curve up until the blue value in the milk equals 209 (Fig 7.7, bottom).

When your adjustments are completed, your Info tool should indicate that all three right-hand values (RGB) are equal (Fig 7.7, upper right).

8c) Midtone neutralization: With the Info tool, measure the RGB values of the tile in the lower left-hand corner of the image. The Info tool will show an elevated red reading: R=244, G=124, B=124 (Fig 7.8, upper left). Note that your values may vary slightly. To correct this elevated red reading, activate the Curve tool (Enhancement tools). We will lower the red value until all three equal ~124. Activate the Red channel. Lock the quartertone portion of the

▼ *Figure 7.9 Raw and Final Images*
The top image was the image created with a raw scan, without corrections. The bottom image is the result of the tone compression, color correction, and unsharp mask performed in this chapter. Note how the top image has a distinct red color cast, and is darker, lower contrast, and appears to be out of focus when compared with the lower, adjusted image. Compare your final image with the results seen here. Remember that an accurate printed version of your RGB scan will depend upon a correct RGB-to-CMYK conversion.
Note: If the top image does not visually appear to have a color cast when viewed on your monitor, then your monitor may be out of calibration. In either case, the numbers measured with and shown in the Info tool will show higher red values.
(See page 304 for color version)

curve by placing a control point at the quartertone. Now, drag the middle part of the red curve down until the red value in the milk equals ~124 (Fig 7.8 bottom).

When your adjustments are completed, your Info tool should indicate that all three values (RGB) are equal (Fig 7.7, middle).

Note: We have performed neutralization on the quartertone and midtone portions of this image. Neutralization can be performed on any portion of an image which contains neutral areas, including highlight, three-quartertone, and shadow portions of images, using the same techniques we have used here.

You may use the Curve tool to adjust overall brightness and contrast of the image using the Master Curve (which controls all three channels simultaneously). To lighten or darken: Move the curve up or down. To adjust contrast: Flatten the curve where you want grayscale values. Flatten the curve in the midtone area to lower overall image contrast. Refer to Figs. 6.8 and 6.9 on page 116. Flatten curve near the highlight and shadow areas to increase overall image contrast. Specific sections of the grayscale spectrum of an image, such as the shadow areas, can be lightened or darkened by raising specific sections of the Master Curve. See Figs. 6.6–6.10, page 116, for instructions on controlling image brightness and contrast.

9) Set the resolution to 200–300ppi, depending upon the line screen at which you intend to print. See the section "Resolution for scanning contone images" towards the end of this chapter for more information on setting scanning resolution for contone images. We will set our resolution at 200ppi for reproduction at 150 lpi.

10) Set the scaling percentage to match your output needs using the Scaling tools in the upper left-hand corner of the image Preview window. Be sure that the horizontal and vertical scaling are the same so that you do not apply any distortion to your image. You should have the scanner perform the scaling whenever possible, rather than perform this scaling in the post scan in Photoshop or other pixel-based imaging software. Your scanner will perform the scaling faster and do a better job.

Note: Your scanning resolution will automatically increase to accommodate any scaling percentage you assign. For example, if you assign the scanner to perform a 200% scaling, then the resolution of the scanner will automatically increase by 200%. This increase in scanning resolution will not appear in your scanner control window, however; it occurs automatically in the background. The resolution you set in the scanner control window will

▼ *Figure 7.10 Unsharp Mask*
If you decide to apply unsharp mask during the scanning process, you can use This scanner's unsharp mask dialog box to adjust the amount of unsharp mask which will be applied. Use medium as a starting point, then try high and compare the results. For post-scan control of unsharp mask try Photoshop's unsharp mask filter.

determine the final resolution of your image at the end of the scan. For more information on the relationship between scanning resolution and scaling, see the sections on resolution and scaling in Chapter 1, and in the "Resolution for scanning contone images" section near the end of this chapter.

11) Double-click the thumbnail image in the Scan Job List window to set your image to be saved as a pixel-based TIFF or EPS (see the section on file formats at the end of Chapter 1).

12) The final step to capturing and correcting an image is sharpening. All scanners soften images during the scanning process. To improve image sharpness, we use a tool called unsharp mask (see Fig. 7.9 for raw and corrected images). This sharpening can be applied during the scan or, if you prefer, you may use the unsharp mask tool in Photoshop to apply unsharp mask to improve image focus.

13a) To apply unsharp mask during the scan with the scan software, click the "Filter" menu in the Scan Control palette. Select "Unsharp mask" at the bottom of the menu. Try the Medium and High choices (Fig 7.10) and see which one gives you the best results for your images.

13b) For a bit more control over your unsharp masking, you can apply unsharp mask through Photoshop after you have scanned your image. Here are some starting values for a 200ppi grayscale portrait image opened in Photoshop: unsharp mask Amount = 100-150, Radius = 1–2, Threshold = 3–6 (Fig 7.11). Unsharp masking may be applied either during the scanning or after the scan in an application like Photoshop. If you know that you will be combining an image with another and/or performing significant image editing, it is generally best to wait until these chores are finished before applying unsharp mask.

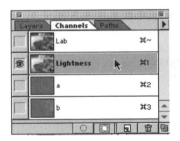

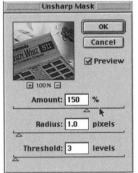

▼ *Figure 7.11 Lab application of Unsharp Mask*
By converting your image to Lab mode and applying unsharp mask (USM) to the "L" channel only, you avoid the risk of having color shifts occurring along high-contrast edges in your color images. The Threshold for the unsharp mask is set here at 3. This is lower than the 4–6 we would have for a portrait image because there are fewer areas which need protection. Note the greater control in this Photoshop USM dialog box compared with the scanner USM dialog box in the figure above. I often apply USM in Photoshop rather than my desktop scanning program for three reasons: 1) Photoshop's USM controls are often superior, 2) I can confine my USM to just the "L" channel, and 3) If I am performing image edits, I like to perform my USM mask after image editing is complete.(See page 304 for color version.)

After each application of unsharp mask on an RGB image in Photoshop, follow with a fade unsharp mask (Filter – Fade – 100% Luminosity) to prevent color shifts along high-contrast edges.

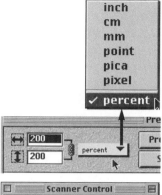

▼ Figure 7.12 Resolution and Scaling Setup

This scanner's scaling controls are found in the upper left-hand corner of the Preview window (top). Units can be chosen to suit your needs. Assign the final resolution you would like your image to have, here 200ppi (bottom), and the scaling which you would like the scanner to perform, here 200%, and the scanner will do the rest. The scan software will direct the scanner to scan at 400ppi, and resize the image 200%. This resizing will lower the image resolution to the requested 200ppi.

Using Lab mode

An alternative Taz-approved method of applying unsharp mask is to convert RGB color images to *Lab* mode, and then apply the unsharp mask only on the "L" channel. The "L" channel contains all of, and only, the grayscale or *luminance* information of the color image. So, any adjustment which is made only to the "L" channel affects only the grayscale values, and none of the color values of the image. Color shift problems along high-contrast edges can be avoided by: 1) performing unsharp mask on individual, lower contrast channels, 2) performing unsharp mask on the "L" channel in Lab mode, or 3) fading unsharp mask to 100% luminosity in Photoshop using the Filter menu as described in the previous paragraph. See Figure 7.10. Converting an image to Lab mode and applying unsharp mask exclusively on the "L" channel is my favorite way to apply unsharp mask. I also use Lab mode whenever I want to make any *luminance*-based adjustments including brightness and contrast, as well as unsharp mask.

14) Scan the image at this higher resolution for the second/final scan.

15) Name and save the image as StillLife_RGB_200.tif.

16) After the scan is complete, open the image in an image editing application such as Photoshop. (If you did not apply unsharp mask during the scan, apply unsharp mask as described in 13b.)

Resolution for scanning color contone images

Resolution requirements for contone color images are identical to those of grayscale contone images, and are therefore generally lower than the resolutions required for line art scanning. While line art scanning resolutions range from 500–1200ppi, grayscale and color contone scan resolutions are usually significantly less than this, generally in the range of 200–400ppi (unless scaling is performed during the scan). Input or scan resolutions for grayscale and color contone images should be controlled by the output resolution at which we will print or otherwise reproduce our image and how much scaling will take place during the scan. For printing, this output resolution is typically defined as the number of halftone dots per inch, also known as line screen, or lpi (lines per inch). A good general formula to use is 1.5 x lpi x scaling factor. For instance, if we intend to print our image at 150 lpi and scale our image 200%, our input scan resolution should be 1.5 x 150 lpi x 2 =450ppi.

As with capturing line art, when scanning grayscale contone images, it is usually a good idea to use the optical resolution of our scanners.

Using the optical resolution of the scanner is a key factor in accurate grayscale reproduction. Using the optical resolution of your scanner will also reduce the *interpolated*-related softening of the image which occurs as a result of scanning, and noticeably decrease scan times. (See Chapter 1, Scanning Challenges for an in-depth discussion of optical resolution.)

All contone scan resolutions recommended in the following step-by-step tutorials are based upon an output print resolution of 150 lpi and an input scan optical resolution of 1200ppi. Therefore in the above example where we are scaling our image 200% (scaling factor = 2) we would round the 450ppi resolution above to 400ppi which equals 1200ppi÷3.

Remember that the resolution requirements for output depend upon the amount of scaling which needs to be performed, the RIP being used for printing, the screening technology, and the intended viewing distance. See chapter 2 for more discussion on AM and FM screening technologies and variation in resolution.

RGB–CMYK note

All scanners capture images in RGB mode. Some scanners can convert your image to another color space, such as CMYK, on-the-fly. If you are planning to print your images on a CMYK printing device, your images must be converted into CMYK. The question is when and where should this conversion occur? If you are sending your files out to have them printed at a service bureau or printing company, ask them for instructions as to who should perform the conversion, and how it should be done. If you are printing to your own in-house color printing device, you will need to first determine what kind of file your printing device accepts. Some accept RGB, and some only CMYK. If your color printer only accepts CMYK, you can have your scanning software perform the conversion for you by using the MagicMatch or binuscan PhotoPerfect software, or you can perform the conversion in an image editing application like Adobe Photoshop.

Poor-quality image note

Properly setting the highlight and shadow points using an editable histogram is a first step to helping to improve poor-quality images. Significant adjustments of an image's brightness and contrast, using a curve tool, may be required to correct images which have initial lightness and contrast problems. Some images require mostly global changes others may need only specific area adjustments, such as lightening shadow regions, while some others will require both. Nearly all scanned images require the use of unsharp masking to improve their sharpness or focus.

PAULINE'S SCAN TIPS

Scan Tip # 7-1

Color photos should be scanned in 24-bit (or higher) mode to capture the three 8-bit+ channels which are required for an RGB image.

Scan Tip # 7-2

Calibrating your scanner for color scanning involves linearizing, similar to what we did for grayscale scanning, but this time on three channels. This three-channel linearization is called neutralization. It not only lightens the response of the scanner, but it removes color cast from the scanner.

Scan Tip # 7-3

For color images with neutral highlights, set highlight and shadow points on individual channels using a histogram. For images with strong color casts, use the master, or composite, RGB histogram to set highlight and shadow points.

Scan Tip # 7-4

Be sure to clearly distinguish between any specular highlights that your image may contain, and the diffuse highlights, which contain the critical highlight image data. The diffuse highlights should be located in the lightest portions of the image which still have detail.

PAULINE'S SCAN TIPS

Scan Tip # 7-5

Making neutral areas of your image neutral is a basic key to color scanning. Use your Info tool to measure neutral areas such as white highlights. Use a curve tool to make adjustments to individual channels to make these neutral areas neutral. This will remove any color cast from your image.

Scan Tip # 7-6

For color contones, as for grayscale contone images, determine the maximum print/reproduction size of an image before you scan, and allow your scanner to perform the scaling duties. This will save you time and result in higher quality images compared to performing these chores in an image editing application after the scan.

Scan Tip # 7-7

When determining the input resolution at which you will scan grayscale photos, use a formula of 1.5 x lpi at which the image will be printed. Remember that this image should not be scaled up after the scan, as there will not be enough pixel data to support the printing.

Scan Tip # 7-8

During the scanning sampling process, your scanner will soften your image. To return an image to its original sharpness/focus, apply unsharp mask to your image. This can be performed during the scan if you do not intend to edit your image. If post-scan image editing is in order, perform the unsharp mask after the scan and image editing processes have been completed. For portrait images in particular, be sure to utilize a threshold value (3–5) to prevent over-sharpening of smooth, low-contrast portions of your image. I prefer to convert my color images to Lab mode and apply the unsharp mask to the "L" channel. This prevents color shifts from occurring along high-contrast image areas.

8

Transparencies Step By Step

As the Byte Turns continues...

Will Danny D'Ziner and Pauline E. Prepress intentions be transparent to each other, or will they have negative impressions?

What are all those marks on my slide images?

Oooh, that doesn't look good!

You're handling your transparencies with your hands rather than with gloves, and you are not cleaning the film before you scan.

TRANSPARENCY SCANNING

What Is a Transparency?

A transparency is an image that exists on film. While most transparencies are contones, a transparency can hold any kind of image, including black and white or colored line art, or grayscale or color contones. Unlike reflective images, where light is reflected off the surface of the image prior to capture, transparent images are captured by passing light through the film. Popular film sizes include 35mm, 2¼" x 2¼", 4" x 5", and 8" x 10". Unlike reflective images, which are nearly all positive images, transparencies exist as both positive and negative images.

Transparency Challenges

Just as with any reflective image, it is the underlying grayscale values that control the composition, quality, and color values in a digital grayscale or color contone image captured from a transparency. When we are capturing and reproducing color contone images from transparencies, our main focus should still be on accurate reproduction of grayscale. If we want to faithfully reproduce a grayscale or a color contone transparent image so that our scanned version is as close as possible to the original, our focus should be on grayscale reproduction. In other circumstances, we may want to alter a transparent contone image from its original form with the intent of improving and/or just changing the image. In either case, whether we are reproducing or altering a transparent contone image, we will focus on the grayscale values of the image.

Two of the most common problems we see with scanned transparent images are, like with reflective images, that they tend to reproduce too dark, and transparent images often have unbalanced color, which leads to obvious color casts in images. Plus, with negative transparencies, we have no original image to refer to. But whether our images are too light, or too dark, or the contrast is poor, or the color balance is wrong, control of our images always boils down to the control of our image's grayscale values. There are four primary factors to which we need to pay the most attention if we want to control our color values, and these are: 1) scanner *calibration (linearization* and *neutralization)*, 2) setting of *highlight* and *shadow* values, 3) controlling the distribution of grayscale data to control *contrast*, and 4) neutralization of images to remove image color cast.

Pixels vs. vectors

All of our scanned images will be initially created as pixel-based images, as this is the only form in which scanners capture images. Like some of the simple reflective line art images we created and discussed in the chapter on line art scanning, simple transparent line art images are good candidates to be converted into vector-based images.

Like their reflective cousins, transparent grayscale and color contone images, which by their very nature contain a great deal of detail, will be captured as, and remain as, pixel-based images.

Resolution for scanning transparent images

Just as with capturing reflective line art and contone images, it is usually a good idea to use the optical resolution of our scanners when capturing transparent images. Using the optical resolution of the scanner is a key factor in accurate grayscale reproduction. Using the optical resolution of your scanner will also reduce the *interpolated*-related softening of the image which occurs as a result of scanning, and noticeably decrease scan times. (See Chapter 1 for an in-depth discussion of optical resolution.) For transparent image scans, we use resolution values similar to those used for line art (500–1200ppi) and contone images, 1.5 x lpi x scaling factor as we did for our reflective scans (refer to the line art, reflective grayscale, and color contone chapters for more details on these basics).

If we are scanning small transparencies, such as 35mm slides, and intend to print them at larger sizes such as 5" x 7" or 8" x 10", then a considerable amount of scaling and therefore higher optical resolution is required to create a high-quality scanned image. For instance, in order to capture a 35mm slide with enough resolution to scale it to print as an 8" x 10" image at 150 lpi, an 8x increase in the scan resolution would be required. Using the 1.5 x lpi x scaling factor formula, we would require: 1.3 x 150 x 8 = 1800ppi minimum optical resolution to capture the image properly.

Film emulsions

Another challenge unique to film scanning is accounting for the differences in exposure characteristics between various emulsions which are used to create films. Negative films especially have large differences between the color characteristics from various manufacturers. Particularly when scanning negative films, it is important to choose scan settings, often called film or emulsion terms, which match the type of negative film emulsion you are scanning.

TRANSPARENCY SCANNING (POSITIVES)

▼ *Figure 8.1 Frame Holder*
Shown here is the frame holder for a 2¼" x 2¾" transparency. The double pattern of the three dots at the top and bottom of the frame is used for the auto recognition feature.

▼ *Figure 8.2 Film Support Choices*
In this scan software, you have the choice of three types of frames: 1) 35mm slide tray for multiple slides, 2) frame holders of various sizes, and 3) a negative holder.

Calibration of your Scanner

Linearization and/or neutralization for grayscale or color scanning

The same calibration techniques for scanning grayscale and color reflective images, discussed earlier in this book, apply to scanning transparencies as well. The only difference is that a transparent target with known grayscale values should be used. Separate transparent targets (positive and negative) are needed because a different light source is generally used than what is used for a reflective scan, and that light will be transmitted through, rather than reflected off, the target and images to be scanned.

Handling transparencies

It is a good idea to always handle your transparencies with white, lint-free gloves. It is very easy to get fingerprints on transparencies. They are easily damaged, particularly on the emulsion side.

Using one of several film holders which should be provided with your scanner makes handling of your transparencies easier. Besides easier and cleaner handling, the scan software may also provide an auto-detect feature which automatically locates images placed inside the provided film holders. The scan software shown here (Fig 8.2) provides three choices: 1) *35mm Slide Tray* for mounted slides, 2) *Frame Holder* (Fig 8.1) for unmounted film placed in a custom frame holder, and 3) *Negative Film Holder* for use with strips of film. Note: Your scanner may be shipped with one or more of the following four frame holders: 4"x 5". 2¼" x 2¾" (6cm x 7cm), 2¼" x 2¼" (6cm x 6cm), and/or a holder for negative strips of film.

Step-by-step: positive transparency scanning

1) If you are using a flatbed scanner, clean both the upper and lower scanner glass beds by wiping them with a lint-free cloth which has been lightly sprayed with a mild optical glass cleaner. (See the section on scanner maintenance at the end of this book for more information on cleaning and maintaining your scanner.)

2) Place the transparency image squarely in a transparency holder.

▼ *Figure 8.3 Scan Control*
This PowerLook 3000 supports a high optical resolution of 3048 x 3048ppi, which can be used for high-quality scaling of small images like 35mm slides. Having the scanner perform the scaling will result in higher quality images.

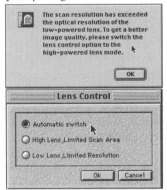

▼ *Figure 8.4 Dual Lens Systems*
Some scanners, like this UMAX PowerLook 3000, have a dual lens system with both low and high resolution (1220ppi and 3048ppi). If you get a warning message like this, be sure to check the scanning software to adjust the lens properly.

3) Clean your transparency by blowing off the image with a can of compressed air.

4) Place the transparency holder with the image on the scan bed. Note: To take advantage of the maximum optical resolution of some scanners, you must place the frame holder so that the image is inside the area of the scan bed designated as the maximum resolution area. When using a negative holder, it may be necessary to place a cover on top of the holder to flatten and hold the negatives securely during the scan.

5) Close the scanner cover.

6) Launch the scan software.

7) If you are using a scanner which has the ability to control the focus, now is the time to either activate the auto-focus feature of your software or perform a manual focus. Consult your software manual for instructions.

8) Select the appropriate source image choice (frame holder or tray, if you are using one) from the source image menu (Fig 8.2).

9) Perform the calibration and image setup steps. Linearization and neutralization will need to be performed. You can use the gamma curve tool to provide a rough, three-channel linearization, and then fine-tune the neutralization calibration with a color cast adjustment tool. Remember that any tool which you use to perform a calibration adjustment should not be used again except to perform a recalibration.

Note: To perform a calibration for scanning a transparency, you will need to use a film-based grayscale target. Contact your scanner manufacturer to determine a source for a film target. Be sure that you obtain the grayscale values for the swatches on the target. Also, be sure that the grayscale values you receive are in units you can relate to, such as RGB (0–255) or percent grayscale (0–100%K), such as the values which are used on the Taz Tally calibration target used in the previous reflective grayscale and color contone scan exercises.

For adjusting your scanner settings to capture your transparency-based grayscale and color contones, use the same tools and follow the same procedures that we used to adjust the tone compression and neutralization for reflective grayscale and color contones. Highlight and shadow adjustments should still be performed on individual channels using an editable histogram. Neutralization of neutral (gray) portions of your transparent image can be accomplished through adjustment of a curve tool on individual channels. Unsharp masking can be applied either during the scan or in the post scan in an image editing application such as Photoshop.

Your scanned transparencies, which will be initially created in an RGB mode, can, like scanned reflective color contones, be converted into Lab mode. Once in Lab mode, the "L" channel can be used for applying unsharp mask without fear of color cast shifts along high-contrast edges. I also like to use the "L" channel for performing other *luminance* adjustments such as brightness and contrast adjustments. See Part III: After the Scan for more details on techniques for editing scanned images.

Note: Remember that the resolution requirements for output depend upon the amount of scaling that needs to be performed, the RIP being used for printing, the screening technology, and the intended viewing distance.

Scaling transparencies

In many cases, when we scan transparencies, and in particular if we are scanning 35mm slides and 120-size film, we need to significantly scale our images to adjust them to a useful print size. For instance, scaling a 35mm slide up to print at 11" x 14" requires a 10x increase in size and resolution. This scaling often requires high optical resolution to maintain image quality after scaling. The scaling can be done either during the scan or after the scan. By far, the best approach is to have the scanner perform the scaling, as the scanner will perform the scaling faster and with better quality. If you do not have your scanner perform the scaling, you will need to scan your images at a high enough resolution to accommodate the scaling of your images in an image editing application such as Photoshop. For instance, if you scan a 35mm slide at 300ppi, but you intend to scale the image after the scan by a factor of ten (10), you would need to scan your original image at 3000ppi to accommodate the post-scan scaling without decreasing the resolution and therefore the quality of the image (Fig 8.3). Your scanner will perform this scaling by setting the resolution at 300ppi and scaling at 1000%. See Chapter 3 for more information on scaling during a scan.

TRANSPARENCY SCANNING (NEGATIVES)

▼ Figure 8.5 Negative Emulsion Choices

If the manufacturer of your negative emulsion is listed, select the negative emulsion which matches your film.

Setup Specifics for Negative Scanning

Negative scanning is performed the same way as positive transparency scans, but with a few setup details specific to negative images.

1) Be especially careful when cleaning your negative images, as their emulsion (image) side is particularly susceptible to scratching.

2) Mount your negative images in frame holders as you would with positive transparencies, but if you use the negative strip holder with multiple images, be sure that there is some method or tool which can be used with the strip holder to help keep your negative strips, which tend to curl, flat during the scanning process.

3) When selecting your source image in the scanner control palette, be sure to choose a basic film/emulsion type of the negative images you are scanning from the Negative Film Holder sub menu (Fig 8.5). Every film manufacturer uses a different film emulsion to create their negative transparency films. As a result, each film emulsion has different color characteristics or sensitivities. Your scanning software should provide you with the ability to choose from any one of the most common negative film emulsion types. Your negative transparency calibration targets should be made from the same film type which you generally scan. If you typically scan a variety of negative films, you will obtain the best and most predictable scan results by creating and using film emulsion-specific calibration targets for each type of negative film emulsion you scan.

TRANSPARENCY PROBLEMS

Dirty Transparencies

The most common problems found with scanned transparencies are dirty images, which can be prevented by carefully cleaning your scan bed(s) with a lint-free cloth, and cleaning your images with canned air prior to scanning.

Newton Rings

▼ **Figure 8.6 Newton Ring**
Newton ring circles can be caused by the bending and separation of light which occurs when light passes through the glass/air/image boundaries.

An annoying problem sometimes encountered with scanning transparencies is the occurrence of circular patterns of light known as Newton rings (Fig 8.6). Newton rings are caused by the bending and separation of light as it moves through any glass/air/image boundaries. These multi-surface transitions exist when transparencies are scanned using scanners which require that the image be mounted on a glass substrate such as a drum scanner or a flat, glass bed scanner. This problem can be especially common on flatbed scanners which have overhead transparency units. These multi-purpose scanners create six different transition surfaces through which light must pass between the light source and the light collector. This problem can be avoided by using a dedicated film scanner which holds your transparency between a light source and collector without the use of an intervening surface. If, however, you do not have access to a dedicated substrate-free film scanner, there are several ways of preventing and/or solving this problem.

1) If this problem occurs intermittently, it may be prevented by simply remounting the image in its holder or using a new holder.

2) Mount your image using a mounting oil. Use of a mounting oil significantly decreases the likelihood of dispersion problems by lowering the difference in optical density, and therefore the amount of dispersion which occurs, between the film and the substrate.

3) If this problem occurs consistently, but intermittently, you should evaluate your scanning environment. A consistently cool, dry area is best. You can find out more about anti-Newton ring products, such as film mounting oil, from your local photography shop.

Note: See the section on creating and maintaining a professional, high-quality scanning environment at the end of Chapter 11.

PAULINE'S SCAN TIPS

Scan Tip # 8-1

Dedicated film scanners will generally provide better results than multi-purpose scanners. Dedicated film scanners have no glass–air interfaces which can interfere with the passage of light through and from the image.

Scan Tip # 8-2

Small transparencies, such as 35mm slides, require significant enlargement to print at standard sizes such as 5" x 7" or 8" x 10". This enlargement requires high resolution. It is best to use high optical resolution rather than interpolated resolution; therefore, scanners with high optical resolution ($\geq$ 2000 ppi) are preferred for scanning small slides.

Scan Tip # 8-3

Due to the high enlargement factor involved in the scanning of small transparencies, it is necessary to take extra precautions with cleaning your slides. Cans of dry air are excellent for this purpose.

Scan Tip # 8-4

When scanning negative transparencies, it is critically important to pay close attention to, and adjust for, the specific film emulsion used on your film. Each manufacturer has its own emulsion with its own sensitivities. Your software should have built-in adjustments for the major manufacturer emulsions.

PAULINE'S SCAN TIPS

Scan Tip # 8-5

Newton rings can be avoided through the use of dedicated film scanners with no glass–air interfaces. Newton rings can be avoided when scanning with flatbed scanners by using scanning oil to mount your images.

Scan Tip # 8-6

The calibration of film scanners requires the use of film targets (positive and negative) to linearize and neutralize the scanner. Be sure to acquire film targets which are themselves neutral. Also be sure that the film targets are accompanied by grayscale values with useful units, such as RGB or percent gray, rather than the less useful density and/or L* values common on some targets.

9
Screened Images Step By Step

As the Byte Turns continues...

Will Danny D'Ziner and Pauline E. Prepress be able to SCREEN each other properly, or will they follow the same old PATTERN?

PREVIOUSLY PRINTED/SCREENED IMAGES

▼ Figure 9.1 Previously Printed Image

The challenge is to remove the scan pattern created by the printed pattern of halftone dots without softening the image so much that its quality is destroyed.

A printed/screened color version of this image can be found in the "Practice Images" pages at the back of this book.

What Is a Screen Pattern?

Printed photographic images, such as images from books and magazines, are constructed from patterns of halftone dots called screens. These screened patterns, usually constructed from very evenly spaced halftone dots, often form easily recognizable patterns. While these dots and their patterns, typically screened at 65–250 lpi, may not be easily recognized by the human eye, they are easily "seen" by a scanner, which is typically capturing the screened image at 200–300ppi. When scanned, this pattern of halftone dots is captured by the scanner. If this pattern is not removed prior to reprinting, a moiré pattern will likely result (Fig 9.1). Scanning images printed at lower line screens, 65 –120 lpi, will typically produce the most obvious patterns. The process of removing the captured halftone dot pattern from a scanned image is called descreening. See Chapter 3, "Printing Scanned Images," for more details on how these screen patterns are created during the RIPing and printing processes.

Descreening Challenge

Our challenge is to convert this scanned pattern of high-contrast, halftone dots into a lower contrast, smoother pattern of grayscale pixels. So, we need to convert dots into pixels and lower the small-scale contrast to remove the original dot pattern. It is important to remove this halftone dot pattern so that it will not be reproduced as a moiré pattern when it is reprinted after it is scanned.

The process of scanning itself begins to remove the dot pattern, because, as we have seen in other exercises, scanning tends to soften high-contrast edges, in this case, the edge of the halftone dots. So, all we need to do is help that contrast lowering process along by further softening the image. This image softening, to remove this dot pattern, can be accomplished by using one or more softening tools and/or techniques which lower the contrast pattern created by original halftone dots. Care needs to be taken, however, that the image is not softened too much. Over-softening an image may lower its quality to unacceptable levels. Although over-softening can be used as an artistic effect by a designer, our goal is usually to soften the image just enough to rid the image of its latent halftone dot pattern, and no more. Any creative addition of softening may be added on top of this.

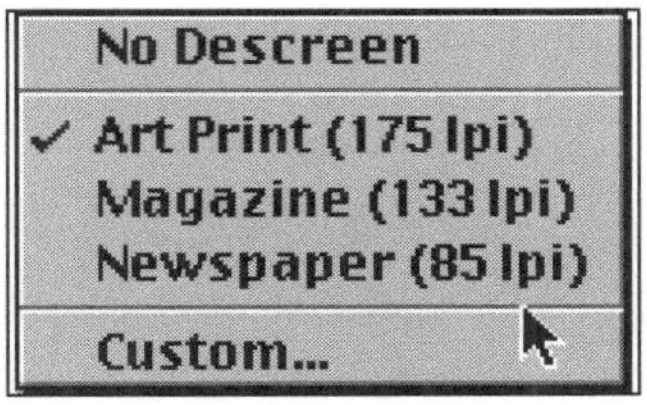

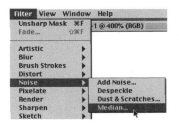

▼ Figure 9.2 Descreen Filter
When scanning previously printed images, activate the Descreen Filter in the Scan Control palette to help with the removal of the scan pattern which often results from the scanning of printed materials. Configure your scanner's descreen filter to match the line screen at which the image was printed.

Step-by-step: descreening procedures

Any printed/screened grayscale or color contone image needs to be treated with the same proper scanning procedures we have previously covered, including: scanner calibration (linearization for grayscale images and linearization and neutralization for color contones); tone compression by setting proper highlights and shadows (using an editable histogram); contrast adjustments (using a curve tool); and color correction (neutralization) for color contone images. After these fundamental adjustments have been made on a preview image in preparation for the final scan, there are numerous tools and techniques which can be used to aid in the descreening of a printed image. Listed below are some which can be applied during the scanning process and some which can be applied afterward.

Descreening tools applied during the scan

After a fundamental preview scan has been adjusted for the final scan, here are the various tools which can be used individually or together to aid in the descreening process:

A) Throw your scanner slightly out of focus if your scanner has this capability.

B) If you cannot unfocus your scanner (most flat beds), try placing a 1/16" sheet of plate glass on the scan bed beneath the image.

C) Select the proper scan source/mode, 256 grayscale or TrueColor RGB, and set up the scan as you normally would for grayscale or color contone images as outlined in previous sections.

D) Rotate the image on the scan bed.

E) Scan at a higher resolution (1.5x) than would be needed to print or reproduce the image.

F) Activate the descreen filter from the Scan Control palette and select the line screen (lpi) at which the image was printed, 85 lpi, 133 lpi, 150 lpi, etc. (Fig 9.2).

G) Name and save your image as a TIFF as instructed before using a naming scheme such as TazJaz Hawaii_RGB_200DS.tif. Here the "DS" indicates that the image has been descreened.

After the scan in an image editing application

A) Open TazJaz Hawaii_RGB_200DS.tif and make a copy to work on.

B) View the image in various channels (for color images) to see where

▼ Figure 9.3 Photoshop Noise Filter
On difficult images, descreening can be aided through the careful application of noise filters, such as the Median filter, in Photoshop. Work on individual channels rather than the composite image when descreening color images. This reduces the amount of total damage to an image, thereby preserving as much of the image quality as possible.

most of the patterns are being generated, and plan to work on the individual channels.

C) Sample the image down to its proper resolution.

D) Rotate the image to its proper position.

E) Apply Noise Filters: Median, De-speckle, or Dust & Scratches to individual channels for color images as needed (Fig 9.3).

F) Blur individual channels.

G) Apply noise and blur to the entire image if necessary (avoid this in color images whenever possible).

H) Convert the image to Lab mode.

I) Apply unsharp mask to the "L" channel to sharpen the image. Be careful not to bring back any residual pattern. Apply the filter in 50% increments. Alternatively, you can apply "Fade" on the Luminosity after each unsharp mask if you apply unsharp mask to a composite RGB image.

J) Name and save your image as a TIFF as instructed before using a naming scheme such as TazJaz Hawaii_RGB_200DS2.tif. Here, the "DS2" indicates that this is the second descreened version of the image.

Naming note: You may want to simplify the naming of the final version of an image once you produce an acceptable descreened and sharpened image. I like to keep careful track of my image versions with sequential numbers, especially if I have multiple working versions of an image, or numerous intermediate steps.

Some descreening tips

Tip #1

View each effect on the whole image and up close at the pixel level to help you judge the effect of the current move and provide guidance for the next adjustment you may want to make. Usually, one of the RGB channels will show the original halftone dot pattern less than the other channels. This less-affected channel will require fewer repairs than the other channels. Repair this channel by itself with the minimum amount of alterations possible. Then use this channel to help maintain the sharpness and integrity of the final image. Descreening of color images should be done on a channel-by-channel basis rather than on the composite image to prevent excessive image softening.

Tip #2

When you find a descreening sequence that works for a type of image, record the sequence of alterations as a Photoshop action. This action can then be easily played back on other images. If you are not familiar with this function in Photoshop, please refer to Adobe's Photoshop manual and Help file.

Additional Corrections after the Scan

You may want to save the Unsharp masking and RGB-to-CMYK conversions of an image for Photoshop, depending upon how much image editing you plan to perform in the post scan in Photoshop. The more editing and correction you intend to do, the more appropriate it is to work in RGB (or Lab) mode and save the mode conversion and unsharp masking for Photoshop.

Note: Since the grayscale value adjustment which occurs during the application of an unsharp mask tool affects not only the contrast but the color values as well, color shifts can occur along sharpened edges within an image. Color shift problems along edges can be avoided by: 1) performing unsharp mask on individual lower contrast channels, 2) performing unsharp mask on the "L" channel in Lab mode, or 3) fading unsharp mask to 100% Luminosity in Photoshop Filter menu (Filter–Fade unsharp mask–100%–Luminosity).

PAULINE'S SCAN TIPS

Scan Tip # 9-1

When scanning previously screened (printed) images, it is useful to scan at a somewhat higher resolution than you would finally like to have. Down-sampling to your final target resolution in an image editing application will tend to interpolate the captured halftone dot pattern, thereby reducing its visibility.

Scan Tip # 9-2

When evaluating scanning software, look for the presence of descreening algorithms, and use them when scanning previously printed images.

Scan Tip # 9-3

Post-scan additions of noise and gaussian blur filters can help remove captured screen patterns. But, it is nearly always best, when working with color images, to apply these effects on individual channels rather than on the composite image. Some channels usually need more work than others, and the less-damaged channels can be spared the heavy application of correction filters, thereby helping to maintain the sharpness and focus of the image.

Scan Tip # 9-4

The process of descreening usually noticeably softens an image. The application of unsharp mask can return some of an image's focus and sharpness. However, when applying unsharp mask to a descreened image, apply it a bit at a time (~50%) and check to make sure the sharpening is not reactivating the screen pattern you have just removed.

10
Color Management

As the Byte Turns continues…

Will Danny D'Ziner and Pauline E. Prepress MANAGE to color their images of each other in the proper light?

*Hey!
Why doesn't my monitor match my printer?! And why do my two printed images look different?*

*What's wrong with some creative variation??…
Oops!
WRONG answer!*

Your monitor is difficult to match to your printer, and each printer requires a separate RGB-to-CMYK conversion.

AUTOMATED COLOR MATCHING AND CORRECTION

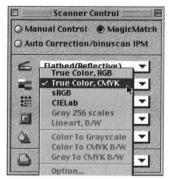

▼ Figure 10.1 Automatic Scanning
MagicMatch, seen here, is an example of an automatic scanning software. It is selected by clicking the MagicMatch button in the upper right-hand corner of the Scanner Control palette. When activated, MagicMatch, like many auto scanning/conversion software applications, offers several color space conversion options not available while in Manual Control.

Concept

In addition to the manual scanning controls which we have been using thus far, many scanning software applications also offer automatic scanning capabilities. There are a wide variety of automatic scanning packages covering a wide range of capabilities, including programs which do simple tone compression and contrast adjustments, to those which offer fully automated scanning as well as color space conversion. The quality of the various automatic scanning programs runs the gamut from poor to excellent.

Color Space Conversion

Many high-quality scanning software applications offer color space/gamut conversion. When you view the scan mode pull-down menu (Fig 10.1), you will see some examples of color space conversion, including CMYK, sRGB, and CIE Lab. These three menu choices are really a combination of scanning and color space conversion selections, and not just scan modes. Your scanner will still capture your image as an RGB image, and will then convert it on-the-fly to the color space you have selected. All you need to do is select the portion of the image which you want scanned and the automatic portion of the scan software sets up and performs the scan and then converts your RGB image to the color space you have selected. When you choose to utilize an automatic scan/conversion mode, you will often lose the manual setup and image enhancement controls we have utilized in the previous chapters. You should also note that some automatic scanning software does not support the scanning of negative images.

If you like the setup and scan choices which the automatic scan software offers, then use this scan mode. If, however, you want to take more control of the scanning setup, then choose the Manual Control mode.

Following is a brief description of several common color spaces and some notes on their use.

CMYK

A CMYK selection like the one shown in Fig 10.2 is used to convert your images directly into a CMYK color space after your scanner captures them. CMYK is used for the printing of your images on CMYK desktop color printers and commercial printing presses. If you select the CMYK conversion choice, you will notice that a printer's menu appear at the bottom of the Scanner Control palette (see Fig 10.2). If you use the CMYK conversion choice, it is important for you to select from this menu the printer description which is closest to the device on which you will be printing your image. If you intend to print your image on one device, that device appears in the printer's list, and if you do not intend to use your image for other purposes (a Web page, printing to a film recorder, or CMYK printing device), this CMYK conversion choice may be a good method to use. If, however, you intend to reproduce your image on several different devices, converting your scanned image immediately to a specific CMYK color space may not be the best approach. Converting an image to a specific CMYK color space will tend to restrict the color values in the image to that specific device and reduce the number of colors which can be reproduced on other devices. (See the discussion of multi-purposing of images below.)

▼ Figure 10.2 CMYK Conversion
If you select the CMYK conversion choice in this scanning software, MagicMatch, it is important to select a printer which most closely resembles your printing device from the "Printers" menu at the bottom of the Scanner Control palette. Selected here is the 3M MatchPrint proofing device, which is a common proofing device used in commercial offset printing.

RGB

RGB is a very restricted monitor color space. This conversion mode should be chosen only if you intend to use your images for projection on 8-bit (256 color) color monitors or projectors. If you intend to print your images on CMYK or other RGB devices, such as 16-bit (thousands of colors) or 24-bit monitors (16.7 million colors), do not choose this conversion mode.

CIE Lab

CIE Lab is a large color space defined by the limits of human vision, and it is used by numerous color management systems. It is a wonderful, although not widely used, image editing/color correction space. If your color management software utilizes this color space, or you happen to have the ability to work in Lab mode with your post-scan images, this is a good color space. CIE Lab is also a good archive color space in which to save your images if you intend to use them for multiple purposes. (See the following discussion on multi-purposing of images.)

Multi-purposing of images

During most of the history of professional scanning and commercial printing, and in the early days of desktop publishing, most of our scanned images were converted directly to CMYK, and most often during the scanning process. This is still a viable approach if you intend to print to only one type of device, such as a commercial printing press. The recent and continuing explosion of electronic publishing into all areas of graphic communications allows us to reproduce our images on many different types of devices, including RGB film recorders, Web pages, and a dizzying array of desktop color printing devices. Many of these new devices are able to reproduce a wider range, or *gamut*, of colors than standard commercial printing presses. As a result, it is not always appropriate to convert directly to CMYK, as in doing so you may inadvertently reduce significantly the range of colors which you may be able to reproduce on other devices. And if you work exclusively in the world of RGB (Web pages, film recorders, monitors and projectors), conversion to CMYK is totally unnecessary.

If you intend to multi-purpose your images, that is, use them on multiple devices, a good approach is to capture/create your images initially in a large color space such as TrueColor RGB or CIE Lab. This initial image can be saved as a wide-gamut color archive image from which copies can be made to reproduce on a wide variety of devices. For instance, RGB-to-CMYK (for printing) or RGB-to-Index (for Web use) conversion can be accomplished through Photoshop or other image editing/correction applications.

Color Management Software

Most automatic scanning/conversion software applications require the addition of color profiles, such as ICC profiles, and an operating-level color management engine, such as ColorSync, to work properly. These components must be properly installed in order for these automatic color space conversion capabilities to function properly. The proper creation of the color profiles, which should match the specific devices you are using to scan, view, and print your images, is one of the most important keys to accurate and predictable color space conversion. Some people prefer to perform their color space conversions in an image editing application such as Photoshop, where they may have more control over the conversion, rather than utilize generic profiles shipped with many scanners.

PAULINE'S SCAN TIPS

Scan Tip # 10-1

Each output device has its own color space, or gamut. So, when we prepare a scanned image for output on a specific device, we should use the color characteristics of that device to guide this preparation, or gamut conversion. If you are preparing your images to be printed at a printing company or service bureau, ask their production manager for guidance in setting up an RGB-to-CMYK gamut conversion which will match their production process.

Scan Tip # 10-2

Being linear and neutral is the foundation of all good color management. Even if you do no more than engage in making your devices and images linear and neutral, you will be taking a big step toward properly and predictably controlling your color.

Scan Tip # 10-3

If you need to multi-purpose your images, you will want to scan your images into a large color space, CIE or RGB, which encompasses all of the output devices you intend to use. Then you can convert copies of your images into the device-specific gamut for each output device.

11

Miscellaneous Scanning Issues

As the Byte Turns continues...

Will Danny D'Ziner and Pauline E. Prepress be able to MONITOR their use of their printed images?

I need to use my images for several different purposes...I need to use them for multiple print devices as well as the Web.

Way over my head...Let's ask Pauline. Hopefully she can help explain the solution.

When multi-purposing an image, you need to create it for the largest size, highest resolution, and largest color space with which you intend to work.

CONTONE SCANNING RESOLUTIONS

▼ *Figure 11.1 Scan Resolution and Scaling Dialog Box*
Use your scanner's software to determine the final resolution of your image. And, whenever possible, let the scanner perform your scaling chores as well. Your scanner will do a better job, and do it faster, than a post-scan image editing application like Photoshop.

Concept

Output resolution in lines per inch (known as lpi or line screen) should control the input scan resolution in pixels per inch (ppi). When multi-purposing images, use the resolution of the most demanding device (usually a printing press) to perform your scan. Then, make copies of your original image and down-sample the image resolution to match the requirements of less demanding devices (laser printers, Web images, etc.).

Commercial and desktop halftone printing

Standard halftone (AM) screening:

Formula: 1.5 x lpi x scaling factor

Example 1, no scaling: 1.5 x 150 lpi x 1 (no scaling) = 225ppi

Example 2, with scaling: 1.5 x 150 lpi x 2 (doubles image dimensions from 4"x5" to 8"x10") = ~450ppi

Best results will occur if you perform scaling during the scan. For instance, you would set your scanner resolution for 200ppi at 200% for example 2 above (see Fig. 11.1 and Fig. 11.2). The exception to this is when you scan previously screened/printed images. These should usually be scanned at a higher and odd resolution, with the expectation that the resolution will be lowered in Photoshop after the scan.

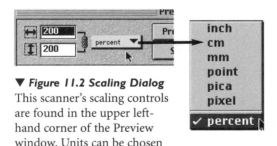

▼ *Figure 11.2 Scaling Dialog*
This scanner's scaling controls are found in the upper left-hand corner of the Preview window. Units can be chosen to suit your needs.

Stochastic (FM) screening

There are no line screens in FM printing, so we use final resolution to help determine input scan resolution. For printing to large-format inkjet printers, final resolution should be between 100–150ppi after scaling. A good average is 125ppi. For finer-grained FM printing on offset presses, higher resolutions, 150–175ppi, may be required. Consult your printing company or service bureau for their specific guidelines.

Note: See Chapters 2 and 3 and the glossary for more in-depth discussions of *AM* vs. *FM* screening. Also, remember that the resolution requirements for output depend upon the amount of scaling that needs to be performed, the RIP being used for printing, the screening technology, and the intended viewing distance.

Other output devices

In addition to the standard dot printing devices such as commercial presses and laser printers that use dots to reproduce images, there is an increasing array of desktop output devices, such as dye sublimation and ink jet printers, that do not use standard dots for image reproduction. In addition, there is a proliferating array of software drivers which may supply scaling functions to images during the printing process. Because of this wide variety of printing technologies available to us, it is difficult to offer specific advice for scanning resolution for all desktop devices. But, here are some guidelines:

1) Most desktop printing devices require resolution in the range of 100–300ppi in the pixel-based image.

2) Test your output device at a number of resolutions. For instance, you might try printing with 100, 150, 200, 250, and 300ppi. Then experiment to judge which resolution is the one that you need. Choose the lowest resolution that gives you satisfactory results. Often you will find that you will not see any improvement in image quality past a certain resolution. You may be surprised how low you can go with some of the new printers and their technologies. If you are sending your files out to a service bureau for printing, be sure to consult them for advice on image resolution.

The RIPs used by different manufacturers may have various capabilities such as scaling and interpolation. The resolution for most FM printers is significantly lower than typical commercial print resolutions of 200–300ppi. Required image resolution will vary with the screening technology and intended viewing distance. For instance, large-format printers that create images which are intended to be viewed from many feet away produce much larger and more widely spaced dots, requiring much looser resolution, (often well below 100ppi) than standard commercial print material, which is intended to be viewed from a distance of 10"-16". Be sure to become familiar with your RIP's capabilities and the intended use of the images you scan.

DOT GAIN

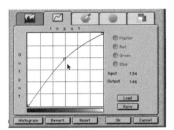

▼ *Figure 11.3 Dot Gain Correction Curve*

A curve that overall lightens an image prior to printing it should be applied to each image to compensate for dot gain. The amount of lightening, or dot gain adjustment, required depends upon several variables, including the ink or toner to be used and the paper or other substrate on which the printing will occur. For example, uncoated papers tend to require more dot gain correction than coated papers.

Note: It is a good idea to contact your printing company to discuss who will perform the dot gain correction on your grayscale images, and where it will be formed. This will help prevent the dot gain from being ignored or from being double-applied.

Concept

Images tend to print darker than they scan. This is because ink and toner tend to spread out when they are applied to paper, making our halftone dots larger and our grayscale values darker. This spreading out of ink and toner when it is applied to printing substrates is known as dot gain. In general, we need to lighten our images prior to printing them so that they print and view at their proper grayscale values.

Dot gain correction

Correction for dot gain can occur in any number of places, including: during the scan, in an image editing application like Photoshop, during gamut conversion for color images, or even during the RIPing process itself. Regardless of when the correction occurs, the typical tool used is nearly always the same. Dot gain correction usually involves applying a curve to lighten the image prior to printing. If you are multi-purposing your images, it may be best to apply the dot gain correction lightening curve after the scanning process so that you can accommodate the dot gain requirements of more than one output device. Post-scan application of a dot gain correction curve will also allow you to avoid the creation of non-print images which appear too light.

1) To apply a dot gain correction during the scanning process, you can create or load a curve similar to the one in Fig 11.3 with the Curve tool (Image Enhancement tool window). Click the Load button to select a saved curve. You can download Photoshop curves or ones created in the scan software.

2) Alternatively, you can increase the midtone number on the gamma curve to effect dot gain correction lightening. But be aware that by applying dot gain correction through your gamma curve, you would be linearizing your scanner to a specific output device rather than to your monitor. This can be a helpful, time-saving procedure if you are printing to only one device, but can create problems if you are outputting to several devices.

3) Dot gain correction can be applied in Photoshop or other image editing applications through the creation or loading process and application of curves or transfer functions.

4) If you are sending your graphic images out to a service bureau or printing company, call and ask them if they will be applying dot gain correction to your images. If they want you to apply the correction, ask them how much of a curve you should apply.

5) If you are printing in-house on your own printers, you may want to experiment with several curves to see which one gives the best results.

Note: It is always a good idea to archive original, non-dot gain corrected images somewhere, in case you need to use your images again on other devices which require different, or no, dot gain correction.

MULTIPLE SCANS

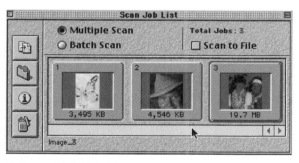

▼ Figure 11.4 Multiple and Batch Scans
The scan software allows you to scan more than one image at a time, or scan the same image several different ways. Separate frames are set up for each scan made.

You can improve your productivity through multiple and batch scanning. These scanning tools allow you to scan more than one image at a time, or scan the same image in multiple ways. To take advantage of these scan tools, activate the Scan Job List tool from the Window menu (see Fig 11.4). Multiple or batch scan settings are set by creating additional scan frames. This can be done by creating a new scan frame from the Image menu, or by using the scan frame tool in the Preview window.

Multiple-Image Scanning

Multiple-image scanning involves setting up a scanner to capture multiple images during one scanning pass, using individual scanner setups for each image. With multiple-image scanning, you get the highest quality because the scanner will calibrate before capturing each image.

Batch-Image Scanning

Batch-image scanning also captures multiple images during one scanning pass, using the same individual scanner setups for each image. With batch-image scanning, you get the fastest speed because it does just one calibration upon starting the project. In either case, separate frames are created for each scan frame.

SCANS FOR WEB IMAGES

Two Approaches to Scanning for Web Imaging

Scan for print and then convert a copy for the Web

A good approach is to start by scanning an image for the highest resolution needed, which is usually print. Then, make a copy of the image and prepare that image for the Web. This Web preparation usually involves down-sizing, resolution reduction, mode and color space adjustment, and a file format change. This is a good procedure to use because images are often and sometimes unexpectedly used for multiple purposes.

Scan directly for the Web

If you know that you will only use an image for the Web, use the same techniques for line art, grayscale photographs, and color photographs discussed earlier, keeping the following in mind:

1) Scan the images at the largest format size that you will need for use on a Web page. Note: You can always copy and down-size your images later without loss of image quality.

2) Scan the images at 72ppi, but make sure that you create them at the size at which you will use them. No scaling up will be possible without noticeable image degradation. You may choose to scan at a much higher resolution if you are working in a real-time, high-resolution image editing software, like Live Picture.

3) Do not go through any gamut conversion to CMYK. Capture your images in RGB or CIELab mode.

4) If you are scanning directly for the Web, final image preparation for the Web still usually involves a mode and color space adjustment and a file format change. Take this more direct approach if you are working on a Web-only project.

TECHNICAL SUPPORT

If you have trouble with your scanner, or trouble getting your software drivers to access your scanner or work correctly, try following these steps:

1) Take the time to consult your manual for proper setup and installation tips. I know, you hate manuals, but many problems can be easily solved without having the hassle of a telephone call and a long wait. See if your manual has a troubleshooting, common problems, or frequently asked questions (FAQ) section. You may be surprised to find your problem, and its solution.

2) Open and read the "Read Me" files which came with your scanning hardware and software. These "Read Me" files, while admittedly being dull as dishwater to look at, often contain numerous pearls of wisdom including lists of known conflicts and solutions or work-arounds.

3) Consult the "Help" menu which may be available in your scanning software. You may be surprised to find the answer to your problems right there in front of you.

4) Contact your scanner manufacturer. Look in your scanner manual for a phone number, or better yet, try contacting your manufacturer via the Web. If you cannot find a specific Web address, try www."the company name".com, then look for likely help areas called "Support", or "Technical Support." Most companies' Web addresses are pretty straightforward, at least to get to the main home page. After you locate the technical support page, save that Web address as a bookmark so that you can return to it quickly at any time. I have done this for all the hardware and software manufacturers whose products I own and use. If you cannot directly find the answers to your questions you can often leave questions for Technical Support to answer via email or a call-back.

5) Contact a local VAR or service provider for help. Don't be afraid to pay for good-quality technical advice. But, don't let them leave or pay them before they fix your problem.

6) Provide some choice expletives while hurling your equipment and software manuals out the window. This will provide immense emotional satisfaction, if not a solution to your technical problem. :-)

TRAINING SUPPORT

Consulting Help and Custom Training

If you would like my advice on scanning problems, or you would like to arrange for custom training for you or your staff, contact me via email at ttallyphd@aol.com for more information.

Training Seminars

If you are interested in obtaining first-hand training on scanning and other image creation and editing techniques, you may attend a Taz Tally Seminar. You may obtain a discount for seminar attendance by mentioning that you saw this information in a Taz Tally publication when you sign up for a seminar. Contact Taz Tally Seminars at 941-433-0622, or visit the Web site at www.tazseminars.com.

Educational Materials

If you are interested in obtaining other training materials such as interactive training CDs, videos, and books, as well as mini-courses and online training, visit www.tazseminars.com. Also, check out the Prentice Hall Web page ar www.phptr.com for a list of all of my Prentice Hall educational materials.

SCANNING ENVIRONMENT

Cleaning Your Scanner and Images

If you are using a flatbed, be sure to clean your scan bed with a lint-free cloth prior to each use. Keep your mitts off the glass while you are handling your images. It is so easy to put fingerprints on the scan bed glass. The easiest way to keep both your scanner and your images clear of smudges and fingerprints is to wear white cotton gloves while handling your images. While there are many cleaning solutions available, I recommend the Vision Eye Care solution, which can be purchased at Walmart for ~$3.00US. This solution comes with a small packet which holds a lint-free (very important) silk cloth. It is generally a good idea to spray the solution on the cloth rather than directly on the scan bed.

This will prevent any solution from dripping into the "works" of the scanner.

It is just as important to clean your images as it is to clean your scanner. However, care needs to be taken when cleaning images to prevent damage from occurring during the cleaning process. Prevention is better than cure in this case. Always use white cotton gloves when handling images, and particularly when handling film-based images such as positive transparencies and negatives.

The best method of cleaning dust off images is to use canned air. But, be careful when using canned air because sometimes you'll blow the transparency right out of your hand onto the floor. And then to add insult to injury, you will probably end up stepping on it while you are trying to find it. Oops! Then what will you tell your client? So, it is best to firmly place your image in its scanning film holder prior to treating it with canned air.

If your images need to be cleaned with a cloth, be sure to use a soft, non-abrasive, lint-free-cloth. I recommend silk. In some cases, with the dirtiest of images which may have spills or other difficult grunge on them, I have actually had to wet them down to clean them. Do not use any solution other than distilled water, and let the images air-dry completely prior to handling them. DO NOT try to speed up the process by using a hair dryer or similar tool. Film emulsions are very sensitive to temperature and can be easily warped or destroyed by excess heat.

A Professional Imaging Environment

If you intend to perform high-quality scanning, and especially if you will be working with transparencies, you will probably find that you will be well-served by creating a clean scanning environment. If your scanning environment is dusty and dirty, trying to clean your scanner and your images may prove to be an exercise in frustration. For no sooner do you clean your image, than new dust settles on your newly cleaned images. While you are at it, why not just set up a total professional imaging environment for both scanning and printing. Following is a short list of environmental conditions to control to create a clean, consistent imaging environment:

• Filtered air with positive air pressure

• Constant temperature and humidity

• Control of static electricity

• Clean, dedicated electricity

• Neutral-colored walls and monitor backgrounds

• Indirect 5000K lighting

SCANNER MAINTENANCE AND SAFETY

One key to having a scanner perform consistently is to follow a few simple maintenance and safety precautions.

Maintenance

A clean scan bed is a first step to high-quality scanning. At the beginning of each scan session, you should clean the glass surfaces that will be in contact with your images. If you are scanning reflective art, you need to clean the lower glass scan bed. And, if you are scanning transparencies, you will need to clean both the upper and lower glass plates. The PowerLook 3000 has only one glass surface to clean. Use a lint-free cloth (I recommend silk) and a streak-free optical cleaning solution. Spray a bit of the solution on the silk cloth and then clean the glass surface(s). Do not spray any liquid directly on the scanner surface. It is also a good idea to have your scanner in a dust-free environment with constant temperature and moisture, if possible. Dust-heavy environments may eventually lead to dust getting into the scanner and settling on the inside of the glass, perhaps affecting scanner operation.

Cleaning the outside of the scanner should also be done with a cloth on which you have sprayed a non-corrosive cleaner such as pure water or water with a mild cleaner. Be sure to unplug your scanner before cleaning.

Safety

Electrical safety is of primary importance. DO NOT plug your scanner into an outlet which does not have a grounding plug. Three-prong sockets are grounded and should be used. It is also a good idea to attach your scanner to your computer before you plug it into an electrical outlet. Plug both devices into their electrical outlets before you turn them on.

The easiest way to damage your scanner is to treat it roughly when you move it. First, never move your scanner while it is operating. Prior to moving your scanner, and particularly if you intend to travel any distance, be sure to lock the optics in place. This is done by turning the lock slot(s) into its locked position. Reflective-only scanners will have one lock slot. If your scanner has a transparency adapter, there will be one or more additional locks. There is no lock on the PowerLook 3000. Please refer to your hardware manual for the location of the lock slot on your particular scanner.

PAULINE'S SCAN TIPS

Scan Tip # 11-1

It is good to be clear on the type of halftone dot being used to print your scanned image. While most commercial printers continue to use standard AM dots, some use FM dots, and many desktop devices employ FM screens to print images. AM and FM screens have different resolution requirements, with FM typically requiring less resolution than AM. Consult your service bureau for specific resolution guidelines.

Scan Tip # 11-2

Dot gain occurs whenever ink or toner is put on paper and can create significant darkening of your images. Dot gain can be corrected during printing or in the post scan in an image editing program. Post-scan correction is best for multi-purposing.

Scan Tip # 11-3

Images which are scanned for use on the Web can be set for size and resolution directly during the scan. But, if you intend to multi-purpose your images, it is best to scan for print and then convert, with down-sizing, sampling, and color space conversion for the Web on a copy of the scanned image.

Scan Tip # 11-4

Much time can be saved by scanning more than one image during each scan pass. Be sure that your scanning software supports individual scan settings for each image.

Scan Tip # 11-5

Maintain a consistent scanning environment to obtain consistent scan results.

PART II REVIEW

Step-by-Step Line Art Scans

The key issue when scanning line art is to pay attention to edge reproduction. Simple line art can be scanned at 500–600ppi and then converted to vectors. Detailed black and white line art should be scanned in 8-bit+ (GS) mode and at a resolution in the range of 1000–1200ppi (depending upon the optical resolution of your scanner). The grayscale scan will provide you with the ability to precisely control the density of the detail in a post-scan image editing application such as Photoshop. Be sure to convert all grayscale versions of line art images to 1-bit black and white if you want the line art edges to print crisply.

Colored line art should be scanned in 24-bit (RGB) mode. This produces three grayscale versions of your images with varying contrast, which can be used to separate the various colored line art areas after the scan.

Remember to always work on a copy of your image, never the original. Keep the original as an untouched archive image to which you can return later. This is particularly important with detailed and/or colored line art images scanned in 8-bit grayscale and/or 24-bit color mode.

Step-by-Step Grayscale Scans

The key issue to address when scanning grayscale photos is grayscale reproduction. We usually want to faithfully reproduce the original image's grayscale values. Nearly every setting and adjustment we make on a grayscale scan is made to meet this end. The key settings we adjust are scanner calibration, highlight and shadow, brightness and contrast, scaling, resolution, and sharpening.

Grayscale photos should be scanned in 8-bit (or higher) mode to capture the necessary number of grayscale values. Most scanners capture images darker than they really are. So, prior to scanning a grayscale photo image, you should calibrate your scanner. You need to have a grayscale chart which has known grayscale values. The purpose of this exercise is to linearize your scanner. See the back of this book for information on where to obtain a 10-step grayscale chart made specifically for desktop scanners.

Setting highlight and shadow points are two critical adjustments to make when setting up a scan. Use a histogram to place your highlight and shadow points as it will allow you to see the distribution of grayscale data in your image. Be sure to clearly distinguish between any specular highlights which your image may contain, and the diffuse highlights which contain the critical highlight image data. The diffuse highlights should be located in the lightest portions of the image that still have detail.

A curve tool, rather than linear sliders, should be used to adjust image brightness and contrast. Using a curve tool tends to maintain a higher percentage of image grayscale data, and allows you to protect the highlight and shadow values you may have set.

When adjusting the scaling, determine the maximum print/reproduction size of the image you may need before you scan, and allow your scanner to perform the scaling duties. This will save you time and result in higher quality images compared to performing these chores in an image editing application after the scan.

When determining the input resolution at which you will scan grayscale photos, use a formula of 1.5 x lpi at which the image will be printed. Remember that this image should not be scaled up after the scan, as there will not be enough pixel data to support the printing.

During the scanning sampling process, your scanner will soften your image. To return an image to its original sharpness/focus, apply unsharp mask to your image. This can be performed during the scan if you do not intend to edit your image. If post-scan image editing is in order, perform the unsharp mask after the scanning and image editing processes have been completed. For portrait images in particular, be sure to utilize a threshold value (3–5) to prevent over-sharpening of smooth, low contrast portions of your image.

Step-by-Step Color Scans

As with grayscale images, the key issue with color scanning is grayscale reproduction. This is because underlying grayscale values control color values in a digital image. Color photos should be scanned in 24-bit (or higher) mode to capture the three 8-bit+ channels which are required for an RGB image.

Calibrating your scanner for color scanning involves linearizing, similar to what we did for grayscale scanning, but this time on three channels. This three-channel linearization is called neutralization. It not only lightens the response of the scanner, but removes color cast from the scanner.

For color images with neutral highlights, highlight and shadow points should be adjusted on individual channels using a histogram. For images with strong color casts, use the master, or composite, RGB histogram to set highlight and shadow points.

Be sure to clearly distinguish between any specular highlights which your image may contain, and the diffuse highlights which contain the critical highlight image data. The diffuse highlight should be located in the lightest portion of the image which still has detail.

Making neutral areas of your image neutral is a basic key to color scanning. The Info tool should be used to measure neutral areas such as white highlights. A curve tool can be used to make adjustments to individual channels to make neutral areas neutral. This will remove any color cast from your image.

For color contones, as for grayscale contone images, you should determine the maximum print/reproduction size of the image you may need before you scan. Allow your scanner to perform scaling duties. This will save you time and result in higher quality images compared to performing these chores in an image editing application after the scan.

When determining the input resolution at which you will scan grayscale photos, use a formula of 1.5 x lpi at which the image will be printed. Remember that this image should not be scaled up after the scan, as there will not be enough pixel data to support the printing.

During the scanning sampling process, your scanner will soften your image. To return an image to its original sharpness/focus, apply unsharp mask to your image. This can be performed during the scan if you do not intend to edit your image. If post-scan image editing is in order, perform the unsharp mask after the scan and image editing processes have been completed. For portrait images in particular, be sure to utilize a threshold value (3–5) to prevent over-sharpening of smooth, low-contrast portions of your image. I prefer to convert my color image to Lab mode and apply the unsharp mask to the "L" channel. This prevents color shifts from occurring along high-contrast image areas.

Step-by-Step Transparency Scans

When scanning transparencies, dedicated film scanners will generally provide better results than multi-purpose scanners. Dedicated film scanners have no glass–air interfaces which can interfere with the passage of light through and from the image.

Small transparencies such as 35mm slides require significant enlargement to print at standard sizes such as 5" x 7" or 8" x 10". This enlargement requires high resolution. It is best to use high optical resolution rather than interpolated resolution; therefore, scanners with high optical resolution, ≥ 2000ppi, are preferred for scanning small slides. Due to the high enlargement factor involved in the scan of small transparencies, it is necessary to take extra precautions when cleaning your slides. Cans of dry air are excellent for this purpose.

When scanning negative transparencies, it is critically important to pay close attention to, and adjust for, the specific film emulsion used on your film. Each manufacturer has its own emulsion with its own sensitivities. Your software should have built-in adjustments for the major manufacturer emulsions.

Step-by-Step Screened Image Scans

When scanning previously screened (printed) images, your scanner will tend to capture and reproduce the halftone pattern from which the image is constructed. It is useful to scan at a somewhat higher resolution than you would finally like to have. Down-sampling to your final target resolution in an image editing application will tend to interpolate the captured halftone dot pattern, thereby reducing its visibility.

When evaluating scanning software, look for the presence of descreening algorithms, and use them when scanning previously printed images. In addition, post-scan additions of noise and gaussian blur filters can help remove captured screen patterns. But, it is nearly always best, when working with color images, to apply these effects on individual channels rather than on the composite image. Some channels usually need more work than others, and the less damaged channels can be spared the heavy application of correction filters, thereby helping to maintain the sharpness and focus of the image.

The process of descreening usually noticeably softens an image. The application of unsharp mask can return some of the image's focus and sharpness. However, when applying unsharp mask to a descreened image, apply it a bit at a time (~50%) and check to make sure the sharpening is not reactivating the screen pattern you have just removed.

Color Management Issues

In an electronic publishing system, each output device has its own color space, or gamut. So, when we prepare a scanned image for output on a specific device, we should use the color characteristics of that device to guide this preparation, or gamut conversion. If you are preparing your images to be printed at a printing company or service bureau, ask their production manager for guidance in setting up an RGB-to-CMYK gamut conversion which will match their production process.

Being linear and neutral is the foundation of all good color management. Even if you do no more than engage in making your devices and images linear and neutral, you will be taking a big step toward properly and predictably controlling your color.

If you need to multi-purpose your images, you will want to scan your image into a large color space, CIE or RGB, which encompasses all of the output devices you intend to use. Then you can convert copies of that image into the device-specific gamut for each output device.

Miscellaneous Scanning Issues

Both AM and FM dots are used to print contone images. It is good to be clear on the type of halftone dot being used to print your scanned image. While most commercial printers continue to use standard AM dots, some use FM dots, and many desktop devices employ FM screens to print images. AM and FM screens have different resolution requirements, with FM typically requiring less resolution than AM. Consult your service bureau for specific resolution guidelines.

Dot gain occurs whenever ink or toner is put on paper. Dot gain can create significant darkening of your images. Dot gain can be corrected during printing or in the post scan in an image editing program. Post-scan correction is best for multi-purpose images.

Images which are scanned for use on the Web can be set for size and resolution directly during the scan. But, if you intend to multi-purpose your images, it is best to scan for print and then convert, with down-sizing, sampling, and color space conversion, for the Web on a copy of the scanned image.

Much time can be saved by scanning more than one image during each scan pass. Be sure that your scanning software supports individual scanned settings for each image.

Maintain a consistent scanning environment for consistent results.

Part III

After the Scan

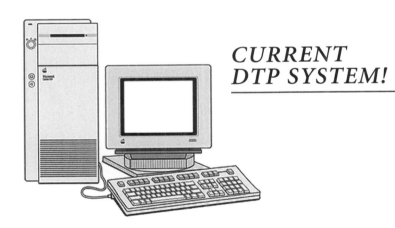

*CURRENT
DTP SYSTEM!*

*THE ORIGINAL
DTP SYSTEM!*

Part III After the Scan

As the Byte Turns continues...

Will Danny D'Ziner and Pauline E. Prepress be satisfied after they finish their scans, or will they need to edit their images of each other?

Hey! What's all this after the scan stuff? Haven't I already learned all that I need to know?

Everyone always seems to want changes!

Once we have created a high-quality scanned image, we often get requests for altering that images. If we are not careful, we can destroy our images during the editing process.

And then there are the poorly scanned images which you seem to get stuck with and become responsible for as well...

AFTER THE SCAN

Why Discuss "After the Scan?"

You might be wondering why we have devoted an entire part of this scanning book to discussions and techniques which do not directly involve scanning. There are several good reasons to do this.

First, even if we produce high-quality images during the scan, we can ruin our images during most scan image editing procedures if we are not careful. If an adjustment, such as changing the size and/or resolution of a scanned image, is performed improperly, it can demonstrably reduce the quality of a previously high-quality scanned image.

Second, scanning should most often be done with a final product in mind, and it is helpful to know some post-scan techniques which will allow us to dress up and/or improve the flexibility and usability of our scans. For instance, knowing when and how to properly convert line art images from pixel-based into vector-based images can dramatically enhance the scalability, skewability, and editability of our scanned line art images. Knowing how and when to properly convert a scanned RGB image into a CMYK image will make the difference between good- vs. poor-quality results during printing.

Third, in the real world of production, as scanner operators, we are often called upon to fix the poor scan results of others. Many of the tools and techniques we learned and applied to our scanning challenges can be used to improve the images that others may have butchered. Working in image editing applications such as Photoshop, and using tools such as editable histograms, curves, and unsharp masking, and techniques such as properly resetting highlight and shadow points, making brightness and contrast adjustments, affecting color correction, and improving image sharpness or focus, can allow us to noticeably improve, if not entirely fix, many poorly captured images.

Fourth, if you are not fortunate enough to have access to scanner driver software which has all the necessary tools and controls required to effect a good-quality scan, you may be forced, at least temporarily until you acquire better software, to perform many of your image correction procedures during the post scan in an image editing application such as Photoshop. If you are forced to perform these post-scan corrections, it will become quickly apparent why you need to have access to higher quality, more capable scanner software.

Avoiding Destroying your Images

One of the easiest ways to destroy your well-scanned, high-quality images is to start indiscriminately adjusting the crop, size, scale, and/or resolution of your image. The print size, pixel dimension, and resolution of your image are all determined during the scan. All three of these variables are linked to and proportional to one another. If you go about changing any of these variables without proper care, your image may be interpolated; that is, new pixel values and/or new pixels will be generated. Any time interpolation occurs, the original pixel values, which we worked so hard to create during the scan, will be altered. The alteration of the original pixels nearly always results in reduced image quality. In this section, we will address post-scan techniques for cropping, scaling, canvas size, resolution adjustments, and border additions.

Enhancing your Images

When we create high-quality scanned images, we provide good-quality images which can be altered and/or enhanced to improve their flexibility or suitability for specific purposes.

Simple pixel-based line art images can be converted into vector-based line art images to improve their scalability, skewability, editability, printability and even reduce their files sizes. When properly scanned, detailed line art can be adjusted to control image details. Both line art and contone images can be altered from their original conditions if we want to change their image characteristics. If we like, we can change line thickness and detail density of line art images. Colored line art images can be separated and edited. Line art images which have low-quality edges can be dramatically improved with post-scan image editing.

We can alter a contone image's brightness, contrast, and focus. All our images can be adjusted for specific output devices. Our grayscale photos need to be dot gain corrected for various printing devices. Our scanned RGB color images need to be converted into CMYK as well as dot gain corrected for printing on specific devices. If we output to multiple devices, we need to be able to manage our color for each device. To use our scanned images in Web pages, we usually need to adjust our image's size, resolution, file format, and sometimes even their bit depth, and these adjustments need to be made in the proper order. All of these post-scan image adjustments can be made, but care must be exercised to perform these image changes with decisions and techniques which minimize the loss of image data and quality.

Improving Poor or Unfinished Images

As scanner operators, we are often called upon to fix the mistakes of others. We are not infrequently handed images which are too dark or too light, have too little or too much contrast, or the image may be too soft or appear out-of-focus. Often, our color images have color cast to them which needs to be removed. If we can put our hands on the original images, it is usually prudent to just re-scan these images with proper tools and techniques. So, always ask for access to the original image first! You might be surprised to get it! But in the absence of the original image, we can use image editing tools such as editable histograms, curves, and unsharp mask filters, similar to those found in good scanning applications, to rework the damaged images.

Sometimes, if our image editing applications have better tools than our scanning applications, or we need to perform some image editing tasks before we provide our finishing touches, we may decide to wait until we have opened the image in our image editing application to perform these tasks. A good example of such a scenario might be a scanned image to which we want to add some type and a drop shadow, or perhaps add another image to form a collage. In such cases, we would not want to apply our unsharp masking adjustments until after we had completed all of our image editing and combination changes. So, we would choose to apply the unsharp mask not during the scan, but in a post-scan image editing application such as Photoshop.

Regardless of the reasons for any post-scan image editing, we must take care to wield our editing tools with skill and discretion, so as to actually enhance our images while minimizing any deleterious effects.

12
Line Art Editing

As the Byte Turns continues…

Will Danny D'Ziner and Pauline E. Prepress be able to LINE up their art after they finish their scans?

I need to edit my line art after I scan it. What do I need to do?

Let's ask Pauline. She can help explain the details.

Editable line art begins with making the right scan decisions. Then you need to know just a couple of effective techniques. The key is being able to visualize where you want to go.

PIXEL-TO-VECTOR CONVERSION

Why Pixel-to-Vector Conversion?

There are two kinds of image building blocks from which we construct digital images, pixels and vectors. Scanners create pixel-based images. Often, with simple and intermediate detailed line art, it is advantageous to convert pixel-based versions of our line art images into vector-based images. Vector images typically have sharper, smoother edges; are more easily scaled, skewed, rotated and edited; and usually have significantly smaller files sizes than their pixel-based equivalents (Fig 12.1).

Since pixel-based images are constructed from a specific number of pixels, they have a specific resolution, such as 600ppi. If a pixel-based image is scaled, the size of the pixels changes and the resolution of the image changes, hence the concept of a resolution-dependent image. In addition, rotating a pixel-based line from a vertical or horizontal position usually lowers the quality of the edge due to the creation of "stair stepping" by the offset pixels. Also, since pixel-based images are filled with pixels throughout, and not just on their edges, they tend to have relatively large file sizes. And finally, because pixel-based images have fixed resolutions, printing them on higher resolution output devices does not significantly improve an image's edge quality. A 300ppi line art image doesn't look much better printed at 2400 dpi than it does at 300 dpi because the size of the pixels does not change.

▼ *Figure 12.1 Pixel vs. Vector Edge*
Even the highest quality pixel-based line art edges cannot compete with vector-based line art edges. On the left is a line art edge captured using the optical resolution of the scanner (600ppi). On the right is the same edge converted to a vector. It is clear that the sharpness and quality of the edge has been improved by the conversion. The keys to gaining this kind of edge quality improvement is scanning at the optical resolution of the scanner and then choosing the proper conversion setup values in pixel-to-vector conversion applications like Adobe Streamline.

When converted to a vector-based image, line art edge quality can be significantly improved. Because vector-based images are constructed from lines, they are, unlike pixel-based images, resolution-independent. Therefore, vector-based images can be scaled, skewed, and rotated without any loss of edge quality. Due to the fact that vector-based images only require a vector edge along the outside of an image, contrasted with pixel-based images which require that an entire image be filled with pixels, vector images tend to be significantly smaller. It is not unusual to witness an 80% to 90% reduction in file size when a line art image is converted from pixels to vectors. It is also worthwhile to note that the resolution of a vector-based image is not determined until the image is output. This means that vector-based images can be used to take advantage of higher resolution output devices. So, it should be clear that for low-detail images, there are significant advantages to converting pixel-based line art images to vector-based images. The key to superior results is to scan the original line art using the optical resolution of your scanner and using the proper pixel-to-vector conversion application and settings.

▼ *Figure 12.2 Simple Low-Detail Line Art*

Simple line art, like this butterfly, has large areas with few details. Scanning at the optical resolution of the scanner is the key to edge consistency and clean conversion to vector line art. A scan resolution range of 500 – 600ppi is generally sufficient for simple line art which will be converted into vectors. If you intend to leave your line art image a pixel-based image, then scanning at a higher variation of the optical resolution of your scanner (1000–1200ppi) is recommended. Find this image to scan in the "Practice Images" section in the back of this book.

▼ *Figure 12.3 Streamline Setup*
Key Settings:
  Noise Suppression = 10
  Tolerance = Loose (5.0)
  Curved & Straight = Curved (5.0)

Pixel-to-Vector Challenges

There are three primary keys to creating a high-quality, easily editable vector line art images with sharp, smooth edges:

1) Start with a high-quality original line art image with sharp edges. This will provide you with a high-quality edge to reproduce.

2) Scan the line art image at 100% (no scaling), using the optical resolution of your scanner. These two key settings will eliminate interpolation, which will result in a smoother, more consistent edge for the vector conversion program to follow.

3) Control the settings of the vector conversion program to reduce the number of control points created and therefore the complexity of the vector edges.

It should be pointed out that most pixel-to-vector conversion programs, such as Adobe's Streamline which we will use here, have a common personality characteristic; that is, they tend to be very "anal retentive." This means that these programs will, if they are allowed to, follow every little nook and cranny along a pixel-based line art edge. The key to smooth vector-based edges then is to minimize the roughness of the pixel-based edge and to tone down the anal retentiveness of your conversion program. Starting with a smooth original edge, scanning at the optical resolution of your scanner, and not scaling your line art image during the scan will all reduce edge roughness. Below I will make some recommendations for reining in your conversion application.

Step-by-step: pixel-to-vector conversion

1) Scan your simple line art image, such as the simple butterfly image seen in Fig 12.2, as described in the "Step-by-step: low-detail line art" scanning exercise in Chapter 5, using the optical resolution of your scanner at 100% scale. Save your image as a TIFF (.tif).

2) Open the simple butterfly image (Bfly_1bit_600.tif) in Streamline for conversion to a vector-based image. This conversion allows for geometric manipulation such as scaling and rotation without degradation of edge quality, easier editing such as color assignments, and dramatic file size reductions.

3) Choose Conversion Setup from Streamline's Options menu.
(Options menu – Adjust the settings as follows:
Method = Outline
Tolerance = Loose (5)
Lines = Curved & Straight = Curved (5.0) See Fig 12.3.

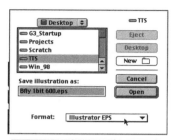

▼ Figure 12.4 Save As Dialog
Save your Streamline vector image as an Illustrator EPS. Also be sure to save your image with a screen preview. Be sure that None is NOT checked. Choose a preview appropriate for your image and computer platform.

▼ Figure 12.5 Intermediate Detail
Scan and convert this intermediate-detail line art image. The challenge here is the accurate reproduction of the thin lines so that they are clean, sharp, and of constant thickness. The keys here again are scanning at the optical resolution of your scanner and choosing the proper conversion values in Streamline.

4) Choose Convert from the File menu.

5) Save the converted image (File–Save) as a vector graphic in Illustrator EPS format. This Illustrator EPS file format is a very generic EPS format which can be easily opened and edited in any vector-based drawing program such as Illustrator, Freehand, Canvas, or Corel Draw. Be sure to save your vector EPS image with a low resolution screen preview. Be sure that None is NOT checked in the Preview dialog box. This preview is required for your vector EPS to be recognized and made visible when it is placed in a page layout application such as QuarkXPress, Pagemaker, InDesign, or Publisher 2000. (See Fig 12.4.)

6) Now open your newly created vector-based image in your choice of drawing applications (Freehand, Illustrator, or Corel Draw) to edit this image (assign colors, scale, rotate, etc.).

7) Repeat this process (1–6) with the intermediate-detail line art image shown in Fig 12.5. The challenge here is the accurate reproduction of the thin lines, and their intersections, so that they are clean, sharp, and the lines are of constant thickness. The keys here again are scanning at the optical resolution of your scanner and choosing the proper conversion values in Streamline. If properly scanned and converted, you should get a crisp, clean image which will have few control points and will be easy to edit and print.

Note: You can adjust the tolerance and curve of your setup to suit the detail of your image. The settings suggested here will provide you with the fewest number of control points and the smoothest edge. I usually start with these settings and alter them if necessary.

Note: If you have a line art image which has areas with distinctly different detail areas, some higher detail and some lower detail, you may want to scan these sections separately and/or set up the conversion values differently for each section. The separate image sections can then be re-combined as vectors in a drawing application such as Illustrator or Freehand.

Note: If you intend to take your images cross-platform from Mac to Windows, or use your images on both platforms, it is usually best to save your images in IBM PC/Windows format as these can be read on both platforms.

Note: Find this butterfly image to scan in the "Practice Images" section on page 306 in the back of this book.

HIGH-DETAIL LINE ART EDITING

▼ Figure 12.6 High-Detail Line Art Image

More detailed line art images like this butterfly often have thinner lines and/or smaller detail points than simple line art images (contrast these images with the simple line art image in Fig 12.2). Again, scanning at the optical resolution of the scanner is the key to edge consistency and accurate detail capture and reproduction.

Two key scan variables are altered for the capture of detailed line art. For detailed line art, it is usual to scan at a higher optical resolution setting (1000–1200ppi), and at an increased capture bit depth (8 bits or higher).

Find this image to scan in the "Practice Images" section on page 306 in the back of this book.

What Is High-Detail?

As we know, there are two kinds of image building blocks from which we construct digital images: pixels and vectors. Scanners create pixel-based images. As previously discussed, with simple- and intermediate-detail line art, it is often advantageous to convert pixel-based versions of our line art images into vector-based images. This is only true for relatively simple line art which does not have a great deal of detail. While vector images are terrific for creating sharp, smooth edges, vector art is not a good choice for rendering lots of detail. Fine detail usually gets lost during the pixel-to-vector conversion, and high-detail images often become too complex to edit and print when they are converted into vectors.

Capturing, editing, and printing high-detail images is the graphic realm where pixel-based images shine. Before the digital age, we had two fundamental types of graphic images: painting and drawing. Painting was usually used to show fine detail and gradations, such as in portrait painting, while drawing was used to work with simpler object-oriented graphics such as logos. Well, as the old saying goes, "There ain't nothin' new under the sun!" In the world of digital imaging, we still paint and draw. But now we paint with pixels and draw with vectors. So, when an image requires the rendering of fine detail, we generally start with and stick with pixels.

Is there a hard line of division as to when and where pixel- and vector-based images should be used? No, there isn't. For some images such as complex photographs of people or landscapes, the choice of pixels is obvious. In other cases, simple line art, such as the butterfly in Fig 12.2, the choice of vectors is obvious. And sometimes, you may experiment with both. But generally, if an image has more than fifty (50) separate areas of detail, such as the butterfly in Fig 12.6, and showing detail is more important than edge smoothness or sharpness, then the image is a good candidate for pixels. With just a little experience, you will be able to quickly choose which type of image, pixel or vector, you want. The key is *visualizing* what the results will be of your scanning and/or image editing before you get there.

High-Detail Line Art Challenges

The basic challenge in capturing and editing detailed line art images is preserving the detail in such a way that the finest points of detail are distinguishable from each other and are editable after they are captured with a scanner. If we *visualize* a detailed line art image, such as the detailed butterfly in Fig 12.6, the way a scanner will "see" the image, we can imagine that a scanner might have some difficulty clearly distinguishing the finer points of detail which are very close together. In fact, some lower quality scanners will tend to merge areas of fine, dark detail together, thereby destroying the differences in detail. And if this fine detail is not captured during the scan, there will be no detail to control in the post scan. So, to enhance the ability of a scanner to distinguish detail and to improve our chances of being provided with editable detail in the post scan, we capture our images at high resolution (usually the optical resolution of the scanner) and in 8-bit (grayscale) mode. (See the high-detail scanning exercise in Part II.)

Step-by-step: high-detail line art editing

1) Open the detailed line art image named Bfly_Detail_GS_1200.tif, which we scanned in Part II, in Photoshop.

2) Make a working copy of this image using the duplicate function (Image–Duplicate) and save this duplicate to disk. Save the original 8-bit grayscale version of the image as an unaltered file so that you can return to it later.

Note: It is always a good idea to make copies of all original images and perform any image editing functions on your copies. This way, you can always go back to your original images.

3) Activate the Threshold tool in Photoshop (Image menu – Adjust – Threshold). A histogram appears with a movable midtone adjustment pointer. Note the strong bimodal distribution of grayscale values toward the highlight and shadow ends (see Fig 12.7). We will use this tool to adjust the line thickness and density of the detail in the image.

Tool note: Be sure to turn on (place a check in) the Preview check box so that you can see the results of any adjustments you make with this tool.

4) Move the Threshold tool's midpoint to adjust the density of detail in the line art image edges (see Fig 12.7 for the results of moving the midtone point to the left and to the right of its default midtone position). Moving the midtone adjustment to the left decreases the density of the detail, while moving the threshold

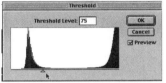

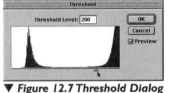

▼ Figure 12.7 Threshold Dialog
Threshold is used here to control the density of detail in the butterfly image above. The threshold pointer is moved right or left to increase or decrease detail density. Note: The top image was adjusted using a Threshold value = 75. The bottom image was adjusted using a Threshold value = 200. Note the greater density of detail in the image adjusted with a Threshold value of 200.

midtone adjustment to the right increases the density of the detail in the image.

5) After thresholding, convert your image to 1-bit black and white mode. In Photoshop, choose (Image menu – Mode – Bitmap). This will convert your image into a 1-bit black and white image, which will reduce your file size by a factor of eight and make it easier and faster to work with. This conversion will also print with sharper edges.

6) Save the final image as a pixel-based TIFF again. There will be no conversion to vector art for high-detail images such as this one. You may want to use a name such as Bfly_Detail_Final_1200.tif. If you have multiple versions of this image, you may want to number them sequentially.

Options

A) Tool note: You may apply different threshold values to various portions of an image by selecting a portion of an image prior to activating the Threshold tool.

B) In Photoshop, you may use the Unsharp Mask tool (Filter menu – Sharpen – Unsharp mask) to control image detail and line thickness. Try various unsharp mask settings to control the thickness of the line art lines. Experiment with Amount = 300–500, Radius= 10–50, and Threshold=0–10. (See the next exercise on working with low edge quality images for more details on this technique.)

C) For softer edges, do not use the Threshold tool and do not convert your image to 1-bit black and white.

What Is Low Edge Quality Line Art?

Low edge quality line art is line art that has a poorly defined edge (Fig 12.8). In both the low-detail and high-detail images we have edited in this chapter, we worked with images that had well-defined edges. In a low edge quality image, the exact edge of the image may be difficult to find or define. Examples of images which often have low edge quality are multi-generational images such as copies and faxes. In these cases, the quality or definition of an image's edge becomes blurred or indistinct during the reproduction process. However, not all poor edge quality images are poor-quality images. For example, in this exercise, we will work with an image which was sketched with a #2 pencil on rough paper. The combination of the pencil against the rough paper created an edge which fades away. This has a very nice softening effect, but makes the edge difficult to pinpoint.

The Challenge of Low Edge Quality Line Art

When we normally think of reproducing line art, we think of reproducing edges. *Edge reproduction* is usually the main focus when we scan an image. However, when an image's edge is difficult to find, edge reproduction becomes a difficult task to accomplish. In the case of poor or low edge quality images, it is often best to think of them as being a hybrid between line art images and contone images, rather than strictly line art images. If we *visualize* the edge of a low-quality line art image as a contone edge, with various shades or tones of gray, our conceptual task becomes a bit easier. As a contone image, at least along the edges, our goal then is to be able to capture and control a gradient edge. During the scanning of the low-quality edge in Part II, we captured our image in 8-bit grayscale mode, thereby providing us with a grayscale gradient edge. Now we will control the thickness and hardness of that edge in an image editing program. The tools we use in this series of examples include the Unsharp Mask tool, the Threshold tool, and the Mode Conversion tool.

Step-by-step: low edge quality line art editing

1) Open TheTaz_GS600.tif, the low quality edge grayscale line art image in Photoshop.

2) Make a working copy of this image using the duplicate function (Image–Duplicate), and save this duplicate to disk. Save the original 8-bit grayscale version of the image as an unaltered file so that you can return to it later.

▼ Figure 12.8 Low Edge Quality Image
This is the raw scanned image of an original low edge quality line art sketch which was made with a #2 pencil on rough stock. The original edges are poorly defined due to the very nature of the soft edge of the #2 pencil on the paper. We scanned this image in 8-bit (grayscale) mode to provide us with a highly editable gradient edge.
Note: Remember the term "low edge quality" is not a judgement of the artistic quality of the image, but rather a technical description of the nature of its edge.
Find this image to scan in the "Practice Images" section on page 306 in the back of this book.

Note: It is always a good idea to make copies of all original images and perform any image editing functions on your copies. This way, you can always go back to your original images.

3) In Photoshop, activate the Unsharp mask tool (Filters – Sharpen – Unsharp mask).

Tool note: A sharpening tool in Photoshop adjusts, usually increasing, the contrast (difference in grayscale value) between adjacent pixels. The Sharpening tool in Photoshop provides three adjustments: Amount, Radius, and Threshold. The Amount adjustment controls the amount of increase in grayscale value which will occur between sharpened pixels. For example, an unsharp mask of 100% will increase the difference in grayscale value between two pixels by 100%. If the two pixels originally had a 5% difference in grayscale value, after the application of 100% unsharp mask, they will have a 10% difference in grayscale value. The Radius adjustment controls the width, in numbers of pixels, of the area which will be affected by the unsharp masking. A Radius of 1 applies the amount of sharpening to one (1) pixel on each side of an edge which is being sharpened. The Threshold adjustment controls which pixels in an image or selection will be sharpened by designating the difference in grayscale value which must exist between two pixels before any unsharp mask will be applied. For instance, a threshold of 5 means that there must be at least a difference of five (5) levels of gray between two adjacent pixels before unsharp mask is applied. Raising the unsharp mask threshold guarantees that only the higher-contrast portions of an image, such as the edges between light and dark areas, will be sharpened.

Here we will use the Unsharp Mask tool in Photoshop to control the image detail and line thickness. You can adjust the unsharp mask setting ranges as follows: Amount = 100–500, Radius = 1–50, Threshold = 0–10 depending upon your desired results (Fig 12.9–12.11).

4) To start try these unsharp mask settings:
Amount = 500
Radius = 5
Threshold = 0

Experiment with various amount and Radius settings to achieve different results in terms of line thickness and abruptness of the edge. See Figs. 12.9 and 12.10 for the difference between the image with a Radius = 5 and Radius = 25.

5) Make a duplicate copy of your image (Image–Duplicate).

6) On the copy of your image, we will increase the contrast further by applying the Threshold tool. If you want to have a bit of softness to your image edges, keep your image in 8-bit (grayscale) mode. If you

want to create a stark, high-contrast black and white-only image with no softening grayscale component on the edge, you can process your image through the Threshold tool (Image menu – Adjust – Threshold) and/or convert the image to 1-bit (black and white) mode (Image – Mode – Bitmap) in Photoshop. Experiment with the position of the threshold midpoint to achieve the look you want. See Fig 12.9 for a thresholded version of this image.

Tool note: It may be a bit confusing discussing the Threshold tool and the Threshold adjustment, which is a part of the Unsharp Mask tool. Be sure to keep the difference between these two thresholds clear in your mind. The Threshold tool (Image–Adjust–Threshold) converts all the pixels in an image to black and white and allows you to control which pixels are converted to black and which ones to white. The threshold adjustment in the Unsharp Mask tool (Filter–Sharpen–Unsharp mask) is used to determine which pixels will be sharpened by this tool and which ones will not.

Options

A) Apply a gaussian blur to the image before application of the unsharp mask. This will further soften and widen the edge of the art and give you even greater edge adjustment control.

B) Adjust the Threshold in the Unsharp Mask tool to fine-tune the application of the unsharp mask.

C) Apply unsharp mask two or more times to create increasingly sharper edges without completely going to black and white as happens when the Threshold tool is applied.

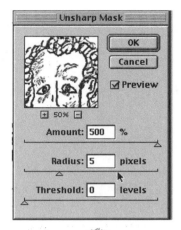

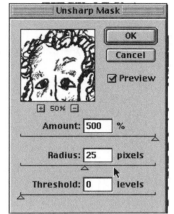

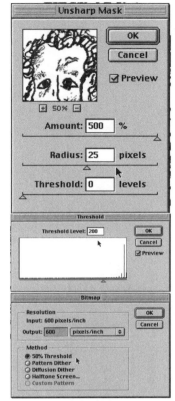

▼ *Figure 12.9 Sharpened with Moderate Radius (5)*
This version of the image was sharpened with a large radius and then thresholded in the Unsharp Mask tool:
Amount = 500
Radius = 5
Threshold = 0

▼ *Figure 12.10 Sharpened with Large Radius (25)*
This version of the image was sharpened with a large radius and then thresholded in the Unsharp Mask tool:
Amount = 500
Radius = 25
Threshold = 0

▼ *Figure 12.11 Sharpened With Large Radius, Thresholded, 1-bit Conversion*
This version of the image was sharpened with a large radius, thresholded and converted to 1-bit mode in Unsharp mask Tool: Amount = 500, Radius = 25, Threshold = 0
Threshold tool: Threshold point = 200
Mode Conversion: Convert to 1-bit Mode (50%)

▼ *Figure 12.12 Colored Line Art*
The key is to scan in 24-bit or higher mode to allow for the creation of color channels, which can be used to select and separate the various colored portions of the image.
Find this image to scan in the "Practice Images" section on page 306 in the back of this book.

Red

Green

Blue

▼ *Figure 12.13 Colored, Separated Line Art*
The above three images are the red, green, and blue versions of the above color logo. Note how the various text characters, which are different colors in the original image, are more easily recognized, and therefore selected and edited, on the different channels.

What is Colored Line Art?

Colored line art is a line art type of graphic image which has color other than black and white, assigned to it (Fig 12.12). Like black and white line art, colored line art images are characterized by solid areas with edges. Typical examples of line art images include logos, pen and pencil drawings, and any other other solid, hard-edged objects. Type characters which you want to capture and edit as graphics may be considered to be, and treated as, line art.

Simple black and white digital line art images are usually scanned in 1-bit (B&W) mode and are therefore composed of pixels with only two shades of gray (black or white) assigned to them. (See the simple line art scan techniques in Part II.) It is the change from black to white pixels which define the edge and therefore the shape of line art images. Detailed black and white line art images are typically scanned in 8-bit (grayscale) mode. Initially, prior to finishing the editing discussed in this chapter, our images are composed of pixels with varying grayscale values and have soft edges. (See the detailed line art scan techniques in Part II.)

Colored line art images are generally scanned in 24-bit (RGB mode) and are therefore composed of three channels of 8-bit (grayscale) pixels. (See the colored line art scan techniques in Part II.) Like their single-channel, 8-bit grayscale cousins, colored line art images scanned in RGB mode initially have soft edges. It is useful to think of colored line art images as sandwiches composed of three grayscale images. Each channel is a different version of the image created by "viewing" the image through three different, red, green, and then blue, filters. The various colored portions of the line art image appear differently in each channel. In Fig 12.13 we see that the various colored letters are more or less visible, depending upon the channel in which they are viewed. We can use this visibility to help us select, and therefore edit, the various colored segments of our colored line art images.

The Challenge of Editing Colored Line Art

Like with any other kind of line art, when reproducing colored line art, we should again think of reproducing edges. *Edge reproduction* is the main focus when we scan and edit colored line art images. With colored line art images, we have the additional challenge of separating the various colored portions of a line art image into separate elements which can be selected and edited, including assigning colors.

We should use the same *visualization* techniques with colored line art as we do with black and white line art. Visualize how the scanner will re-create your colored line art image and how it can be separated and edited. With colored line art, it is very useful to visualize your colored line art image as your scanner and image editing program will see it, as a sandwich of three grayscale images. When I scan a colored line art image, I am not much concerned with the actual color values which the scanner creates. Particularly with spot color logos, a scanner will never be able to reproduce the color accurately during the scanning process. My approach is usually to use my scanner and the RGB image which it reproduces as tools to help me separate the various colored components of the line art. After the various colored segments of a line art image are separated, we can select them and accurately assign any color we desire in our painting or drawing applications. With simple- and intermediate-detail colored line art images, I will often convert the separated portions of my line art image into vector-based images prior to assigning colors. I will then assign colors and perform other editing tasks in a drawing program such as Illustrator or Freehand. For detailed colored line art images, I will usually keep my image as pixels and assign colors in Photoshop or another similar pixel-based image editing application.

In summary, when I analyze a colored line art image, I *visualize* the image as a collection of separate grayscale images. Depending upon the detail in the line art, I will either plan to leave the image as pixels or convert it to vectors. In either case, I enhance the visibility of the various colored portions of my image. These images are provided by the red, green, and blue filtered grayscale versions of my image which help me isolate, separate, select and finally assign color to, and otherwise edit, my colored line art image.

We have the same challenges with colored line art images as we do with black and white line art images. When an image's edge is difficult to find, edge reproduction becomes a difficult task to accomplish. In the case of poor or low edge quality images, it is often best to think of them as being a hybrid between a line art image and a contone image, rather than strictly a line art image. If we *visualize* the edge of a low-quality line art image as a contone edge, with various shades or tones of gray, our conceptual task becomes a bit easier. As a contone image, at least along the edges, our goal then is to be able to capture and then control a gradient edge. During the scanning of the low-quality edge in Part II, we captured our image in 8-bit grayscale mode, thereby providing us with a grayscale gradient edge. If the original image is colored line art , we will scan the image in 24-bit RGB. We can then separate the various colored components using the three grayscale channels. Then we can control the thickness and hardness of that edge in an image editing program using the same unsharp masking, threshold and mode con-

▼ **Figure 12.14 Threshold Adjustment**
On the top is a line art edge captured using the optical resolution of the scanner (600ppi). On the bottom is the same edge captured using an interpolated resolution (1000ppi.) Note the greater "raggedness" of the lower quality, interpolated edge.

▼ **Figure 12.15 Invert Image**
Using the Invert tool in Photoshop, the "Apple" characters are converted to black, making conversion to vectors without a background simpler.

version tools we used before. See the sections on editing detailed and poor edge quality images earlier in this chapter.

In the following step-by step example, we will first separate the various image elements using the RGB channels which were created when we scanned a color logo. Next we will convert the logo into a vector-based image, and then assign color to the various color elements of the logo.

Step-by-step: color line art editing

1) Open the Apple_Logo_RGB_600.tif image.

2) Look through the three (RGB) channels and note how each channel displays the various "Apple" characters as well as the variation in contrast which exists from one channel to another.

Note: Our goal is to clearly and cleanly separate all five "APPLE" charters from their black background. To do this, we will utilize the Threshold tool in Photoshop.

3) Choose the Threshold tool (Image–Adjust–Threshold). The Threshold dialog box appears (Fig 12.14, top).

Note: The default Threshold setting is 128. At this setting, only the first two characters, "Ap," are clearly visible. But you will note that there are numerous well-defined peaks for the other characters. The largest peak on the left of the Threshold dialog box is the black background. We only need to move our threshold slider between the background and the other peaks to separate the characters from their black background.

4) Move the threshold slider from 128 to the left until the Threshold Level reads 75 (Fig 12.14, bottom).

Note: See how the other three characters, "ple," now are clearly and cleanly recognizable.

5) The individual characters can now be easily selected and colorized, or as we will do, simplified, converted to vectors, and colored in a drawing program.

6) Select the Bitmap sub menu choice from the Mode menu selection under the Image menu (Image–Mode–Bitmap). This will simplify the image by changing the mode of the image from RGB to B&W. This mode change will allow the edges to print more crisply, and reduce the file size to make it easier to convert to vectors and/or to print faster.

7) Now, choose Invert from the Adjust sub menu under the Image menu (Image–Adjust–Invert). This will invert all of the pixels val-

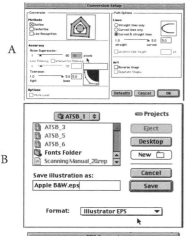

A

B

C

D

Apple®

▼ **Figure 12.16 Streamline Conversion to Vectors**
After inverting the image and saving it as a TIFF, the image is opened in Streamline and converted into a vector image. Note the setup values in Streamline (A):
Noise Suppression = 10
Tolerance = 5
Curves = 5
Save your new vector image as an EPS image (B) with a preview (C).
The result is the creation of a crisp, clean, highly editable vector image (D).

ues, making the Apple characters black on a white background (see Fig 12.15). Once we are done, this will allow us to use Streamline software to convert only the letters to vectors and not the black background. If you want the background converted to vector as well, ignore this step.

If an image is to be converted to a vector graphic, continue with the following sequence

8) Open a pixel-based TIFF image in Adobe Streamline for conversion to a vector-based image. (This allows for geometric manipulation such as scaling and rotation, etc., without degradation of edge quality, easier editing of color assignments, and dramatic reductions in file sizes.)

9) Set the following conversion setup options: Method = Outline, Noise Suppression = 10, Tolerance = Loose (5), Lines = Curved & straight = Curved (5.0) (see Fig 12.16A).

Note: Setting the Noise Suppression up to 10 will allow Streamline to ignore any small blemishes which may be part of the original scanned image. Setting the Tolerance and Curved lines to 5.0 reduces the number of control points which will be created, which in turn creates a smoother edge and a more editable image. Remember, to ensure smooth, consistent edges, scan your line art images using the optical resolution of your scanner.

10) Save the file as a vector graphic using Illustrator EPS format. The image will be saved with the type characters as black-filled outlines (Fig 12.16B).

11) Be sure to save the vector EPS image out of Streamline with an image preview. If your image is not saved with a preview, it will not be viewable when placed in your page layout document.

12) Open the final vector EPS in the drawing application of your choice to edit the following: assign colors, scale, rotate, etc.

Note: Complex colored line art will generally not be separated into vector elements, but will remain as pixel-based graphics for editing. If you prefer to edit an image as a pixel-based image, try applying 0.25 pixels of gaussian blur to your thresholded image prior to selection and colorizing. This will create a smoother, more natural-looking, anti-aliased edge.

PAULINE'S SCAN TIPS

Scan Tip # 12-1

Convert simple- to intermediate-detail, pixel-based line art images to vectors. This conversion to vectors will allow you to take advantage of scalability, skewability, editability, reduced file size, and resolution-independent printing. The two keys to creating editable, printable vector images without creating too many control points are: 1) scan your line art images at 100% using the optical resolution of your scanner to prevent interpolation of line art edge, and 2) reduce the tightness of the vector edge by controlling the preferences of your conversion program.

Scan Tip # 12-2

Detailed line art, which should be scanned in grayscale (8-bit+) mode, can be edited with threshold and or unsharp mask filters to control the thickness of the line art edges and the density of the image detail. Be sure to convert all grayscale versions of line art images to 1-bit black and white if you want the line art edges to print crisply.

Scan Tip # 12-3

Low edge quality images, those with poorly defined edges such as copies, faxes, and pencil drawings, can be improved, controlled, and edited if they are scanned in grayscale or RGB color mode to produce gradient-like edges. Tools such as unsharp mask and threshold can be used separately or together to effect the edge changes desired.

PAULINE'S SCAN TIPS

Scan Tip # 12-4

Colored line art, which should be scanned in 24-bit+ (RGB) mode, can be separated for easy selection and editing. RGB scans produce three grayscale versions (channels) of your images with varying contrast. These variable-contrast channels can be used to separate the various colored line art areas after the scan. Once separated, the individual components of the line art image can be edited or even converted into vectors for editing.

Scan Tip # 12-5

After your line art edits are complete, be sure to convert all grayscale versions of line art images to 1-bit black and white if you want the line art edges to print crisply. Be aware, however, that some line art images, especially some poor edge quality images, may print better if left in grayscale mode. Experiment both ways to test the results.

Scan Tip # 12-6

Before you begin editing a line art image in an application such as Photoshop, make a copy of the image and then work on the copy. This will allow you to return to the original image at any time if you make a mistake or want to try a different approach. It is also a good idea to save copies of intermediate steps, at least until you are satisfied with the final results. When experimenting with various settings and techniques, record your successful approaches so that you do not forget them.

13

Geometric Manipulations

As the Byte Turns continues…

Will Danny D'Ziner and Pauline E. Prepress be able to manipulate the FACETS of their relationship properly?

Many times when I scale my images, their quality drops. How come?

Yea…and we usually get blamed for the output quality problems.

You must avoid interpolation whenever possible. This involves controlling your image's pixel dimensions, print size, and resolution.

GEOMETRIC MANIPULATIONS

▼ *Figure 13.1 Crop Tool*
This tool allows you to select a portion of an image and discard the rest.

▼ *Figure 13.2 Original and Cropped Images*
The top image is the original scanned image. The bottom image is the result after cropping.

What are Geometric Manipulations?

Geometric manipulations are any adjustments which affect or alter the physical characteristics of a digital image. These adjustments include changes to the size, shape, orientation, and resolution of an image. We will cover five basic adjustments: cropping, changing orientation, adding canvas, adding a border, and adjusting the image size and/or resolution without negatively affecting the image quality. We will confine our discussion, however, to editing pixel-based images.

Geometric Manipulation Challenges

There is one key concern when making adjustments to the physical characteristics of an image, and that is maintaining image quality. Some adjustments such as cropping (see Fig 13.2), if properly performed, should not affect image quality. Other adjustment such as changing the resolution of an image can have very damaging impacts on an image. So, our goal is always to minimize the impact we have on an image when we adjust or edit it after the scan.

Cropping

Often after we scan an image, we may not always want to include everything contained in the scanned image. To remove certain portions of the image so that we have just the portion we want to use, we crop the image, using the Cropping tool (Fig 13.1).

Cropping Challenges

The primary challenge in cropping is to maintain image quality and avoid interpolation of an image's pixels during the adjustment. A common cause of image interpolation is changing the magnification and/or resolution of an image during cropping. Changes in magnification and/or resolution usually involve significant interpolation of an image's pixels. Interpolation of an image's pixels in an image editing application such as Photoshop often leads to visible degradation, usually softening, of the image. The addition and/or interpolation of pixels should be minimized during cropping.

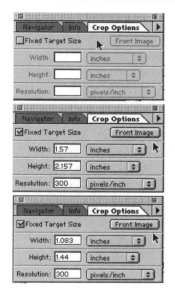

A

B

C

▼ *Figure 13.3 Crop Tool Options*
When the Crop options palette
is first activated, the palette
will appear blank (A). Once
the Fixed Target Size and
Front Image choices have been
checked, the palette will show
the dimensions and resolution
of the starting image (B). After
an image has been cropped,
the Crop tool's options palette
will reflect the new dimensions of the cropped image
(C). Note in the Image Size
dialog boxes how the image
file size is reduced by the cropping (D).
It is important that the Fixed
Target Size check box be
unchecked prior to selecting
and completing a crop, otherwise the image will be interpolated during the crop.

Step-by-step: cropping an image

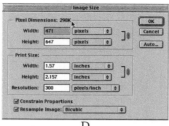

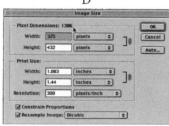

D

1) Open the image Portrait_GS_200.tif.

2) Choose Duplicate from the Image menu (Image – Duplicate) to create a copy of the image.

Note: Always work on a copy of any image you intend to change!

3) Select the crop tool from the Photoshop menu (Fig 13.3).

4) Press the Return key to bring up the Crop tool's option palette (Fig 13.3B)

5) Click the Fixed Target Size check box in the upper left-hand corner of the crop tool's options palette.

6) Click the Front Image button in the upper right-hand corner of the crop tool's options palette. The current image size, 1.57" x 2.157", and resolution, 300ppi, appear Fig 13.3B.

7) Now select the Image size dialog box from the Image menu (Image – Image size). In addition to the current image size and resolution, this dialog box shows the file size of the image, which in this case is 298K (Fig 13.3B). (Note: Your file size will vary depending upon the size and resolution of the area you scanned.)

8) Before you choose your crop area, uncheck the Fixed Target Size check box. If you leave Fixed Target Size checked, you are likely to force the image's pixels to be interpolated.

9) Now with the Crop tool, click and drag across the area of the image you want to retain.

10) To complete the crop of the image, press ENTER, or double-click within the cropped area. Photoshop will complete the crop, and only the crop-selected portion of your image will appear (Fig 13.3C).

11) Once again, check the Fixed Target Size check box and click the Front Image button in the Crop tool's options palette. The new dimensions of the cropped image will appear, 1.083" x 1.44" in this case. Note that the resolution of the image has been maintained; it remains at 300ppi.

12) Open the Image Size dialog box again (Image – Image Size). Note how the file size of the image has been reduced from 298K to

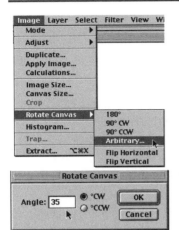

▼ *Figure 13.4 Rotate Canvas Menu*
In the Rotate Canvas dialog box, the 90°, 180°, and Flip choices will not result in any significant additions or interpolation of the image. The Arbitrary choice provides more flexibility, but more opportunity for significant image change as well.

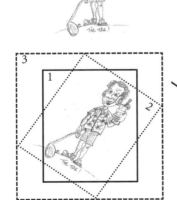

138K. This reduction in file size is due to the discarding of the portion of the image which was outside of the crop area.

Note: It is important that the Fixed Target Size box remain unchecked prior to the selection and completion of the cropping function. If the Fixed Target Size box is checked during a crop, the pixels within the image will be interpolated during the cropping event, and image quality will suffer as a result.

Changing Orientation

Often after we scan an image, we may want to use the image in an orientation that is different from how it was scanned. To change the orientation of an image, we rotate the image. Image rotations can be performed in page layout applications, but it is far better to perform them in a graphics application, such as Photoshop, as this will provide us with better image control and faster printing.

Orientation Challenges

The primary challenge of image rotation occurs when we rotate an image through an angle other than a multiple of 90°. Non-90° (nonorthogonal) rotation usually involves the addition of a significant amount of image data, and results in at least a slight softening, through interpolation, of high-contrast edges.

▼ *Figure 13.5 New Canvas Created*
A 30° rotation creates areas which must be filled in with pixels. A significant increase in file size results.

Step-by-step: canvas rotation

1) Open the image Taz_GS_600.tif.

2) Choose Duplicate from the Image menu (Image – Duplicate) to create a copy of the image.

Note: Always work on a copy of any image you intend to change!

3) Select Rotate from the Image menu (Image – Rotate) (see Fig 13.4).

Note: There are several sub menu choices available under the Rotate menu selection. Any of the sub menu selections which apply a multiple of a 90° orientation change (orthogonal) around any axis, such as 180,° or 90° CW, or a Flip, will not result in significant changes to or interpolation of an image. However, any orientation change which is not orthogonal, such as a 35° rotation, will usually involve significant addition of pixels and often some interpolation as well.

4) Select "Arbitrary" from the Rotation sub menu. The Rotate Canvas dialog box will appear (see Fig 13.4).

5) Assign a 35° rotation to the Rotate Canvas dialog box (see Fig 13.4)

Note: The 35° rotation will result in the addition of a significant amount of image data to the image. When the image is rotated through something other than a multiple of 90°, blank spaces will be created by the rotation of the corners of the original image. These blank spaces must be filled in with pixels, since all pixel-based images must be square.

Fig 13.5 shows the increase in image area and file size which results from a 30° rotation of the Taz drawing. The original image (top) and position, shown as position 1 in the lower image, has an image dimension of 4.5" x 5.917", and a file size of 9.15MB. The rotated image, position 2, shows the offset of the corners, which results in the addition of enough background pixels to create image 3, which has an image dimension of 7.08" x 7.428" and a file size of 18.1MB. The edges of the line art will also be slightly softened. This slight softening can be offset by the application of some unsharp mask. (See the section on editing poor edge quality line art in Chapter 12 for information on applying unsharp mask to sharpen soft edges.)

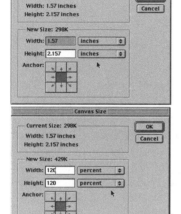

Increasing Canvas Size

Sometimes after we scan an image, we want to add more background area around the edge of our image. This is easily done in an application such as Photoshop by adding more canvas.

Canvas Challenges

There are no quality problems resulting from adding canvas. But, there are a few tips on controlling the addition of canvas which can make it an easy and predictable process. When we add canvas, we typically want to control the width, placement, and color of the canvas. It is a good idea to think through what we want before we start making the additions, as this will help us make the proper choices in the canvas addition dialog boxes.

Step-by-step: canvas increase

1) Open the image Sid_GS_200.tif.

2) Choose Duplicate from the Image menu (Image – Duplicate) to create a copy of the image.

Note: Always work on a copy of any image you intend to change!

3) Select Canvas Size from the Image menu (Image – Canvas size) (see Fig 13.4).

Note: When the Canvas Size dialog box appears, you will notice that there are two adjustments which can be made: 1) adjusting the width and height, and 2) setting the anchor. The default units of measurement for width and height is inches. There are other units which can be used such as pixels and percent. Choose the units based upon your needs. I often use percent, particularly if I am adding canvas to multiple sizes of images which I want to appear to have similarly proportioned canvas additions.

▼ **Figure 13.6 Adding Canvas**
A canvas border can be added to any side or all around depending upon how the Canvas Size dialog box is configured. I like to use percentage units rather than absolute units when I create a proportional border.

4) Change the Width and Height units to percent.

5) Type in 120 percent for the Width and Height.

6) Click in the central square of the Anchor area. This will force Photoshop to add canvas equally all around the image.

Note: If you want to add canvas on just one side, choose one of the outside anchor points and adjust just the width or height.

7) Click OK. A canvas border will be added to your scanned image (see Fig 13.6).

Adding a Border

There are several ways to add borders to our scanned images. One way is shown in the previous segment on "Increasing canvas size." Another way is making and filling a selection around the edge of an image.

Border Challenges

Increasing canvas size to add a border works well if you do not mind adding area to your image. If, however, you want to keep your image the same size and still add a border, then you need to add a border to the image within the boundary of the existing image. Foremost in our minds when we do this should be to create a consistent border.

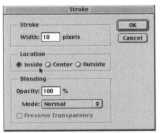

Step-by-step: border addition of a black border

1) Open the image Sid_GS_200.tif.

2) Choose Duplicate from the Image menu (Image – Duplicate) to create a copy of the image.

Note: Always work on a copy of any image you intend to change!

3) Make sure that black is set as the foreground color in the Photoshop tool palette. This is easily done by pressing the "D" key.

Note: You can assign any color you choose to be used as the border color by double-clicking on the foreground color in the tool palette or by using the color palette (press F6).

3) Choose Select All from the Select menu (Select – All).

4) Choose Stroke from the Edit menu (Edit – Stroke). The Stroke dialog box will appear (see Fig 13.7).

5) Type in a 10-pixel width under the Stroke area.

Note: The width in pixels required to create a border of a specific linear width will vary with the resolution of your image. The higher the resolution of your image, the greater the pixel width required to create a given linear thickness.

▼ *Figure 13.7 Adding a Border*
Adding a consistent border to your scanned image can be done by stroking the inside of your image. You can control the width, color, and appearance of your border.

6) Choose Inside from the Location portion of the dialog box.

7) Select 100% Opacity and Normal under Blending.

8) Click OK. A black border will be added to your scanned image.

Note: Experiment with various widths, opacities, and blending modes to create different border effects.

A

▼ *Figure 13.8 Still life Grayscale*

This is a grayscale version of the color still life image we scanned. The starting pixel dimensions, print size, and resolution of this image are shown in the Image Size dialog box below the image.

Scaling your Scanned Images

Often we need to change the size of our scanned images. This can be done easily in Photoshop and other image editing applications. However, if we are not careful, we may significantly reduce the quality of our images in the process.

Scaling Challenges

There are two primary challenges when scaling an image after it has been scanned: interpolation and loss of resolution. To scale an image in the post scan, you have two options: the first does not change the number of pixels, the second does. The first involves no change in the number of pixels; the pixels merely change in size to accomplish the scaling. This is often the best way to scale an image, particularly if an image is being scaled down, as no new pixels are created or interpolated. The danger here becomes evident when we scale an image up in size. When scaling an image up without interpolation, pixel size may increase to the point where there is not enough image resolution to support the printing of that file. On the other hand, scaling with interpolation, while maintaining an image's resolution, nearly always reduces the quality of an image. We are therefore often forced to balance the image quality loss which results from interpolation against the output resolution requirements. These challenges created by scaling are the reasons why it is best to perform scaling chores, and in particular scaling up, during the scan.

Step-by-step: scaling

1) Open an image such as the still life in Fig 13.8.

2) Choose Duplicate from the Image menu (Image – Duplicate) to create a copy of the image.

3) Select Image size from the Image menu (Image – Image size). A dialog box displaying the current pixel dimensions, file size, print size and resolution of the image will appear (see Fig 13.8-A).

B) Scaling without interpolation

4) First we scale the image 50% without interpolation. To do this, make sure that the Resample Image check box is UNCHECKED (see Fig 13.9-B)

5) Make sure the Constrain Proportions check box is checked.

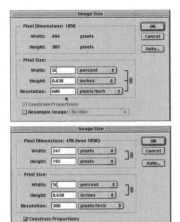

B

C

▼ *Figure 13.9 Image Scaling*
There are two choices when scaling an image in Photoshop after the scan. If the image resolution is allowed to change during the scaling, here 300ppi to 600ppi, no interpolation takes place and image quality is maintained (B). If image resolution is held constant during scaling, here at 300ppi, interpolation of the image's pixels occurs and image quality will suffer (C). Note how the pixel dimensions and file size change when interpolation is allowed to occur.
It is generally best to allow image resolution to change. But beware that scaling an image up may reduce the resolution too much to maintain image quality during printing. This is why it is best to allow your scanner to perform the scaling, and why you should scan at the largest size at which you will use your image.

6) Set the Print Size units to percent.

7) Now type 50 into the Width data area under Print Size.

Note: The Height value should change automatically to one-half of its initial value if the Constrain Proportions check box is checked. It is not necessary to change the Height units to percent for the proper proportional adjustment to be made.

Note: The Resolution of the image, shown under the Print Size area, will increase to 600ppi. This is the result of making the pixels smaller by 50%. The pixel size decreases and the image resolution increases.

Note: The pixel dimensions and file size of the image remain unchanged. This is because we have not allowed Photoshop to interpolate our image.

C) Scaling with interpolation

1) Make another copy of the Still Life image.

2) Now we will scale the image 50% *with* interpolation. To do this, make sure that the Resample Image check box is CHECKED (see Fig 13.9-C).

3) Make sure the Constrain Proportions check box is checked.

4) Set the Print Size units to percent.

5) Now type 50 into the Width data area under Print Size.

Note: The Height value should change automatically to one-half of its initial value if the Constrain Proportions check box is checked. It is not necessary to change the Height units to percent for the proper proportional adjustment to be made.

Note: The Resolution of the image, shown under the Print Size area, will remain at 300ppi. This is because we are accomplishing the scaling by constructing new pixels. Instead of just changing the size of the pixels, we are re-creating a new set of pixels, for the older ones, with exactly the same size. Because the new image is smaller than the original one, we will have fewer pixels.

Note: The pixel dimensions and file size of the image have changed dramatically (Fig 13.9-C). The file size has decreased from 185K to 47K, and the pixel dimensions have been reduced from 494 x 383 to 247 x 142. This is because we have allowed Photoshop to interpolate our image. This interpolation will decrease the quality of our image, and we should therefore avoid this if possible. The best way to avoid this interpolation is to perform these scaling chores during the scan rather than after the scan in an image editing application such as Photoshop. If you intend to use your image as several sizes, it is best to scan it at the largest size at which you will be using it and then scale your image down, preferably without interpolation. If you need to interpolate your images, the interpolation involved with scaling images down is generally less deleterious to your images than the interpolation which occurs when images are scaled up.

PAULINE'S SCAN TIPS

Scan Tip # 13-1

When cropping an image in a post-scan image editing application such as Photoshop, it is important that we prevent interpolation of the image if we want to maintain maximum image quality. Allowing the image print size to vary as a result of cropping will generally prevent interpolation. If you want to maintain the same print size after cropping, be aware that your image will be interpolated.

Scan Tip # 13-2

Rotating an image through 90° increments (90°, 180°, 270°) will not result in significant image interpolation or size changes. However, if an image is rotated through any increments other than 90°, all of the image's pixels will be interpolated, and the size of the image will be increased to accommodate the rotation. The interpolation involved with non-90° rotations usually leads to softening of the image.

Scan Tip # 13-3

The size of the canvas on which an image sits can be increased without creating any interpolation of your image's pixels. Care must be taken to choose the correct tool, a canvas tool rather than an image size tool, to effect this increase in image size without interpolation. Canvas can usually be added either symmetrically or asymmetrically to an image. When adding canvas, you can also define the background color at the same time. It is best to determine the background color prior to making a canvas size adjustment.

PAULINE'S SCAN TIPS

Scan Tip # 13-4

A border can be added to an image in several ways. Adding canvas of a particular color can be an effective way to add a border while increasing the image size at the same time. If you want to add a border to your image, but maintain the current print size, you can stroke the edge of your image with the color you desire.

Scan Tip # 13-5

An image can be scaled after it is scanned; however, it is important to specifically control how this scaling is accomplished. If image resolution is maintained during scaling, interpolation of the pixels will occur, which usually results in softening of the image. If resolution is allowed to vary during scaling, image quality can be maintained, but the physical print size will vary. Scaling an image up while maintaining resolution will generally result in more deleterious interpolation than scaling an image down in size. Always scale a copy; never scale the original image.

14
Correcting Scanned Images

As the Byte Turns continues…

Will Danny D'Ziner and Pauline E. Prepress need to correct their initial impressions of each other?

Now that I've learned how to scan properly, I get consistently good results. But I don't scan all my own images, and many of the ones I get in are poor-quality!

Just say NO! – to bad images, that is. Wouldn't that be nice?

Fixing poor-quality images is always a struggle between holding onto the image information while you try to re-distribute it. I like the just say NO! concept!! I wish I could…

INTRODUCTION

What Are Common Image Corrections?

Image corrections are any adjustments that affect or alter the look or quality of a scanned image. The most common adjustments include changes to image brightness, contrast, sharpness, and color balance. We will be confining our discussion to editing pixel-based images.

Image Correction Challenges

One key concern when making correction adjustments to an image is maintaining image quality. Any image correction functions which we perform have the potential to lower the quality of the image data we have. Some corrections may fix one problem but cause another. For instance, if we have to make large corrections to improve the brightness and/or contrast of an image, we may end up posterizing the image in the process. Many adjustments we make in the post scan tend to remove image data, and therefore threaten the quality of the image. Our goal therefore is to minimize the impact we have on an image when we adjust or edit it after the scan.

ADJUSTING IMAGE BRIGHTNESS

Many images require overall image brightness adjustments because they view and/or print too light or too dark. There are generally two image features which need to be checked and possibly changed to adjust overall image brightness: 1) the highlight and shadow points, and 2) the distribution of grayscale data between the highlight and shadow points.

Brightness Challenges: Grayscale Images

The primary challenge when adjusting image brightness is to avoid or at least minimize the loss of data. The problem is that most post-scan corrections of brightness lead to significant loss of image data. We will use two tools to adjust an image's brightness in Photoshop. We will use Levels to adjust the highlight and shadow points, and Curves to adjust the distribution of grayscale values between the highlight and shadow.

A

B

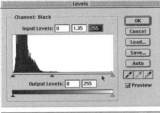

C

D

E

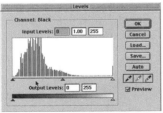

▼ Figure 14.1 Low-Key Image
We use an editable histogram called Levels in Photoshop to correct the placement of the highlight and shadow values of this low-key image. Large adjustments may create image posterization.

Step-by-step: brightness adjustment of grayscale

1) Open the image Low Key Image.tif. (See Fig 14A)

2) Choose Duplicate from the Image menu (Image – Duplicate) to create a copy of the image.

Note: Always work on a copy of any image you intend to change!

3) Select the Levels tool from the Adjust sub menu under the Image menu (Image – Adjust – Levels). The Levels toolbox will appear with an editable histogram showing the distribution of grayscale in the image (Fig 14.1B).

Note: You will notice that most of the image data is clustered at the far right-hand end of the histogram. There is a long flat section of data starting at the midtone and terminating at the highlight end with a little blip of data at the highlight end. To lighten the image, we must redistribute the grayscale data more evenly across the image and have more data closer to the highlight end. We will begin by properly setting the highlight and shadow points, using the Levels tool, and then distribute the grayscale data between these two points with a curve tool.

4) To reset the highlight and shadow points, we need to move the highlight pointer (located under the far right end of the histogram in Fig 14.1B) up where the significant image data begins near the middle of the histogram (Fig 14.1C).

Note: The input value for the highlight changes from 255 to 118 when the highlight pointer is moved.

5) Click OK. The resultant image is seen in Fig 14.1D, which is an improvement, but we can still improve the image more.

6) Activate the Levels tool again to re-examine the histogram in Fig 14.1E (Image – Adjust – Levels).

Note: You will see in the new histogram that there are many blank lines across the histogram indicating missing data areas. You may also note that while the placement of the highlight point has improved, the midpoint pointer of the image, located under the middle of the histogram, is still well to the right of the middle of the image data. Most of the image data is still to the left of the midtone pointer, that is, toward the shadow portion of the image. Most of the image data is clustered around the three-quartertone, which is why the image still appears too dark.

Note: To further brighten the image, we will need to continue to redistribute grayscale data more toward the midtone and highlight ends. To accomplish this, we will use the Curve tool in Photoshop.

A

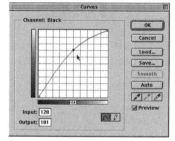

B

C

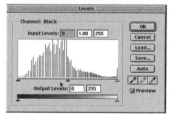

D

▼ Figure 14.2 Brightness Control
After highlight and shadow values are properly set, a curve tool may be effectively used to effect an overall change in image brightness. Here again, large adjustments to the distribution of image data may result in more image posterization.

7) Activate the Curve tool by selecting it from the Adjust sub menu under the Image menu in Photoshop (Image – Adjust – Curve) The dialog box in (Fig 14.2A) will appear.

Note: Make sure that the grayscale ramp along the bottom of the graph has the highlight end on the right side as shown in Fig 14.2-A. If it does not, click the little arrows in the middle of the gray ramp to change the direction.

8) Be sure that the Preview check box is checked so that the effect of the curve adjustment will be visible prior to clicking the OK button.

9) To effect a lightening of the image, move the curve up by clicking and holding on the middle of the curve and moving it up (Fig 14.2B). The amount of movement depends upon how much lightening you want to accomplish.

Note: While we have made a substantial adjustment to the central portion of the curve, you will notice that the highlight and shadow points have remained untouched. By using the Curve tool, we can effect dramatic redistribution for data within an image without destroying the highlight and shadow points.

10) Click OK. The results of the adjustment of the Curve tool can be seen in Fig 14.2C.

11) Now, re-activate the Level tool and histogram once more (Image – Adjust – Levels). The histogram seen in Fig 14.2D will appear.

Note: We now have a good news/bad news story. With the dramatic adjustment we made using the Curve tool, we see two primary changes. First, we see that the image data has been moved more toward the highlight end. The midtone point is closer to the middle of the image data. That's the good news! The bad news is that the amount of missing data, as seen by the blank lines in the histogram, has dramatically increased. There are large sections with little or no image data, which leads to posterization and loss of image detail.

Note: While we have certainly accomplished a lightening of a very dark image, we have also significantly lowered the quality of the image by increasing the amount of lost image data and therefore posterization. This loss of image quality is typical of images which have had large adjustments applied to them after the scan. It is just this sort of image degradation which supports the notion that most image adjustments, in particular the major adjustments such as highlight and shadow point assignment and brightness control, should be performed during the scan, rather than being performed after the scan where there is often limited data with which to work, and that much of the data that is there is often discarded during major post-scan adjustments.

A

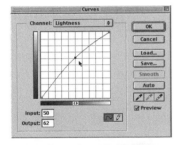

B

C

D

▼ **Figure 14.3 Brightness Control**
After highlight and shadow values are properly set, a curve tool may be used to effect an overall change in image brightness. Here again, large adjustments to the distribution of image data may result in image posterization.

Brightness Challenges: Color Images

The image quality challenges which we discussed for applying brightness adjustments to grayscale apply equally well to color images, since color images are just sandwiches of three grayscale images (see Chapter 2, "Scanned Image Fundamentals").

In addition to the image quality challenges already discussed for grayscale images, adjusting image brightness for color images has an additional challenge, and that is color shift which can occur when the overall brightness of an image is adjusted. To prevent color shifts from occurring during brightness changes in color images, we will make these adjustments while in Lab rather than RGB color mode.

Step-by-step: brightness adjustment of color

1) Open the image Still Life Start RGB_300.tif (Fig 14.3A).

2) Choose Duplicate from the Image menu (Image – Duplicate) to create a copy of the image.

Note: Always work on a copy of any image you intend to change!

3) Convert the image to Lab mode by selecting the Lab mode choice from the Mode menu under the Image menu in Photoshop (Image – Mode – Lab).

Note: This conversion places all the color image data in the "a" and "b" channels, and all the grayscale or luminance data in the "L" channel.

4) Activate the Channels palette by selecting the Show Channels choice under the Windows menu (Window – Show Channels) (Fig 14.3B).

5) Activate the Lab channel by clicking the Lightness channel in the Channels palette (Fig 14.3B).

Note: The Lightness, or luminance, channel is the channel which contains only the grayscale portion of the image. Any grayscale-only manipulation such as brightness, contrast, or sharpening can be applied to this channel without fear of any unwanted or unintended color adjustments occurring.

6) Activate the Curves tool (Fig 14.3C) by selecting the Curves sub, sub menu choice from the Adjust sub menu under the Image menu (Image – Adjust – Curves)

7) Move the middle of the Curves tool up or down to lighten or darken the image. Here we will lighten the overall image (Fig 14.3C). Figure 14.3D results from the application of the curve to the Lightness channel.

Note: You may return to RGB mode if you like, or convert directly to CMYK if you are ready to go to print. (See Chapters 10 and 15 for more information.)

ADJUSTING IMAGE CONTRAST

A

Even if an image has been scanned with proper highlight and shadow points and with good overall image brightness, we sometimes want to adjust the contrast of an image. Adjusting contrast involves redistributing the grayscale data around an image. We adjust contrast by changing the location of concentrations of grayscale data in an image.

Contrast Challenges

B

There are two primary challenges in adjusting image contrast. The first challenge is to avoid the loss of too much image data. Most postscan correction of contrast leads to loss of image data. The second challenge involves protecting the placement of properly assigned highlight and shadow values. It is generally a good idea to stay away from using slider-type contrast controls as these often excessively degrade image quality. We will use a curves tool to adjust the distribution of grayscale values to change image contrast and to protect our highlight and shadow values.

C

Step-by-step: contrast adjustment for grayscale

1) Open the image TazJaz Hawaii.tif (Fig 14.4A)

2) Choose Duplicate from the Image menu (Image – Duplicate) to create a copy of the image.

Note: Always work on a copy of any image you intend to change!

3) Select the Curves tool from the Adjust sub menu under the Image menu (Image – Adjust – Curves). The Curves toolbox will appear (Fig 14.4B).

▼ **Figure 14.4 Curve Tool: Increase Contrast**
Curve tools can also be used to adjust image contrast. Here we are increasing contrast across the entire image. Contrast the bottom image with the original image above.

4) Be sure to check the Preview check box so that you will be able to see any adjustments interactively (Fig 14.4B).

5) To increase the contrast of the image, create an "S"- shaped curve (Fig 14.4C).

6) To decrease the contrast of the image, apply a curve which is flattened in the area of the midtone (Fig 14.5).

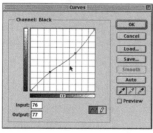

Note: A good rule to remember is that image data is concentrated where the curve is flattened.

▼ **Figure 14.5 Curve Tool: Decrease Contrast**
Here we are decreasing contrast across the entire image by flattening the curve in the midtones. Contrast with the original image above.

Contrast Challenges: Color Images

The image quality challenges which we discussed for applying contrast adjustments to grayscale images apply equally well to color images, since color images are just sandwiches of three grayscale images (see Chapter 2, "Scanned Image Fundamentals").

In addition to the image quality challenges already discussed for grayscale images, adjusting contrast for color images has an additional challenge–color shift, which can occur when overall contrast of an image is adjusted. To prevent color shifts from occurring during contrast changes in color images, we will make these adjustments while in Lab, rather than RGB, color mode.

Step-by-step: contrast adjustment for color

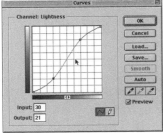
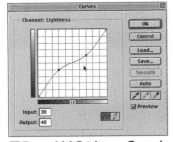

A

B

C

D

1) Open the image Still Life Start RGB_300.tif (Fig 14.6A).

2) Choose Duplicate from the Image menu (Image – Duplicate) to create a copy of the image.

Note: Always work on a copy of any image you intend to change!

3) Convert the image to Lab mode by selecting the Lab mode choice from the Mode menu under the Image menu in Photoshop (Image – Mode – Lab) (Fig 14.6B).

Note: This conversion places all the color image data in the "a" and "b" channels, and all the grayscale or luminance data in the "L" channel.

▼ *Figure 14.6 Brightness Control*
After highlight and shadow values are properly set, a Curve tool may be used to effect an overall change in image brightness. Here again, large adjustments to the distribution of image data may result in more image posterization.

4) Activate the Channels palette by selecting the Show Channels choice under the Windows menu (Window – Show Channels) (Fig 14.6-B)

5) Activate the Lab channel by clicking the "Lightness" channel in the Channel palette (Fig 14.6B).

Note: The Lightness, or luminance, channel is the channel which contains only the grayscale portion of the image. Any grayscale-only manipulation such as brightness, contrast, or sharpening can be applied to this channel without fear of any unwanted or unintended color adjustments occurring.

6) Activate the Curve tool (Fig 14.6C) by selecting the Curve sub, sub menu

choice from the Adjust sub menu under the Image menu (Image – Adjust – Curves).

7) Move the right side (highlight end) of the curve up and the left side (shadow end) of the curve either up or down to increase (Fig 14.6C) or decrease (Fig 14.6D) the contrast of the image.

Note: You may return to RGB mode if you like, or convert directly to CMYK if you are ready to go to print. (See Chapter 15 for more information.)

ADJUSTING IMAGE SHARPNESS

A

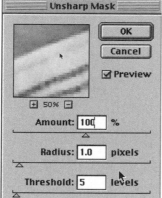

B

The scanning process, because it involves sampling and interpolation of image information as the scanner progresses across an image, usually results in the softening of an image. This softening is most pronounced along high-contrast edges, or on sharp edges between light and dark areas in an image in contone images (Fig 14.7A). If a contone image is not sharpened after it is scanned, it will appear softer than the original image.

Sharpness Challenges

There are two primary challenges in adjusting image sharpness. These involve deciding when to sharpen, and how much to sharpen. Sharpening can be applied to an image at the end of the scanning process itself or after the scan in an application like Photoshop. Many scanning applications contain their own sharpening tools and allow you to apply sharpening to the image as soon as it is captured. Allowing the scanner to apply the sharpening is certainly the fastest, most efficient way to apply sharpening, but it is not always the best choice. Sharpening of an image, which can also be thought of as improving the focus of an image, is accomplished by increasing the contrast, or grayscale values, between adjacent pixels.

▼ *Figure 14.7 Sharpening Choices*
Determining how much sharpening to apply is critical to good sharpening results:
A = Unsharpened
B = Good sharpening
C = Too much edge sharpening; note formation of edge haloes (see next page).
D = Not enough threshold, note mottling in background

There are two variables which control when we sharpen an image. The first is the quality of the sharpening tools and the second is how much image editing we intend to apply to an image after the scan is complete. The sharpening tools that some desktop scanners have are not very sophisticated and therefore do not allow us much control. The common sharpening tool of choice is called unsharp mask, a strange

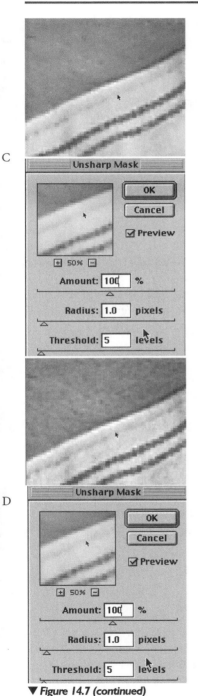

C

D

▼ *Figure 14.7 (continued)*

name for sure, but a tool which usually allows us more control over sharpening than standard sharpening tools. A good unsharp mask tool should allow us to control how much sharpening is applied and where it is applied in an image. Since scanners tend to preferentially soften the higher contrast areas of an image, our unsharp masking tools should allow us to preferentially sharpen higher contrast areas. As a minimum, you will want to be able to control the amount of sharpening, the width of the sharpened area, and the threshold of when sharpening is applied. The Amount and width, or Radius, controls allow us to control how much sharpening will be applied by allowing us to specify the amount of increase in contrast that will occur and the width over which that increase in contrast will be applied. A threshold tool will provide us with control over where the sharpening will occur in an image by allowing us to specify the minimum grayscale value difference (the Threshold) which must exist between adjacent pixels before sharpening will be applied.

Some scanner-based sharpening tools do not provide us with enough control over the sharpening, and therefore sharpening should be performed in the post scan for best control and results. But even if a scanner provides superior control, we may sometimes choose to apply sharpening to an image after the scan.

Sharpening, as we have discussed here and in Chapter 1, is accomplished by increasing the contrast between adjacent pixels. While this serves to improve the focus of an image, it also tends to decrease the occurrence of intermediate grayscale values in the sharpened areas of the image. The problem is that we may need to make additional changes after the scan. Any sort of smoothing process, such as touching up images or creating gradients or shadows, requires intermediate grayscale values for good results. Particularly if we intend to combine our scanned image with other images in collages, we need to have a full spectrum of grayscale values to allow us to effect smooth transitions along image edges. Sharpening tends to increase the abruptness of edge transitions and can hinder the creation of smooth transitions where our combined images meet. Therefore, it is a good idea to apply unsharp mask to an image only after we are done editing it. Sharpening should be the last step prior to output. If we scan an image that we know we will be using in many ways, and may well be editing in multiple circumstances, it is a good idea to create an unsharpened archive version of the image to which we repeatedly return to make copies and reuse.

The second issue related to sharpening is how much to apply. It is easy to overdo sharpening. A little bit is good, a bit more may be even better, but past a certain point, too much sharpening can ruin an image.

Too much sharpening can create obvious sharpening haloes, where abrupt black and white edges are created along high-contrast edges (Fig 14.7-C), and mottling, where thresholding has not been employed to protect the lower contrast portions of an image (Fig 14.7D).

Step-by-step: sharpness adjustment for grayscale

1) Open the image Still Life GS.tif (Fig 14.8A).

2) Choose Duplicate from the Image menu (Image – Duplicate) to create a copy of the image.

Note: Always work on a copy of any image you intend to change!

3) Select the Unsharp Mask tool from the Sharpen sub menu under the Filter menu in Photoshop (Filter – Sharpen – Unsharp Mask).

4) Click the Preview check box so that you will be able to interactively preview the results of the unsharp values prior to clicking the OK button.

5) Set the following values: Amount = 150, Radius = 1, Threshold = 2.

6) Click the OK button. The image will appear sharper (Fig 14.8B), but not too sharp.

7) Now make another duplicate from the Image menu (Image – Duplicate) to create a copy of the image.

8) Again select the Unsharp Mask tool from the Sharpen sub menu under the Filter menu in Photoshop (Filter – Sharpen –Unsharp Mask).

9) Click the Preview check box so that you be able to interactively preview the results of the unsharp values prior to clicking the OK button.

10) Set the following values: Amount = 150, Radius = 2, Threshold = 2.

11) Click the OK button. Fig 14.8C will appear sharper than Fig 14.8B. Is this too sharp? I think so, but you have to decide for each image based upon the look you want and the results you expect.

While the amount of sharpening applied to an image varies with each

A

B

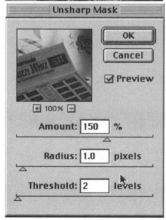

C

▼ **Figure 14.8 Sharpening**
Applying unsharp mask is a critical adjustment to make on a scanned image if we are to replace the softening which was created when the image was scanned. It is critical to match the Amount, Radius, and Threshold with the content and resolution of the image you are sharpening.

A

B

C

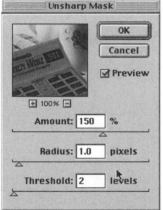

D

▼ *Figure 14.9 "L" Channel*
Sharpening
Converting an RGB color
image to a Lab color image
allows us to apply sharpening
on the "L" channel, thereby
avoiding the creation of color
shifts along high-contrast
edges in our color images.

image's resolution, here are a few guidelines for getting started: Portrait images with resolutions of 200–300ppi which will be printed at 150–200 lpi: Amount = 100–150, Radius = 1–2, Threshold = 3–5. Landscape and product shot images at 200–300ppi printed at 150–200lpi: Amount = 125-175, Radius = 1–2, Threshold = 1–3.

Sharpening Challenges: Color Images

The image quality challenges which we discussed for applying sharpening adjustments to grayscale images apply to color images as well, since color images are just sandwiches of three grayscale images (see Chapter 2).

In addition to the image quality challenges already discussed for grayscale images, adjusting image contrast for color images has an yet another added challenge,– color shift, which can occur when a color image is sharpened. This sharpening-related color shift may occur as a result of more sharpening being applied on one channel than another, due to that channel having higher contrast edges than the other channels. To prevent color shifts from occurring during sharpening of color images, we will make these adjustments while in Lab, rather than RGB ,color mode.

Step-by-step: sharpening adjustment for color

1) Open the image Still Life Start RGB_300.tif (Fig 14.9A)

2) Choose Duplicate from the Image menu (Image – Duplicate) to create a copy of the image.

Note: Always work on a copy of any image you intend to change!

3) Convert the image to Lab mode by selecting the Lab mode choice from the mode menu under the Image menu in Photoshop (Image – Mode – Lab).

Note: This conversion places all the color image data in the "a" and "b" channels, and all the grayscale or luminance data in the "L" channel.

4) Activate the Channels palette by selecting the Show Channels choice under the Windows menu (Window – show Channels).

5) Activate the Lab channel by clicking the Lightness channel in the Channel palette (Fig 14.9B).

Note: The Lightness, or luminance, channel is the channel which contains only the grayscale portion of the image. Any grayscale-only manipulation such as brightness, contrast, or sharpening can be applied to this channel without fear of any unwanted or unintended color adjustments occurring.

Select the Unsharp Mask tool from the Sharpen sub menu under the Filter menu in Photoshop (Filter – Sharpen –Unsharp Mask).

6) Click the Preview check box so that you be able to interactively preview the results of the unsharp values prior to clicking the OK button (Fig 14.9C).

7) Set the following values: Amount = 150, Radius = 1, Threshold = 2.

8) Click the OK button. The image will appear sharper (Fig 14.9D), but not too sharp.

Note: You may return to RGB mode if you like, or convert directly to CMYK if you are ready to go to print. (See Chapter 15 for more information.)

FIXING COLOR CASTS

One of the major challenges we face with scanning color images is color cast. As explained in Chapters 2 and 7, color cast is either the excess or lack of one or more colors, and can be caused by a poorly neutralized scanner, incorrectly exposed images, or both. If color cast is not detected and corrected, color images will print with poor color fidelity. While it is best to remove color cast at the scanning stage by calibrating your scanner and removing any original color cast from your images during the scan, we are faced with making color corrections after the scan.

Color Cast Challenges

There are two primary image components we look for when we set out to perform color corrections on images: neutral and memory colors. As explained earlier in this book, neutralization is the fundamental concept and skill which we use when working with color images. If we make the neutral gray portions of a color image neutral, then the remainder of the colors in an image tend to start falling into place. The second image component we look for is what we call "memory colors," which when they are incorrect, the human eye will easily detect. Examples of memory color are red stop signs and green grass. Orange stop signs and yellow grass call immediate attention to themselves as being wrong. Another common memory color is human skin. While there is no one set of colors that apply to all humans, there are some general color ratios that we aim for which make human skin reasonable-looking. Perhaps the most important habit to acquire when attempting to color correct images is not to trust your monitor and how images look on screen, but rather to use quantitative measurement tools to actually measure and correct images by the numbers.

▼ Figure 14.10 Original Color Image
Many images require color correction. Here we will measure and adjust the white highlights and facial skin tone values.

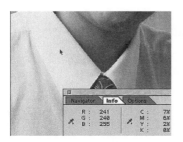

▼ Figure 14.11 Original Highlight Values
Note the 255 value for blue, which is not only not equal to the red and green values, but is too high, or blown out. For the highlight area of this image to be properly neutral, the measured blue values in the white collar must be adjusted down so that it has a similar value (~242) to that of the red and green values.

Remember the first color pictures we made as kids, the original color-by-number kits? This is the older kid's version of that. We will use color Info tools, sometimes called densitometers or intensitometers, to measure our color values.

Step-by-step: neutralization of color cast

1) Open the image Wine Woman RGB 200.tif (Fig 14.10).

2) Choose "Duplicate" from the Image menu (Image – Duplicate) to create a copy of the image.

Note: Always work on a copy of any image you intend to change!

3) Activate the Info tool under the Window menu (Window – Show Info). The Info palette will appear on screen.

4) Set the Info tool to measure RGB values by clicking on the small eye dropper icon next to the left-hand set of values on the left side of the Info tool palette (Fig 14.11).

5) Select the eye dropper from the tool palette, and set the tool to measure 5x5 in the Tool Options dialog box by pressing the return or ENTER key.

Note: Be sure to return to the Info tool palette before you proceed.

6) Move the Info tool onto the bright, white area of the shirt collar (Fig 14.11).

Note: This shirt collar region should be a neutral highlight portion of this image, which means that the RGB values should be equal, and they should all be around 5% highlight.

Note: The Info tool here uses a scale of 0–255 grayscale values instead of 0–100%, so we must translate from one scale to the other. A 5% value on the 255 scale is 242.

7) Read the RGB values shown in the Info tool palette.

Note: The red and green values are nearly equal and are right at the proper 5% highlight value in this image at 241 and 242, respectively. The blue value, however, is much higher at 255. This blue value needs to be lowered so that it equals ~242. We will use the Curve and Info tools in Photoshop to adjust and re-measure the blue highlight values.

8) Activate the Curves tool in the Adjust sub menu under the Image menu (Image – Adjust – Curves) (Fig 14.12).

9) Select the blue channel by clicking the Channel pull-down menu located at the top of the Curves tool window and dragging down the Blue channel (Fig 14.12).

Note: I place the Info palette, Curves window, and image so that I can see and work with all three without having to move either the inten-

**▼ Figure 14.12 Corrected
Highlight Values**
Note now that the RGB values
are about equal in the white
highlight area of the collar.
This is accomplished by adjusting the blue channel curve
down until the blue value is
lowered to approximately 242,
or the 5% value, to where the
blue will match the red and
green values.

sitometer palette, or the Curves window. I can navigate around the image using Photoshop's navigation keyboard shortcuts.

Note: I take several measurements on various portions of the collar to get an overall sense for what the general RGB values are. I try to locate the lightest portion of the image and measure that as one of the measurement locations. This shirt represents a specular highlight and should therefore print at ~ 5%, or 242.

10) Now move the highlight end of the blue curve lower until the RGB values are approximately equal. I usually do this progressively and sample several portions of the collar as I go.

Note: In the lightest portion of the highlight collar, the RGB values should all measure ~ 242/5% for a SWOP (specifications for web off-set press) press. This way, the white collar will print neutrally at a 5% highlight.

Note: If you are using CMYK values instead of RGB, your C/M/Y ratios should be approximately 7/5/5 to obtain a neutral 5% highlight dot. These uneven CMY values are necessary due to the contaminated nature of most printing inks.

Note: You may want to consult your printing company to make sure that the 7/5/5 ratio is good for their presses and inks.

Note: I generally perform most of these basic color correction chores on an RGB image because the math is easier and the files are smaller. Plus, it is easier to multi-purpose an RGB image than a CMYK image. I adjust for specific CMYK values during RGB-to-CMYK conversion.

Skin tone correction

To continue the correction of this image, let's focus on the skin tone values, as these are important memory color values to make reasonable. We might suspect that since there was such a strong blue color cast in the highlight region that this blue color cast may exist elsewhere through the tonal range of the image. We will measure to find out; we will not trust our eyes to make this determination.

1) Select the Multi-Eye Dropper to measure RGB values on several locations on the face. Click and hold the Eye Dropper tool and drag it over to the second (multiple) Eye Dropper tool (Fig 14.13A).

2) Make four measurements on various portions of the face to get an overall sense for what the general RGB values are. I try to look in lighter, midtone, and darker portions of the face (Fig 14.13B). All four values will appear in the Info tool palette when you use the Multiple Eye Dropper tool.

Note: While facial skin tone values are not nearly as cut-and-dried as

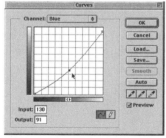

▼ *Figure 14.13 Facial Skin Values*
The multiple eye dropper tool allows you to measure, view, and correct color and/or grayscale values simultaneously. The multiple point values, both the original and the corrected values, are displayed in the eye dropper tool Info palette. The Curves tool is used here for adjusting the blue values in this image.

neutral values, there is a general range of ratio values to which most acceptable healthy skin tones occur. In most humans, RGB skin tone values should have the following relationship: red > green > blue in a ratio of between 5/4/3 to 5/3/2. If the R/G/B ratios deviate significantly from these guideline values, then skin tones will tend to look unnatural or other-worldly.

3) Look at the RGB values for the four eye dropper-measured areas of the image (Figures 14.3A & B).

Note: The blue values in all four measurements are either equal to or only slightly below the green values. The blue values should be significantly below the green values.

4) Activate the Curves tool again in the Adjust sub menu under the Image menu (Image – Adjust – Curves) (Fig 14.13C).

5) Select the blue channel by clicking the Channel pull down menu located at the top of the Curves tool window and dragging down the Blue channel (Fig 14.13C).

Note: I place the Info palette, Curves window, and image so that I can see and work with all three without having to move the intensitometer palette or the Curves window. I can navigate around the image using Photoshop's navigation keyboard shortcuts.

6) Now move the midtone portion of the blue curve lower until blue values in all four measured areas of the face are lowered to the appropriate values. I adjust these curves down until an R/G/B ratio ~5/3/2 is obtained in each of the several locations of the face (Fig 14.13C).

Note: I try to make all my color correction moves at once so I only have to apply the Curves dialog box once.

You can now go from RGB to CMYK depending on your needs, but be sure to set up color preferences first.

7) On the final image, apply unsharp mask: Filter – Sharpen – Unsharp Mask using the following settings: Amount = 100–150, Radius = 1.0, Threshold = 3–5. Here again, I would use the "L" channel in Lab mode to sharpen my image.

Note: Following are some reference skin tone values if you want to work in CMYK instead of RGB mode:

In mid-tone Caucasians: Y = 50–55%, M = 45–50% (5 – 10% lower than Y), C = 1/3 – 1/5 of Y (R–G–B ~5–3–2, E.G., 210, 145, 120) Asians: ~higher in yellow and cyan (green), Africans: generally higher in Magenta (blue and red).

Note: I prefer working in CMYK for skin tone corrections as % values are more intuitive for many people than 0–255 values.

PAULINE'S SCAN TIPS

Scan Tip # 14-1

When making image brightness adjustments on grayscale images, use an editable histogram to adjust the highlight and shadow points of your images. Set your highlight at the beginning of the significant image data in the histogram. The precise position, or grayscale value, of the highlight point can be fine-tuned to match the minimum highlight value of your output device.

Scan Tip # 14-2

Overall brightness of images should be controlled using a curve tool rather than standard brightness sliders. Using a curve tool to adjust brightness will allow you to maintain previously set highlight and shadow points and reduce the amount of image data loss which occurs during the adjustment.

Scan Tip # 14-3

Image contrast adjustments should be done using a curve tool. The contrast can be adjusted by controlling the shape of the curve. Wherever the curve slope is flattened the grayscale values will be concentrated. So, an "S"-shaped curve which flattens in the highlight and shadow regions will result in an increase in overall image contrast, while a flattening of a curve in the midtone region will result in a decrease in overall image contrast. Using a curve tool to adjust brightness will allow you to maintain previously set highlight and shadow points and reduce the amount of image data loss which occurs during the adjustment.

Scan Tip # 14-4

When making brightness and contrast adjustments to color images, it is best to make these adjustments only on the luminance values. An effective way to do this is to convert your RGB color image to Lab mode. Any brightness and contrast adjustments can then be made only to the "L" channel, which contains only luminance or grayscale data.

PAULINE'S SCAN TIPS

Scan Tip # 14-5

Scanning will tend to soften nearly all contone images. To restore image focus, we apply sharpening tools. Usually the best tool to apply sharpening is an unsharp mask tool, which should allow us to control both the amount and placement of the unsharp mask. Scanners tend to preferentially soften high-contrast portions of images, so our sharpening tools should be set to preferentially sharpen these same high-contrast areas. A good sharpening tool should allow us to control the amount of sharpening, the radius, and the threshold of where the sharpening will be applied. Sharpening amounts will usually vary between 100–200%, radius values vary between 1–2 pixels, and thresholds vary from 2–5. A typical setting of unsharp mask starting values for a 200ppi contone photograph of a person's face being printed at 150 lpi might be Amount = 100%, Radius = 1, Threshold = 5. Avoid over-sharpening, as excess sharpening can lead to the creation of black and white haloes along high-contrast edges.

Scan Tip # 14-6

Neutralization is the foundation to color correction. If we make the neutral gray portions of an image neutral, the rest of the color values in an image tend to fall into place. Typical image neutrals to look for are white clothing, paper products, white buildings and walls, and white product backgrounds. An image area will be considered neutral, that is gray, when the RGB values for that area are all equal.

Scan Tip # 14-7

There are numerous tools which can be used to make adjustments to the color values in an image, but all color correction judgements should be made by measuring the color values with an Info tool which measures the grayscale

PAULINE'S SCAN TIPS

values of the pixels rather than making visual evaluations. A curve tool used to adjust the color values on individual channels can be an effective color adjustment tool.

Scan Tip # 14-8

When making color cast corrections in highlight areas, be sure to keep two adjustments in mind. Your white highlight values should not only be equal, but should be adjusted for the printable or minimum highlight values on your output device. Typical highlight values include: commercial printing = 5%, desktop laser printers = 10%, newsprint = 20%.

Scan Tip # 14-9

In addition to adjusting neutrals, we must often pay attention to the color values of key components of an image and/or memory colors. For instance, our skies should be blue, our grass green, and our stop signs red. A very important component of many color images is facial skin tone values. While there are wide variations in human skin tones, most skin tones share a common ratio of RGB colors. In most humans, red is greater than green which in turn should be greater than blue. The specific values will vary depending upon the tonal area of the image, but RGB ratios are typically in the range of 5/4/3 to 5/3/2.

Scan Tip # 14-10

When applying unsharp mask to a color image, try converting your image to Lab mode first, and then applying the unsharp mask to the "L" channel only. Performing "L" channel unsharp masking will prevent any color shifts from occurring along high-contrast edges.

15
Preparing For Output

As the Byte Turns continues...

Will Danny D'Ziner and Pauline E. Prepress be Put Out with one another, or will they be able to get good Out Put of their images?

Now that I have learned how to scan my images, how do I make sure that they look their best when I output them?

I know Pauline has some words of wisdom on this topic.

The key is to know as much about the output device as you can. Then you can address key output issues such as resolution, dot gain, and gamut conversion.

INTRODUCTION

Output-Specific Image Preparation

When we scan our images, it is a good idea to know how they will be used. The ultimate use of our images may well affect how we scan them. For instance, if we know that an image will be printed at twice the size of the original, we can set up the scanner to scale it to 200% during the scanning process. If we know that our image will be printed at 150 lpi, then we can set our scanner input resolution to 1.5 times that line screen. The more we know about the requirements of our output devices, the more closely we can tailor the scan to that device. Printing companies and color trade shops have taken advantage of this concept for years to help speed up the production process and provide maximum image quality by allowing their scanners to perform most of the image correction and preparation functions for them. In the world of desktop publishing, we too can take advantage of this concept, but there are a few twists to consider, particularly if we intend to output our images on multiple devices.

Output Preparation Challenges

When we scan images on the desktop, we face two fundamental challenges: 1) we are often using scanners and software which may not provide us with all the image preparation controls we would like, and 2) we often want to output our images to more than one device. The first challenge, the scan system capabilities challenge, may be met by performing our image preparation chores in a sophisticated image editing program such as Photoshop. While this will generally not produce as good a quality as if we had applied the correction during a scan, it at least allows us to prepare our images more specifically than our scanner and its software did. If you use a low-quality scanner with poor-quality software, then the use of a Photoshop-like tool will be important.

The second challenge, that being the desire to output our images on more than one device, commonly called *multi-purposing* our images, is a bit more challenging. Each device on which we output our images has different output characteristics and capabilities. So, if we prepare an image to be specifically well-suited to be output on one device, it may not be well-suited to be output on another. Even if we have very sophisticated scanning hardware and software which will allow us to prepare an image exactly the way we want it to output on a specific device, we may not want to take advantage of that capability as doing so may compromise our ability to multi-purpose our images on other devices.

A couple of examples will serve to illustrate this concept. Let's say that we prepared a 4" x 5" color contone to print on a commercial printing press at 8" x 10" at 200 lpi. We set up our high-quality scanner to scale the image 200%, at 300ppi, and converted it to a CMYK color space. This image, in other words, was specifically prepared for that commercial print job. If, however, we wanted to next output that image to a Web page, the image characteristics would be all wrong. For the Web, we want a 2" x 3" image, at 72ppi, and in RGB color space. So, the original CMYK image needs to be rebuilt to match these specifications. This can be done in Photoshop, of course, but each color conversion or mode change in Photoshop can lower the quality of the image. In addition, by converting the original scanned image to CMYK right off the scanner, we threw away much of the color saturation which could have been shown in RGB but could not be reproduced in CMYK. Similarly, if we scanned the image for output on the Web and wanted to *repurpose* that image for use in commercial CMYK printing, we would be in even worse straits as sizing an image up and increasing its resolution are usually far more damaging than going down. Even if we intended to just print to CMYK devices, each device has its own range of colors it can reproduce, known as the color *gamut* of that device, so preparing a color image for reproduction on a color laser printer is no guarantee that it will print properly on a commercial press. In fact just the opposite is true. One final example will seal the point. If we prepared a grayscale photo to print specifically on a 600-dpi / 85-lpi desktop laser printer which had 30% dot gain, and then decided to print it at 150 lpi on a commercial press with 20% *dot gain*, our image would not only not have enough resolution, it would print too light due to the large dot gain adjustment which was made to print on the laser.

So, what to do?

Here are some guidelines for scanning images for multiple use:

1) Always perform the basic image correction functions during the scan, including:

   a) Calibrating the scanner

   b) Setting image highlight and shadow points

   c) Adjusting overall brightness and contrast controls

   d) Setting resolution and scaling for the largest and highest resolution use (see #2 and #3)

e) Capturing more than 8 bits per pixel

f) Capturing color images into a large color space (see #4)

g) Applying sharpening during the scan only if you are planing to output the final scanned image (see #5)

2) Scan your images at the largest size at which you will want to use them (this will often be a print size). Scaling digital images down in Photoshop is far less detrimental than scaling up.

3) Scan your images at the highest resolution you will need (this is again often commercial print resolution). Again, lowering resolution is far less damaging than raising resolution.

4) Scan your images into a large color space such as Lab, CIE, or larger gamut RGB so that you will capture enough color to satisfy all of your output devices including your monitor.

5) Apply unsharp mask after all image editing is complete. This can be done during the scan if the scanner provides sophisticated-enough unsharp masking, and you do not intend to perform much editing on the image after the scan.

6) Do not apply dot gain until you are ready to send the image to a specific printing device. If the dot gain adjustment can be applied at the RIP or with a transfer function, so that your original image will not be affected, so much the better. (Talk with your local printing company or service bureau prepress manager to determine which option is best for them and you.)

7) Make a large-gamut archive copy of the original scan so that you can return to it for later conversion and use. Always make a copy of the archive image each time you repurpose it so as to protect the integrity and quality of the original image.

DOT GAIN CORRECTION

Many people have problems with their images printing too dark. There are three major variables that contribute to this: 1) non-linear scanners which capture images too dark, 2) improper placement of highlight and shadow points, and 3) dot gain. We have already covered the first two variables; now we will cover adjusting for dot gain. *Dot gain* is a term which describes how dots grow in size in various processes such as film-to-film transfers and plate making. But, the greatest dot gain occurs when ink or toner spreads out when it is applied to paper. This increase in dot size results in a darkening of our images. See Chapters 1 and 3 for a more in-depth explanation of dot gain.

A

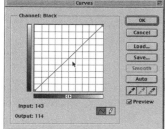

B

▼ Figure 15.1 Dot Gain Correction

All grayscale images will get darker when printed on paper as a result of dot gain. An image can be corrected for dot gain by applying a dot gain correction curve to the image prior to printing.

Dot Gain Challenges: Grayscale Images

Since this is a function only of printing, and dot gain varies widely depending upon the press and paper on which the images will be printed, we most often apply dot gain correction after the scan, but before we print the image, if we are multi-purposing our images. The basic goal is to lighten our images to accommodate the darkening which occurs on the press. For grayscale images, this dot gain correction can be performed through the application of a curve. Once again, we should always perform this curve-based lightening on a copy of the original scan so as to preserve the characteristics and quality of the original image. If we send a dot gain-corrected image to the Web, for instance, it will appear too bright. And remember that each printing device and paper will have different dot gain characteristics. In general, uncoated paper will have more dot gain than coated paper.

Step-by-step: dot gain adjustment for grayscale

1) Open the Sid GS 200.tif image (Fig 15.1-A).

2) Choose Duplicate from the Image menu (Image – Duplicate) to create a copy of the image.

Note: Always work on a copy of any image you intend to change!

3) Select the Curves tool from the Adjust sub menu under the Image menu (Image – Adjust – Curves) The Curves tool window will appear with an adjustable linear curve (Fig 15.1B).

4) Be sure to set the highlight portion of the gradient on the right end of the bottom gradient in the Curves window. This will prevent confusion as we move forward.

Note: You will notice that there are 10 horizontal and vertical lines criss-crossing this graph. Each one represents 10 steps of grayscale. To make a dot gain correction, we will be moving the middle of this curve up from the 50% grayscale position from its starting position. While each printing device/paper combination will have a unique dot gain value, here are some general guidelines. When printing on coated commercial stock, we will generally be moving the midpoint position of the curve up to between the 40–45% location. When printing on uncoated stock, the placement of the midpoint of the curve will be between 30% and 40%. To proceed further, we will need to know how much to adjust the curve. This knowledge may be based upon instructions we receive from our printing company or service bureau, or it may be obtained through trial and error testing. Either way, we need to know how much to move our midpoint.

A

B

C

▼ **Figure 15.2 Dot Gain Correction**
A: Dot gain correction curve.
B: Dot gain-corrected image, prior to printing.
C: Printed image with NO dot gain correction applied. Note how the image is darker and lower in contrast due to the concentration of data toward the shadow end of the image.

Note: We will correct this image to print at 150 line screen on uncoated stock. We received instructions to move the midpoint of the curve to 35%.

5) Place a check in the Preview check box in the lower right corner of the Curves window to allow you to interactively see the preview prior to clicking OK (Fig 15.2A).

6) Click on the midpoint of the curve and drag it up to the 35% position on the chart (Fig 15.2A)

7) Click OK to apply this change.

Note: The lightened-for-dot gain image will appear. This image will look as if it is too light, and it would be if it were not going to be printed. All the image density which we removed will be returned as dot density when we place the inked image on paper. When this image is printed, it will look just like the image in Fig 15.1A.

If we do not apply this dot gain correction and print the image directly, it will print as you see in Fig 15.2B, where the same amount of dot density is added, but to a darker beginning image.

It should be noted that this same correction could be applied during the scan, at the RIP or by attaching a transfer function to this image. It is best to discuss where and how to apply dot gain correction with your printing company so that you don't both forget to do it or duplicate efforts.

Dot Gain Challenges: Color Images

We have the same dot gain challenges when printing color images as we do with grayscale images, with one major additional variable. When we dot gain-correct a grayscale image, we have only one ink to adjust, black. When we create and apply a dot gain correction for color images, we have four inks to adjust, one for each printing ink, cyan, magenta, yellow, and black. Each of these inks gain a little differently than the others, so in order not to create a color shift when we correct for dot gain, we need to adjust each ink separately.

Instead of using the Curve tool to create a dot gain correction curve as we did with the grayscale image, we most often apply a dot gain correction during the RGB-to-CMYK gamut conversion. High-quality RGB-to-CMYK gamut conversion tools will always provide some avenue for accommodating dot gain. See the next section on RGB-to-CMYK conversion.

RGB-TO-CMYK CONVERSION

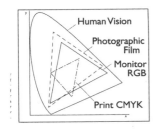

▼ Figure 15.3 Gamuts

Each output device has its own gamut. The commercial CMYK printing device color space is one of the smallest, far smaller than either photographic film or RGB monitors. Our eyes have the largest gamut of any device we work with. This means that there is much more color which we can create, capture, and see than we can print. What the above diagram also tells us is that when we multipurpose our images, we do not want to automatically convert all of our color images into CMYK. If we do, we end up tossing out much of the color we can reproduce on other devices.

When we move from one color space to another, we want to try to match the colors in the starting device, perhaps a scanner, to the final device, perhaps a printing press, as closely as possible. This is called gamut mapping. This gamut mapping requires that we know the color characteristics of both devices.

Gamut Conversion Challenges

The first point to be made in any discussion of gamut conversion is that all output color spaces are device-specific. This means that each device to we output our images, including, but not limited to, monitors, printers, projectors, and film recorders, has its own range of colors which it can reproduce. This range of reproducible color is called that device's *gamut* (Fig 15.3). For the best quality results when we output our images to multiple devices, we should create a separate gamut conversion for each output device. This is true even if we move our image from one monitor to another. We basically want to match our input and output devices to one another as closely as possible. When we talk about matching one device to another, we call this *device matching*. When we include multiple devices and numerous applications across one or more networks, we call this *color management*, or as some would say, a color nightmare.

In the best of all color management worlds, we would use color input, viewing, and output print targets; sophisticated measurement instruments and profile construction software to define the gamuts of, and create a profile for, each device in our publishing system. With these profiles and some sophisticated gamut mapping software we could map one device profile to another. And when we wanted the best possible control over our color, this is what we would need to do.

It doesn't take a rocket scientist to see that this could lead to a whole lot of work, and much hair-pulling as well. I am assuming that most of us do not have the skill or resources to implement the above described type of color management system. Luckily this does not have to be an all-or-nothing battle. There is some middle ground in this battle to control color, and this middle ground is where we will play. I will mention the higher ground at the conclusion of this section, but will leave the details for my book on color management. So to enter the color fray, we will perform a gamut conversion in Photoshop moving the color in a scanned image from RGB to CMYK using a standard commercial press as the target output device. Thankfully, Photoshop provides us with some built-in tools we can use to control our color reasonably well. It is these built-in tools which we will use in the following step-by-step gamut conversion. Other software applications provide similar tools. The setup we perform here will give us insight into other gamut conversion setups, including the full-blown color management systems discussed above.

Step-by-step: RGB-to-CMYK conversion

In Photoshop, it is important to define the monitor color space in which we are working, as well as the final output target space to which we will be printing. If you are sending your files out to have someone else print your images, you will want to ask them for the setup values they recommend for their output devices.

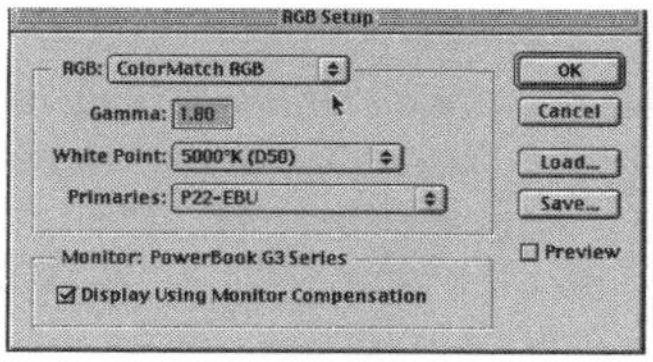

Standard built-in conversion

▼ *Figure 15.4 RGB Setup*
This Photoshop window is used to set up the color space in which we work with and view our images in Photoshop. These settings also have a large impact on what happens during the RGB-to-CMYK gamut conversion process.

1) Open the Still Life 300RGB.tif image.

2) Choose "Duplicate" from the Image menu (Image – Duplicate) to create a copy of the image.

Note: Always work on a copy of any image you intend to change!

3) Select RGB setup from the Color Settings sub menu under the File menu (File – Color Settings – RGB setup). The RGB Setup window will appear (Fig 15.4).

This setup will allow us to define the monitor color space in which we will be viewing and editing our images. The values we establish here will also affect the color that results when we accomplish an RGB-to-CMYK conversion.

4) Click on and drag down through the menu which appears at the top of the window next to the label RGB to select the basic monitor space in which you want to work. The default monitor space in many cases is sRGB. This should be avoided in nearly every circumstance. There are several other viable built-in choices, including Adobe RGB and Apple RGB. If you are working primarily in prepress, I recommend ColorMatch RGB (shown in Fig 15.4). Ask your service bureau for their recommendations.

5) Next you will want to set the White Point Primaries and values. Unless instructed otherwise, leave these on the default settings which appear when you make your RGB monitor choice. If you are working in prepress, 5000°K is the standard viewing color/temperature.

6) Click the Display Using Monitor Compensation check box if you want Photoshop to adjust your image on-screen to match the setting in this dialog box.

The settings you make in this RGB Setup dialog box will be used during the RGB-to-CMYK conversion, whether you activate the monitor compensation check box or not. Sometimes I will deactivate the Monitor Compensation check box to speed up Photoshop's on-screen redraw when I am working on non-color-critical adjustments.

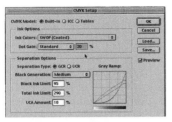

▼ Figure 15.5 CMYK Setup
This Photoshop window allows you to choose from three different ways to control the RGB-to-CMYK conversion: the Built-in method, the ICC profiles, and the Tables method.

7) Next, select CMYK setup from the Color Settings sub menu choice under the File menu (File – Color Settings – CMYK setup). The CMYK Setup window will appear (Fig 15.5).

8) Choose one of the CMYK models at the top of the window by clicking on the button next to it. In the absence of custom setup data, select the Built-in choice.

9) Next to the Ink Colors label, click on the menu. Select the ink color set which most closely matches the device on which you will be printing. If you are printing on a commercial press, you will likely choose one of the *SWOP* (Specifications Web Offset Publications) choices for coated, uncoated, or newsprint. We will choose SWOP (Coated) here.

Note: The choice you make here will affect both the Dot Gain value and the color generation Gray Ramp curves which you see at the bottom of the window.

10) Set the Dot Gain value. If you do not have any specific instructions, use the default value generated when you choose the Ink Colors set, 20% here.

Note: If your color images are consistently too dark when they print, try raising the Dot Gain value in 2% increments until your images print with acceptable lightness.

11) Next, under the Separation Options, choose either *UCR* or *GCR*. This choice will control how much black substitution will occur when the CMYK ink values are generated. Most printing companies prefer one or the other of these. It is best to use the method your printing company is most familiar with. I have selected GCR here.

Note: Select both methods and notice how the color generation graph changes. GCR (Gray Component Replacement) has more black substitution earlier in the gray ramp sequence than UCR (Under Color Removal).

12) If you choose GCR, as we have done here, you will want to control how strong the black substitution will be for the other colors. Click and drag down the pull-down menu next to the Black Generation label. You will generally choose either Light or Medium. We have selected Medium here. Once again, take the lead provided by your printing company.

13) Type in a value for Black Ink Limit. this will vary from 80% for newsprint to 90–100% for commercial printing.

14) Total Ink Limit is next. This will generally vary from 220–230 for newsprint to 290–330 for commercial printing. This value should never be close to 400%. If this number is too high, too much ink

will be placed on the page during the printing process.

15) Finally, you should set the UCA (Under Color Addition), which allows you to further adjust the amount of ink in the shadow portion of an image. This should rarely exceed 10% (shown here). As a default, you can leave this at 0%. If you would like to have the shadow portions of your contone images denser, a little bit of UCA can be added to increase shadow density. But be careful, as it is easy to blot out shadow detail with the application of too much UCA. Use this only under the strict supervision of your prepress manager.

Note: If we had selected UCR instead of GCR, the Black Generation and UCA choices would not be available to us.

16) Click OK. Photoshop has now been prepared to convert your image from RGB to CMYK.

17) Select the CMYK mode from the Mode sub menu under the Image menu (Image – Mode – CMYK). This will convert your image from RGB to CMYK mode using our assigned setup values.

Custom color tables

Some printing companies have constructed their own custom color conversion tables, called *color lookup* tables. These tables have generally been constructed using the specific set of press setup conditions that exist for a particular press or printing company. These tables may represent very high-quality gamut maps for that particular press. If your printing company has custom color lookup tables, they can give you a copy of these tables, and you can use them for your RGB-to-CMYK conversion.

Once you obtain custom color tables from your printer:

1) Copy the custom color tables onto your hard drive and place them in a folder where you will remember where they are.

2) Next, select CMYK setup from the Color settings sub menu choice under the File menu (File – Color Settings – CMYK setup). The CMYK Setup window will appear (Fig 15.6A).

3) Now, click Tables in the CMYK Mode choice section. The tables window (Fig 15.6B) will appear.

4) Click the Load button. A Finder or Windows navigation dialog box will appear.

5) Navigate through your hard drive to locate the custom color tables you copied onto your hard drive.

6) Load these custom tables into Photoshop.

7) Click OK. Photoshop has now been prepared to convert your image

A

B

▼ *Figure 15.6 Custom Tables*
If you select the Tables option in the CMYK Setup window (A), the Tables dialog box will appear (B). Custom color lookup tables can be loaded to control the RGB-to-CMYK conversion.

from RGB to CMYK.

8) Select the CMYK mode from the Mode sub menu under the Image menu (Image – Mode – CMYK). This will convert your image from RGB to CMYK mode using our loaded setup values.

ICC profile use

In addition to standard and custom setup, Photoshop also supports the use of color profile to control RGB-to-CMYK conversion. To use the ICC color profile to control this type of conversion, configure the CMYK Setup window in the following way:

1) Select CMYK setup from the Color settings sub menu choice under the File menu (File – Color Settings – CYMK setup). The CMYK Setup window will appear (Fig 15.7A)

3) Now, click ICC (International Color Consortium) in the CMYK Mode section. The ICC options window (Fig 15.7B) will appear.

4) Next to the Profile label, click and drag down on the menu to select the output device you want to convert your file to.

Note: You can choose an RGB device here as well as CMYK output devices, if you just want to change monitors instead of printing the image.

5) Next, click and drag down next to the Engine label to select the color engine, or processing, software you would like to use. I have chosen Apple ColorSync here.

6) Finally, you will want to select an Intent to match the kind of image you are converting. Perceptual (Images) is selected here for use with color contone photographs.

Note: Here again, you will want to seek the advice of your printing company or service bureau for instructions on how to configure this ICC options dialog box. Your service company may even have their own ICC profiles which they can give you to use in this setup. In this case, you would copy the profiles onto your hard drive and use the Load button on the right side of the dialog box to access their profile information.

7) Click OK. Photoshop has now been prepared to convert your image from RGB to CMYK.

8) Select the CMYK mode from the Mode sub menu under the Image menu (Image – Mode – CMYK). This will convert your image from RGB to CMYK mode using the assigned ICC options.

Note: Which method you choose above will depend upon the workflow and capabilities of your service company. Using the ICC profile options is certainly easier than configuring the built-in values. However, not all service companies use a profiling system, and the profile system is less flexible in terms of making easy adjustments to output. Discuss your options with

A

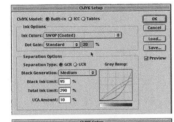

B

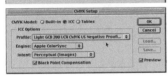

▼ Figure 15.7 ICC Profile Use
If you select the ICC option in the CMYK setup window (A), the ICC Options dialog box will appear (B). Here you will control the output Profile that will be used, the conversion Engine, and the Intent to control the RGB-to-CMYK conversion.

your service company. If you are printing in-house, try both methods and see which gives you the best results. If you use the built-in method, you will be able to make adjustments easier than if you use the profile method.

Profiling controls

While it is beyond the scope of this book to delve much deeper into the profiling system, it is worth mentioning that Photoshop provides even more options for controlling images with profiles. For instance, using the Profile Setup window (Fig 15.8) (Color Settings – Profile Setup), we can ask Photoshop, using the Assume Profile menus, to assign a color profile and convert an image upon opening. We can also control, using the Profile Mismatch Handling menus, how Photoshop handles images that already have color profiles assigned to them that do not match the assumed profiles. Profiles are often used as part of an integrated *color management* system, which is designed to make color more predictable and reliable.

▼ *Figure 15.8 Profile Controls*
Using this profile control window in Photoshop, we can control the profile assignment and conversion of images when they are opened in Photoshop.

Exporting images with profiles

Increasingly, we are gaining the ability to assign color characteristics to our images when we create them and have those color characteristics preserved, even if we send them to another location for output. An example of this is Photoshop's Export TIFF with ColorSync Profile capability (File – Export – Export TIFF with ColorSync Profile). When we choose this export function from Photoshop, the ColorSync Export Module window in Fig 15.9 appears. With this module, we can assign and embed a series of color profile characteristics into our image when we export it. This profile-based color description can then be used to reproduce this image wherever it goes.

▼ *Figure 15.9 Profile Export*
Images can be saved with embedded color profile information which can be used to open and output your images on other remote stations. Be sure that the receiving station knows that this profile information is there and how to take advantage of it.

Note: It is important to point out that not everyone uses color profiles at this time. Before you send an image with embedded profile information, be sure that your receiving output station knows that the profile information is embedded and that they know how to use that information. If someone opens and prints your image and either ignores or overrides your profile information, all of your hard profile efforts will be for naught.

Scanning profiles controls

So far, we have been controlling the RGB-to-CMYK conversion in Photoshop after a scan is complete. It is increasingly possible to control the conversion to CMYK during the scan process. In fact, the same profile system we have been discussing can be used to make this conversion on-the-fly during the scanning process. All that is required is scanning software that has the capability of accepting color profiles. Figure 15.10 shows a UMAX MagicScan scanner software interface which provides the ability to convert a scanned image on-the-fly to CMYK. This conversion feature is

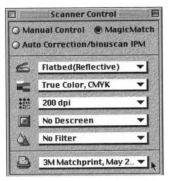

▼ Figure 15.10 Scanner Profiles
Images can be saved with embedded color profile information, which can be used to open and output your images on other remote stations. Be sure that the receiving station knows that this profile information is there and how to take advantage of it.

activated as follows:

1) The scanner interface is launched. The Scanner Control interface window in Fig 15.10 appears.

2) The MagicMatch button at the top of the dialog box is checked. This activates the conversion capabilities of this particular software. Other scanning software will have a similar button.

3) Next, TrueColor, CMYK is chosen from the scan mode menu.

4) The output profile, in this case 3M MatchPrint, is chosen from a list of profiles at the bottom of the Scanner Control window.

Note: This profile is a generic model profile which, while better than no profile, is inferior to a custom profile which you might construct for your specific 3M MatchPrint in your production system.

5) Set up the scan using all the procedures discussed earlier.

6) Once the final scan is initiated, the scanner will capture the image in RGB and then convert the image on-the-fly to CMYK using the profile information assigned in the Scanner Control window.

Note: This is certainly the fastest and most efficient way to convert an image. And if the output profile is of high quality, that is, it is a custom profile which closely matches the final output device, this type of conversion can be of very high quality. So why don't we use this method? Printing companies and scan houses have been doing this for years. It works great as long as you are going to output on only one CMYK device. But remember our discussion of gamuts. If we save directly into CMYK off the scan, we are severely restricting the color gamut of the image. In addition, a CMYK file is 33% larger than an RGB file, which means that all manipulations including opening, closing, saving, editing, etc., will require 33% more time. Furthermore, color correction is easier to understand and perform on an RGB image, particularly if you are new to the color correction game. And finally, if we intend to perform much creative image editing, there are numerous Photoshop filters which only work in RGB. So if we intend to multi-purpose our images, we are usually better off scanning into RGB and converting to a device-specific CMYK (or other color space) when we are ready to output the images.

Proofs

Regardless of which method you choose to perform your gamut conversion, if you are going to have someone else print your images, you should always request a color proof before final output. And always ask the output technician if they can match the proof. If you do not request and ask about the proof, you may be in for a surprise on the final print.

CONVERTING IMAGES FOR WEB USE

A

B

C

▼ Figure 15.11 Reducing File Size
Original image (A) is an 8"x5", 200ppi, 5.2MB RGB image. Reduction of pixel dimensions and resolution lowers its file size from 5.2MB to 90K (B). Creation of a medium-quality (compression) JPEG image (C) further reduces the file size to a Web-appropriate 6.8K. The choice of JPEG allows us to retain the 24-RGB quality of the image.

Image Requirements for the Web

When we scan images, as we have already discussed, we should create them at the largest size, at the highest resolution, and with the greatest number of colors that we think we will ultimately use. Commercial print purposes usually set the requirements for image size and resolution. On the Web, however, we can often see more colors than we can reproduce on a printing press, which is one of the reasons why we capture into RGB instead of CMYK if we intend to use our images on the Web as well as in a commercial printing environment. Repurposing our images for use on the Web nearly always requires that we reduce the dimensions and resolution of our images, and often requires that we reduce the bit depth of the images and therefore the number of colors in our images. We perform all this diminution in the interest of dramatically reduced file size. Small file size is king over the Internet. The smaller your files are, the faster they will be transferred across the Internet and viewed by the recipient. In this case, your output device is someone else's monitor.

File dimension and resolution can be handled through the use of the Image Size window in Photoshop. Significant reductions in file size can be accomplished through reducing the dimensions and resolution of an image. In Fig 15.11, we see a reduction in file size from 5.2 MB (Fig 15.11A) to 90K by reducing the dimensions of the image from approximately 5" x 8", to 2" x 3" and lowering the resolution from 200ppi to 72 ppi (15.11B). Further reductions in file size can be attained through the application of compression and/or bit depth reduction. Saving this initially reduced-sized image out as a medium-quality JPEG file further reduces the file size to a tiny 6.8K (15.11C), a very acceptable Web file size.

File Formats

Pixel- and/or vector-based images can be saved in many different file formats. It is useful to think of a file format as a container in which image components, pixels, and/or vectors, are stored. Scanned images will of course be constructed from pixels. The file format we choose for an image should be determined by how the image will be used. For example, if we are to use our images for printing to a PostScript printer, then a pixel-based TIFF or EPS would be most appropriate. If, how-

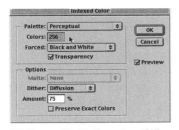

▼ *Figure 15.12 Creating GIFs*
GIFs are used for Web images, and support 8 bits or less information. Image quality and load speed can be controlled through color and dithering choices.

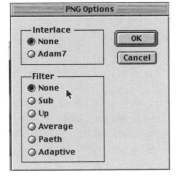

▼ *Figure 15.13 Creating PNGs*
PNGs are used in Web images, and support 8 or 24 bits. Image quality and load speed can be controlled through color and dithering choices.

ever, our images will be used for placement on a Web page, then a GIF, JPEG, PNG, or SWF file format would be most appropriate. Some file formats such as PCX, PICT, and WMF tend to be more platform-specific and less flexible than TIFFs and are therefore less desirable for use as a standard file format. For print, I recommend that you initially save your images in the TIFF format. The TIFF format is a flexible, pixel-based file format which is compatible with use on Mac, Windows, and UNIX systems for print. If you reuse and/or re-create your images for other purposes, you may change the file format of an image. Below is a review of file formats, color spaces, resolutions, and use.

Flash: ShockWave (.swf) is an emerging vector file format developed by Macromedia which can be used on the Web. This is a good format for line art images and other simple graphics, and is excellent for animations. The ShockWave format has all the advantages of standard vector images such as small size, scalability, skewability, editability and resolution-independence.

GIF: GIF (Graphic Interchange Format) (Fig 15.12) is a common pixel-based image format used on the Web. The GIF format supports 8-bit (or lower) grayscale and Index color images, typically at 72ppi.

JPEG: JPEG (Joint Photographic Expert Group) is a pixel-based format commonly used on the Web for viewing and image transfer. This type of image file format is used mainly for grayscale and 24-bit RGB images. JPEG can also be used in CMYK format for storage and printing of high-resolution files, but a JPEG image should be converted into a CMYK, TIFF, or EPS prior to printing.

PNG: PNG (Portable Network Graphic) (Fig 15.13) is a pixel-based format commonly used on the Web for viewing and image transfer. This type of image file format is used mainly for grayscale and RGB images.

SWF: SWF (Shock Wave Format) is a vector-based format commonly used on the Web for animation graphics. This type of image file format can be grayscale, 8-, or 24-bit RGB images. SWF can also be used for printing high-resolution files, but should be converted into a spot or CMYK color space, TIFF, or EPS prior to printing.

PDF Graphics: Any file which you can print to a PostScript printer can be converted on-the-fly for use in a PDF file. Configure the Job Options in Distiller (Settings – Job Options). Set the image resolution to match the final output device: 72ppi for Web viewing, 125ppi for 600-dpi laser, 200ppi for printing at 150 lpi, and 300ppi for printing at 200 lpi. I recommend turning off compression of your contone images to assure them the highest possible printing quality.

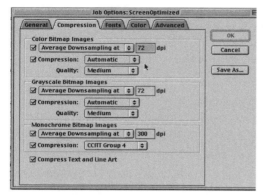

▼ Figure 15.14 PDF Job Options

Converting graphic images for use in PDF can be as simple as setting the Job Options in Adobe Distiller. Match the image resolution to the final output device.

PDF Images

Instead of creating your images as separate graphics which can be placed in a Web page, your images can be incorporated into a PDF (Portable Document Format) file. PDF documents are designed to be application-, platform-, and operating system-independent and Web-safe. Entire pre-existing documents can be re-created through Acrobat Distiller as PDF documents. During this process, the included graphic images can be reformatted on-the-fly while the document is being re-created as a PDF. The key to controlling the graphics in a PDF document is in setting up the Job Options properly. You can create PDF documents for just about any use, from prepress to Web. You have full control over the size and quality of the graphics files though the Job Options settings. In Fig 15.14 we see the Job Options setup window for a Web-specific PDF document. Each of the included graphics will be down-sampled in resolution and compressed per the instructions set up in the Job Options dialog box.

Scanned images which are included as part of a PDF document will be controlled by the Job Options that are configured in Adobe Distiller. Be aware that Distiller by default is set to both down-sample the resolution of your images as well as compress them with lossy compression. Lossy compression results in loss of image data. The higher the compression ratio, the more image data is lost and the lower the quality of the image. Sometimes, lossy compression does not have much impact on how the image may look on screen, but significant image quality reduction becomes apparent when the image is printed. Distiller provides complete control over the amount of down-sampling and compression. For the highest quality results, you may want to turn off all contone image down-sampling and compression. However, you may also want to experiment with using some down-sampling and/or compression to reduce file size. Print testing is the only way to really check the ultimate impact down-sampling and compression may have on an image.

Also remember that PDF images which will be used strictly for viewing do not have the resolution and image quality requirements of print images, and can usually be significantly down-sampled and compressed without a great deal of visual deterioration. In many circumstances, you may want to create one highly down-sampled and compressed PDF version for displaying across the Web and one full-resolution, uncompressed version for downloading, which can be used for printing.

File Naming

For most flexible use, it is a good idea to place a proper three-charac-ter, lowercase format identification extension or suffix at the end of your file names. Examples include: .tif for TIFF files, .eps for EPS files, .gif for GIF files, and .jpg for JPEG files. This three-character extension is not only important for the visual recognition of the file format, but is necessary for some computers to recognize the file format. Windows computers require the three-character extension, and Macs do not. Regardless, it is useful to have that three-character extension as it helps to quickly and easily identify the file format of a graphic at a glance. Photoshop provides you with the ability to automatically add this extension. I recommend using this capability. To configure Photoshop to do this, do the following (Fig 15.15):

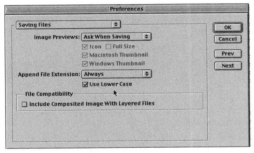

▼ Figure 15.15 Photoshop's File Saving Preferences
Photoshop can be configured to save a proper three-character, lowercase extension at the end of each file by configuring the Saving Files Preferences.

1) Select the Saving Files from the Preferences sub menu under the File menu (File – Preferences – Saving Files).

2) Select Always from the Append File Extension pull-down menu.

3) Place a check in the Use Lower Case check box.

4) Click OK. Now Photoshop will add a proper three-character, lowercase extension to each file which is saved out of Photoshop.

If you are sharing your images with others on other platforms and/or across the Internet, it is good prac-tice to get into the habit of limiting your file names to eight (8) characters. If you do not, the other platforms and/or Internet will do the limiting for you, usually indiscriminately.

PAULINE'S SCAN TIPS

Scan Tip # 15-1

Contone images should have their resolution adjusted for output on specific output devices. For standard AM printing devices, such as most commercial presses, the rule of thumb is 1.5 x lpi of the print device. For FM printing devices, such as many large-format inkjet printers for which there are no lpi values, resolution requirements vary widely, with many being below 100ppi. You should consult your service bureau for resolution guidelines specific to their devices. You may find it useful to run tests on your own FM devices to determine the best target resolutions. For monitor output, the standard resolution is 72ppi.

Scan Tip # 15-2

Nearly all images will experience dot gain, and therefore darkening, when they are printed on paper. The amount of dot gain depends largely on the paper on which it is printed. Uncoated stocks have more dot gain than coated stocks. A curve tool can be used to create a dot gain adjustment. While this curve adjustment can be applied during the scan, it is usually preferable to apply the dot gain either during printing or just before, as the specific adjustment will depend upon each individual press and paper.

Scan Tip # 15-3

Dot gain adjustments for color images are usually made when an RGB image is converted into a CMYK image for printing.

PAULINE'S SCAN TIPS

Scan Tip # 15-4

Mode conversion from RGB to CMYK should be done specifically for each device to which you print, due to the fact that each printing device has its own color gamut and therefore its own CMYK setup values. Typical RGB-to-CMYK setup variables include: ink set, dot gain, choice of UCR or GCR total ink limit, black ink limit, and sometimes, UCA.

Scan Tip # 15-5

If you output to multiple devices, it pays to employ color management tools. While being linear and neutral is the foundation to all color management, sophisticated color management tools allow us to more closely match the color gamuts of various devices by giving us control over gamut mapping.

Scan Tip # 15-6

High-resolution print images usually need to be reformatted for use on the Web. Web adjustments typically include reductions in size and resolution, application of compression, and sometimes reduction of the bit depth. Contone images will typically be saved in 24-bit compressed JPEG (.jpg) format, while flat-color, pixel-based line art images are usually saved as ≤ 8-bit GIF (.gif) images. Vector-based line art images can be saved in Flash Shockwave (.swf) file format to take advantage of the small file size and editability inherent in vector-based images.

PAULINE'S SCAN TIPS

Scan Tip # 15-7

Scanned images which are included as part of a PDF document will be controlled by the Job Options, which are configured in Adobe Distiller. Be aware that Distiller, by default, is set to both down-sample the resolution of your images as well as compress them with lossy compression. Distiller provides complete control over the amount of down-sampling and compression. For the highest quality results, you may want to turn off all contone image down-sampling and compression. However, you may also want to experiment with using some down-sampling and/or compression to reduce file size. Also remember that PDF images which will be used strictly for viewing do not have the resolution and image quality requirements of print images, and can usually be significantly down-sampled and compressed without a great deal of visual deterioration. In many circumstances, you may want to create one highly down-sampled and compressed PDF version for displaying across the Web and one full-resolution, uncompressed version for downloading, which can be used for printing.

PART III REVIEW

After the Scan

This part focused on what we can do to change an image after it has been scanned and how we should go about performing these changes. The changes included altering images to suit our creative needs, fixing someone else's poorly scanned images, and preparing images for output. We need to pay just as much attention to our images after we scan them as we do to how we scan them, because a poorly adjusted or edited image can ruin a perfectly good scan.

Line Art Edits

Convert simple- to intermediate-detail, pixel-based line art images to vectors. This conversion to vectors will allow you to take advantage of scalability, skewability, editability, reduced file size, and resolution-independent printing. The two keys to creating editable, printable vector images without creating too many control points are: 1) scan your line art images at 100% using the optical resolution of your scanner to prevent interpolation of line art edge, and 2) reduce the tightness of the vector edge by controlling the preferences of your conversion program.

Detailed line art, which should be scanned in grayscale (8-bit+) mode, can be edited with threshold and or unsharp mask filters to control the thickness of the line art edges and the density of the image detail. Be sure to convert all grayscale versions of line art images to 1-bit black and white if you want the line art edges to print crisply.

Low edge quality images, those with poorly defined edges such as copies, faxes, and pencil drawings, can be improved, controlled, and edited if they are scanned in grayscale or RGB color mode to produce gradient-like edges. Tools such as unsharp mask and threshold can be use separately or together to effect the edge changes desired.

Colored line art, which should be scanned in 24-bit+ (RGB) mode, can be separated for easy selection and editing. RGB scans produce three grayscale versions (channels) of your images with varying contrast. These variable-contrast channels can be used to separate the various colored line art areas after the scan. Once separated, the individual components of the line art image can be edited or even converted into vectors for editing.

After your line art edits are complete, be sure to convert all grayscale versions of line art images to 1-bit black and white if you want the line art edges to print crisply. Be aware, however, that some line art images, especially some poor edge quality images, may print better if left in grayscale mode. Experiment both ways to test the results.

Before you begin editing a line art image in an application such as Photoshop, make a copy of the image and then work on the copy. This will allow you to return to the original image at any time if you make a mistake or want to try a different approach. It is also a good idea to save copies of intermediate steps, at least until you are satisfied with the final results. When experimenting with various settings and/or techniques, record your successful approaches so that you do not forget them.

Geometric Manipulations

When cropping an image in a post-scan image editing application such as Photoshop, it is important to prevent interpolation of the image if you want to maintain maximum image quality. Allowing the image print size to vary as a result of cropping will generally prevent interpolation. If you want to maintain the same print size after cropping, be aware that your image will be interpolated.

Rotating an image through 90° increments (90°, 180°, 270°) will not result in significant image interpolation or size changes. However, if an image is rotated through any increments other than 90°, all of the image's pixels will be interpolated and the size of the image will be increased to accommodate the rotation. The interpolation involved with non-90° rotations usually leads to softening of the image.

The size of the canvas on which an image sits can be increased without creating any interpolation of your image's pixels. Care must be taken to choose the correct tool, a canvas tool rather than an image size tool, to effect this increase in image size without interpolation. Canvas can usually be added either symmetrically or asymmetrically to an image. When adding canvas, you can also define the background color at the same time. It is best to determine the background color prior to making a canvas size adjustment.

A border can be added to an image in several ways. Adding canvas of a particular color can be an effective way to add a border while increasing the image size at the same time. If you want to add a border to your image, but maintain the current print size, you can stroke the edge of your image with the color you desire.

An image can be scaled after it is scanned; however, it is important to specifically control how this scaling is accomplished. If image resolution is maintained during scaling, interpolation of the pixel will occur, which usually results in softening of the image. If resolution is allowed to vary during scaling, image quality can be maintained, but the physical print size will vary. Scaling an image up while maintaining resolution will generally result in more deleterious interpolation than scaling an image down in size. Always scale a copy, never the original image.

Image Corrections

When making image brightness adjustments on grayscale images, use an editable histogram to adjust the highlight and shadow points of your images. Set your highlight at the beginning of the significant image data in the histogram. The precise position and grayscale value of the highlight point can be fine-tuned to match the minimum highlight value of your output device.

Overall brightness of images should be controlled using a curve tool rather than standard brightness sliders. Using a curve tool to adjust brightness will allow you to maintain previously set highlight and shadow points and reduce the amount of image data loss which occurs during the adjustment.

Image contrast adjustments should be done using the Curves tool. The contrast can be adjusted by controlling the shape of the curve. Wherever the curve slope is flattened, the grayscale values will be concentrated. So, an "S"-shaped curve which flattens in the highlight and shadow regions will result in an increase in overall image contrast, while a flattening of the curve in the midtone region will result in a decrease in overall image contrast. Using the Curves tool to adjust brightness will allow you to maintain previously set highlight and shadow points and reduce the amount of image data loss which occurs during the adjustment.

When making brightness and contrast adjustments to color images, it is best to make these adjustments on the luminance values. An effective way to do this is to convert your RGB color image to Lab mode. Any brightness and contrast adjustments can then be made only to the "L" channel, which contains only luminance or grayscale data.

Scanning will tend to soften nearly all contone images. To return image focus, we apply sharpening tools. Usually the best tool to apply sharpening is an unsharp mask tool, which should control both the amount and placement of the unsharp mask. Scanners tend to preferentially soften high-contrast portions of images, so our sharpening tools should be set to preferentially sharpen these same high-contrast areas. A good sharpening tool should allow us to control the amount of sharpening, the radius, and the threshold of where the sharpening will be applied. Sharpening amounts will usually vary between 100–200%, radius values between 1–2 pixels, and thresholds from 2–5. A typical set of unsharp mask starting values for a 200ppi contone photograph of a person's face being printed at 150 lpi might be Amount =100%, Radius =1, Threshold = 5. Avoid over-sharpening as excess sharpening can lead to the creation of black and white haloes along high-contrast edges.

Neutralization is the foundation to color correction. If we make the neutral portions of an image neutral, the rest of the color values in the image tend to fall into place. Typical image neutrals to look for are white clothing, paper products, white buildings and walls, and white product backgrounds. An image area will be considered neutral, that is, gray, when the RGB values for that area are all equal.

There are numerous tools which can be used to make adjustments to the color values in an image, but all color correction judgements should be made by measuring the color values with an Info tool, which measures the grayscale values of the pixels rather than making visual evaluations. A curve tool used to adjust the color values on individual channels can be an effective color adjustment tool as well.

When making color cast corrections in highlights, be sure to keep two adjustments in mind. Your white highlight values should not only be equal, but should be adjusted for the printable or minimum highlight value on your output device. Typical highlight values include: commercial printing = 5%, desktop laser printers = 10%, newsprint = 20%.

In addition to adjusting neutrals, we must often pay attention to the color values of key components of an image and/or memory colors. For instance, our skies should be blue, our grass green, and our stop signs red. A very important component of many color images is facial skin tone values. While there are wide variations in human skin tones, most skin tones share a common ratio of RGB colors. In most humans, red is greater than green, which in turn should be greater than blue. The specific values will vary depending upon the tonal area of the image, but RGB ratios are typically in the range of 5/4/3 to 5/3/2.

When applying unsharp mask to a color image, try converting your image to Lab mode first, and then applying the unsharp mask to the "L" channel only. Performing "L" channel unsharp masking will prevent any color shifts from occurring along high-contrast edges.

Preparing for Output

Contone images should have their resolution adjusted for output on specific output devices. For standard AM printing devices, such as most commercial presses, the rule of thumb is 1.5 x lpi of the print device. For FM printing devices, such as many large-format inkjet printers for which there are no lpi values, resolution requirements vary widely, with many being below 100ppi. You should consult your service bureau for resolution guidelines specific to their devices. You may find it useful to run tests on your own FM devices to determine the best target resolutions. For monitor output, the standard resolution is 72ppi.

Nearly all images will experience dot gain, and therefore darkening, when they are printed on paper. The amount of dot gain depends largely on the paper on which it is printed. Uncoated stocks have more dot gain than coated stocks. A curve tool can be used to create a dot gain adjustment. While this curve adjustment can be applied during the scan, it is usually preferable to apply the dot gain either during printing or just before, as the specific adjustment will depend upon each individual press and paper.

Dot gain adjustments for color images are usually made when an RGB image is converted into a CMYK image for printing.

Mode conversion from RGB to CMYK should be done specifically for each device to which you print, due to the fact that each printing device has its own color gamut and therefore its own CMYK setup values. Typical RGB-to-CMYK setup variables include: ink set, dot gain, choice of UCR or GCR, total ink limit, black ink limit, and sometimes, UCA.

If you output to multiple devices, it pays to employ color management tools. While being linear and neutral is the foundation to all color management, sophisticated color management tools allow us to more closely match the color gamuts of various devices by giving us control over gamut mapping.

High-resolution print images usually need to be reformatted for use on the Web. Web adjustments typically include reduction in size and resolution, application of compression, and sometimes reduction of the bit depth. Contone images will typically be saved in 24-bit compressed JPEG (.jpg) format, while flat-color pixel-based line art images may be saved as ≤8-bit GIF (.gif) images. Vector-based line art images can be saved in Flash Shockwave (.swf) file format to take advantage of the small file size and editability inherent in vector-based images.

Scanned images which are included as part of a PDF document will be controlled by the Job Options which are configured in Adobe Distiller. Be aware that Distiller by default is set to both downsample the resolution of your images as well as compress them with lossy compression. Distiller provides complete control over the amount of down-sampling and compression. For the highest quality results, you may want to turn off all contone image down-sampling and compression. However, you may also want to experiment with using some down-sampling and/or compression to reduce file size. Also remember that PDF images which will be used strictly for viewing do not have the resolution and image quality requirements of print images, and can usually be significantly down-sampled and compressed without a great deal of visual deterioration. In many circumstances, you may want to create one highly down-sampled and compressed PDF version for displaying across the Web and one full-resolution, uncompressed version for downloading, which can be used for printing.

Part IV

Appendices

CURRENT
DTP SYSTEM!

THE ORIGINAL
DTP SYSTEM!

Appendix A

Glossary

AM dot: Amplitude Modulation dot. Image reproduction building block where a pattern of dots with varying sizes, or amplitudes, are used to simulate grayscale values. See *Halftone (AM) dot.*

bit depth: The number of bits of image information in an image. Black and white images have 1 bit per pixel. Grayscale images typically have 8 bits per pixel. RGB images usually have 24 bits per pixel (eight in each of the three RGB channels), while CMYK images typically have 32 bits per pixel. If the bit-per-pixel value increases in an image, the total image bit depth increases as well. For instance, an 8-bit-per-pixel RGB image has a total image bit depth of 24 bits, while a 10-bit-per-pixel image has a total image bit depth of 30 bits per image. See *Capture bit depth.*

Bitmap: A type of file, usually photos or artwork of some sort, that is composed of pixels. This type of format allows for a continuous tone and fine detail to be possible on the computer. Examples: TIFF, Paint, PICT.

Calibration: The adjustment that must be done to make sure that a scanner or digital camera will properly capture an image. Fundamental calibration techniques usually involve linearization and neutralization.

Capture bit depth: The number of bits per pixel which an image capture device, such as a scanner or digital camera, can capture. Typical capture bit depths are 8, 10,12, and 14 bits per pixel. The higher the bit depth, the more image information is captured. Often, capture bit depth is expressed as the total number of bits captured in a three-channel RGB image, where a 10-bit-per-pixel capture bit depth is expressed as a 30-bit capture bit depth for the combination of all three channels.

Channel: A single, usually 8-bit grayscale portion of an image. There are two kinds of channels: color and selection channels. Color channels are the fundamental building blocks of color images, while selection channels are created from selections. Channels are often saved.

CMYK mode: A color mode which is constructed out of four grayscale channels. This mode is used for printing color images to color printing devices such as commercial printing presses and desktop color printers. Scanned images must be converted into this mode to print them.

Color cast: The presence of color when none should be there. Color cast is typically identified when a neutral or gray portion of an image has unequal amounts of red, green or blue. Fixing a color cast is called neutralization. There are two types of color cast, scanner and image casts, which should be adjusted separately. See *Neutralization.*

Color lookup table: The file that contains a set of data which describes how the color data in an image from one color space should be converted to the color data in another color space. An example of a common color lookup table would be one which contains information on converting RGB to CMYK data. These color lookup tables are often created for specific devices such as a specific printing press.

Color management: The process of controlling color from one device to another through various applications and even computer systems. Color management frequently involves the use of color targets for the creation of color profiles for each device used in an electronic publishing system. The goal of a color management system is to provide consistent and predictable color values. See *Profile* and *ICC.*

Contone: Abbreviation for continuous tone image. Contone images typically contain a variety of gradually changing grayscale values, unlike line art images which are typically flat-looking with few if any shades of gray. A photograph is a typical example of a contone image. Contrast with *Line art.*

Curve: A line graph which controls the ratio of input to output values for grayscale values in an image. A curve is often used to control the brightness and contrast of images and is used to adjust the distribution of grayscale values in individual color channels to accomplish color correction.

Diffuse highlights: The lightest portions of an image which still have detail. These are the most important highlight portions of an image to be captured and preserved. See *Specular highlights.*

Digital image: An image that is captured and/or edited with the use of a digital computer. Digital implies that the image is constructed from two values, 0's and 1's, which are the only two values a digital computer "understands." These 0's and 1's are used to construct and control pixels and vectors, the basic blocks of digital images.

Digitizing: The conversion of images into 0's and 1's so that they may be recognized and manipulated on a digital computer. Images which are digitized are converted into pixels.

DMax (maximum density): This measurement is often used to state the darkest shade of gray which an image capture device can distinguish. An instrument with a high dynamic range usually has a high DMax as well. See *Dynamic range.*

Dot (halftone dot): The building block of continuous tone-printed images. Halftone dot resolution is usually commonly referred to as line screen or lpi (lines per inch). Typically, line screens in commercial printing vary from 133 lpi to 150 lpi. See *Output resolution.*

Dot gain: The tendency for halftone dots to "grow" or enlarge when they are printed. This dot gain occurs because ink and toner tend to spread out when they are applied to printing substrates. Dot gain results in images that print darker than they scan and view.

Dot gain adjustment: The lightening of an image, usually through the application of a lightening curve, to pre-compensate for the darkening that will occur when a halftone dot-based image is printed.

dpi: A commonly used general term for *resolution*. The term *dpi* is often used when other terms are more accurate and useful. See *ppi, Spot, Dot,* and *Res.*

Dynamic range: The range of grayscale values, from black to white, which can be captured by a scanner or digital camera. The dynamic range scale is a logarithmic scale ranging from 0 to 4.0, with 4.0 being the highest. Image capture devices which have high dynamic range can distinguish wider ranges or grayscale values than devices which have low dynamic range. Low dynamic range devices, with dynamic ranges <3.0, typically have a difficult time distinguishing shadow details in images.

Edge reproduction: The main focus of scanning line art. Reproducing the edge of line art is the key to good line art scans. Using the optical resolution of the scanner is often a key to accurate reproduction of line art edges.

Final scan: A scan performed at high resolution after an image has been viewed, cropped, analyzed, and set up using a low-resolution preview scan. See *Preview scan.*

FM dot: Frequency Modulation dot. Image reproduction building block where a pattern of dots with varying spacings, or frequency, are used to simulate grayscale values. See *Halftone (FM) dot.*

Gamut: The range of reproducible colors which a device has available. A color monitor usually has a larger color gamut than a CMYK printer; therefore, there are colors which we can see and produce on a color monitor which we cannot reproduce on a CMYK printer.

Gang or batch scan: Scanning multiple images in one pass with all images having the same identical settings.

GCR: Gray Component Replacement. One of two major descriptions of how black ink (K) is substituted for cyan, magenta, and yellow inks in process commercial printing. GCR typically substitutes black ink throughout the gray ramp of an image from the quartertone through the shadow portions of an image. See *UCR* and *UCA*

Gray map: A chart, usually a histogram, which shows the distribution and frequency of the grayscale values in an image.

Grayscale reproduction: The main focus of scanning contone images, such as grayscales and color photographs. Scanner calibration, linearization, and neutralization, as well as the setting of proper highlight and shadow points, are keys to accurate reproduction of grayscale values.

Halftone: An image built out of a pattern of halftone dots. Continuous tone images such as photographs cannot be printed as continuous tones on a printing press, so they are reconstructed out of patterns of dots. These dot patterns are small enough so that they appear as continuous tone images when viewed at the proper distance.

Halftone (AM) dot: The building block of a printed contone image. Halftone dots are variable-sized dots which are constructed through the combination of a various number of laser spots. The size, or amplitude (A), of halftone dots is changed, or modulated (M), to produce a simulated change in grayscale value.

Halftone cell: The cell in which a halftone dot is created. The size of the halftone cell is determined by the line screen (lpi) of the output device. The number of building block squares of a halftone cell is determined by the output resolution of the imaging device, which in turn determines the number of shades of gray which can be reproduced.

Halftone (FM) dot: The building block image printed with stochastic screening. FM dots are fixed-size dots which are constructed from a small number of laser spots. The spacing, or frequency (F), of dots is changed, or modulated (M), to produce a simulated change in grayscale value.

High-key image: An image which has an overall bright nature, such as a well-lit room with white walls. See the terms *Low-key* and *Medium-key* image.

Highlight point–diffuse: The lightest portion of an image that contains details. A diffuse highlight area contains significant grayscale values or information, and will print as light values of grayscale, which shows details. An example would be the lightest portion of a white shirt. The typical range in which a shadow point will fall is 3–15% grayscale.

Highlight point–specular: The lightest portion of an image that contains NO details. A specular highlight area contains little or no grayscale values or information, and will print as pure white with no details. An example would be a reflection off a chrome bumper. A typical grayscale value for a specular highlight is 0% gray.

Histogram: A chart with highlight, mid-tone, and shadow sliders which displays the frequency and distribution of grayscale values in an image. A histogram is often used for setting the highlight and shadow points in an image.

HSV/L: Hue, saturation, and value/lightness. Used to describe the color of a pixel. Hue is the basic color determined by its frequency or wavelength of light. Saturation is a measure of the intensity or purity of the color, and is controlled by the amount of white color added to the basic color. Value, or lightness, is a measure of the grayscale value of the color.

ICC: International Color Consortium. A group of industry-leading manufacturers who together develop standards for handling color files in open electronic publishing systems. One of the most significant contributions of this group is the creation of the ICC Color Profile system, which is a set of profile standards that allows all manufacturers of color management products to create mutually-compatible profiles.

Info tool: A grayscale measurement tool found in many scanning and image editing applications. Info tools on desktop publishing applications commonly use either a 0–100% (percent grayscale) unit scale, or a 0–255 grayscale value scale.

Input resolution: Resolution terminology used to refer to images captured or created as pixel-based images. Usually expressed as the number of pixels per inch (ppi) or pixels per millimeter (Res). See *Input resolution*.

Intensitometer: A tool, often called a densitometer, which is used to measure the grayscale values of pixel-based images.

Keyness: The overall brightness of an image. See the terms *High-key, Medium-key* and *Low-key image*.

Lab mode: A color mode constructed out of one grayscale channel, the "L" or luminance channel, and two color channels, the "a" and "b" channels. This mode is particularly useful for making grayscale-only adjustments, such as brightness, contrast, and unsharp mask, to color images. By making adjustments only on the "L" channel, color shifts can be completely avoided.

Laser spot: The smallest building block of a printed image. The size of a laser spot is controlled by the resolution of the output device. A 2400-dpi imagesetter produces a laser spot 1/2400" across. Laser spots are printed end to end to reproduce the edges of text and line art. Laser spots are combined together to make halftone and stochastic dots which are used to re-create contone images.

Linearization: Adjusting, or calibrating, a scanner so that it will capture grayscale values with their proper values. For instance, a linear scanner will create a 35% pixel when it "sees" a 35% grayscale value. A non-linear scanner will capture grayscale values other than 35% when it "sees" a 35% grayscale value. Typically, uncalibrated/nonlinear scanners create pixels which are darker than the original grayscale values of an image. For example, an original 50% grayscale area may be captured as 60% gray by a nonlinear scanner.

Line art: Line art images are typically flat-looking with few if any shades of gray. Logos and pencil drawings are typical examples of line art images. Contrast with *Contone image*.

Low-key image: An image that has an overall dark nature, such as a late sunset photo. See the terms *High-key* and *Medium-key* image.

Luminance: The grayscale values of a color image. Luminance adjustments include brightness, contrast, and unsharp mask. In Lab mode, all of the grayscale or luminance values are contained in the "L" or luminance channel, which makes adjustment of these characteristics easier.

Medium key image: An image that has an average overall brightness, such as a well-lit portrait of a person's face. See the terms *Low-key* and *High-key images*.

Midtone: Tonal range of an image which centers around 50% grayscale. Grayscale values in an image roughly in the range of 35% to 65% grayscale are considered to be in the midtone region.

Multiple scan: Scanning multiple images in one pass with each image having its own separate scan settings.

Multi-purpose: To use an image for more than one purpose. For instance, the same image may be used for commercial printing, desktop printing, and Web viewing. Multi-purposing usually requires that we reconfigure the image so as to maximize the image characteristics for each use. The changing characteristics include: image dimension, resolution, pixel depth, file format, and color space.

Neutralization: Adjusting, or calibrating, a scanner so that neutral portions of an image will be captured as neutral, rather than having a color cast. A neutral area will have equal RGB values. A non-neutral area will have unequal RGB values. For instance, a neutral 5% gray area should have RGB values each equal to 5%.

Optical resolution: The true or hardware resolution of an image capture device such as a scanner. Using the hardware resolution of a scanner results in faster and more accurate scans. Scanning at other than the optical resolution of a scanner results in interpolated pixels, which are manufactured and therefore less accurate.

Output resolution: Resolution terminology used to refer to images which have been re-created or printed as spot-based and dot-based images. Usually expressed as the number of spots or dots per inch (dpi) or halftone dots per inch or lines per inch (lpi).

Pixel: Basic building block of a bitmap image.

ppi (pixels per inch): The most common term used to correctly express the resolution of a digital image. ppi refers to the number of pixels per inch, both horizontally and vertically, in an image. See *Input resolution*.

Preview scan: A low-resolution, usually 72ppi, overview scan which is done at the beginning of a scan session. This previewed image is used to locate and crop the image to be scanned and set up the scanner for the final, high-resolution scan. See *Final scan*.

Profile or color profile: A file that contains the color gamut information for a particular device. Color profiles can be created for any input or output device we use for capturing, viewing, or printing images, including scanners, digital cameras, monitors, and printers. Color profiles are used during the process of moving and matching an image from one device to another as part of a color management system. See *ICC*.

Quartertone: Tonal range of an image which centers around 25% grayscale. Grayscale values in an image roughly in the range of 15% to 35% grayscale are considered to be in the quartertone region.

Repurpose: To take an image created specifically for one purpose and use it for another. For instance, an image may be created for use in commercial printing, but we also use or repurpose that image for desktop printing and/or Web viewing. Repurposing of images usually requires that we reconfigure the image so as to maximize the image characteristics for each use. The changing characteristics include: image dimension, resolution, pixel depth, file format, and color space.

Res: A less commonly used input resolution term which designates the number of pixels per millimeter in a digital image.

Resolution: The number of building block components per unit distance, such as dots per inch (dpi) or pixels per inch (ppi), in an image. Resolution should be distinguished as either input or output resolution. See *Input resolution* and *Output resolution*.

RGB mode: A color mode which is constructed out of three grayscale channels. This mode is used for the capture and viewing of color images. Scanners and digital cameras work in RGB mode, as do monitors. RGB images must be converted into CMYK for printing. See *CMYK mode*.

RIP: Raster Image Processor. The hardware and/or software device through which all document components, including line art, contone images, and text, are processed to convert them into printed images.

Scan mode: Determines the pixel depth and color space into which an image will be captured or converted, including: 1-bit (B&W line art), 8-bit (grayscale), 24-bit (RGB), and 32-bit (CMYK).

Scanner: Capture device which converts analog images into digital pixels.

Shadow point: The darkest portion of an image that still has details in it. The typical range in which a shadow point will fall is 85–100% grayscale.

Specular highlight: A featureless highlight portion of an image containing no details. See *Diffuse highlight*.

Spot: The smallest building block of a printed text or line art image. Often expressed as dpi (dots per inch). A 300-dpi laser printer has spots which are 1/300" across, while a 2400-dpi imagesetter has spots which are 1/2400" across. See *Output resolution*.

Stochastic or (FM) dot: The building block of a printed contone image. Stochastic dots are constructed through the combination of a various number of laser spots. The spacing, or frequency (A), of halftone dots are changed, or modulated (M), to produce a simulated change in grayscale value.

Streamline: A program from Adobe Systems, Inc., which is used to convert pixel-based images into vector-based line art. Sometimes used as a verb such as in "streamline an image."

SWOP: Specifications Web Offset Publications. An agreed-upon set of industry standard printing conditions used by commercial printers. There are SWOP standards for various kinds of paper such as SWOP coated, SWOP uncoated, and SWOP newsprint.

Three-Quartertone: Tonal range of an image which centers around 75% grayscale. Grayscale values in an image roughly in the range of 65% to 85% grayscale are considered to be in the quartertone region.

Tone compression: Setting the highlight and shadow points of an image which will determine where the captured grayscale values will be placed in an image.

UCA: Under Color Addition. The addition of extra amounts of cyan, magenta, and yellow inks to the shadow regions of a CMYK-printed image so as to increase the ink density in the shadow regions to produce a denser-looking black. See *GCR* and *UCA*.

UCR: Under Color Removal. One of two major descriptions of how black ink (K) is substituted for cyan, magenta, and yellow inks in process commercial printing. UCR typically substitutes black ink primarily in the shadow regions of an image. See *GCR* and *UCA*.

Unsharp mask: A software filter used to increase the sharpness or focus of an image. Most digitally-captured images need to have sharpening applied to return to their original sharpness.

Appendix B

Taz's Top Ten Scanning Tips

TAZ'S TOP TEN SCANNING TIPS

Scan Tip # 1

Always clean your scanner's imaging surface prior to starting a scan session. This should be done using a mild solution and a lint-free cloth.

Scan Tip # 2

Perform basic image correction functions, such as calibration, setting highlight and shadow points, and adjusting image brightness and contrast, during the scan rather than after the scan in an image editing application such as Photoshop.

Scan Tip # 3

Calibrate your scanner at the beginning of each scan session. Linearize for grayscale, and linearize and neutralize for color images, to improve image brightness and reduce color cast problems.

Scan Tip # 4

Use the optical resolution, or 1/2 the optical resolution, of your scanner when scanning line art which you intend to convert to vector-based images. Use 1.5 x lpi x scaling factor for AM screen printing. FM screen printing resolutions vary from 25–100ppi, depending upon the RIP, scaling, and viewing distance.

Scan Tip # 5

Use an editable histogram when setting your highlight and shadow points in a contone image. Highlight values should be set so that the lightest portion of an image that has detail will print as its proper grayscale value. Shadow values should be set so that the darkest portion of the image which still has detail will not fill in and print black. Typical highlight and shadow values for commercial printing are 5% highlight and 90% shadow.

TAZ'S TOP TEN SCANNING TIPS

Scan Tip # 6

Use a curve tool when adjusting image brightness and contrast. This brightness and contrast adjustment should be performed after the highlight and shadow points are set. Do not adjust the endpoints of the curve during brightness and contrast adjustment as this will destroy the highlight and shadow settings.

Scan Tip # 7

Apply unsharp mask to both grayscale and color contone images to improve the sharpness of those images. On a color image, it is a good idea to apply unsharp mask to only the grayscale portions of the image, to prevent color shifts along high-contrast edges.

Scan Tip # 8

Scan detailed line art images in greater than 1-bit black and white mode. Use 8-bit+ grayscale for detailed black and white images, and 24-bit+ RGB for colored line art images. Scanning detailed line art in multi-bit modes allows for more flexible post-scan control and image editing.

Scan Tip # 9

When setting highlight and shadow points for color contones, for best results, adjust the placement of the highlight and shadow pointers on individual channels rather than on the composite channel.

Scan Tip # 10

Neutralize grayscale portions, such as white highlights in color images, to remove color cast from color images and improve overall color balance.

Appendix C

Resolution and Grayscale

LINE SCREEN, RESOLUTION, AND GRAYSCALE

Contone images are constructed out of patterns of halftone dots when they are reproduced through the conventional offset printing process. The number of shades of gray that can be rendered in this process is a function of the ratio of the number of halftone dots per inch to the resolution of the imaging device used to create those halftone dots.

The number of halftone dots per inch is known as the line screen or screen frequency, and is designated by the units lpi (lines per inch). lpi values vary from a low of 50 lpi on some laser printers to 200+ lpi for commercial presses.

The resolution of imaging devices is determined by the size of the image spot which the device can create. These image spots range in value from 1/300" for some laser printers to over 1/3600" for some imagesetters. Imaging device resolution is usually stated in terms of the number of these image spots that are printed per inch, and is commonly, if mistakenly, referred to in terms of dots per inch (dpi). A laser printer which creates an image spot 1/300" in diameter will have a resolution of 300 dpi.

Halftone dots are larger than, and in fact are constructed from, the much smaller image spots. The number of shades of gray which a printing device can reproduce is directly determined by how many of these image spots can be placed inside a halftone dot. This number is determined by the ratio of the size of the halftone dot to the size of the image spot. The number of image spots which can fit in a halftone dot horizontally and vertically defines the halftone cell, which in turn defines the number of shades of gray which can be produced.

An example will serve to demonstrate this principle:

Printing device resolution (lpi) = 100 lpi

Image device resolution (dpi) = 1200 dpi

shades of gray equals $(1200 \div 100)^2 = (12 \times 12) = 144$ shades of gray

Halftone Dots, Image Spots and Shades of Gray

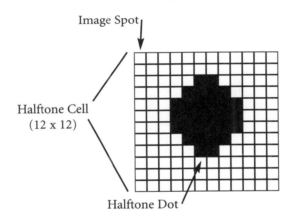

Image Spot

Halftone Cell
(12 x 12)

Halftone Dot

Vary the number of image spots which fill in the halftone cell squares to vary the size of the halftone dot and the shade of gray that is represented.

lpi = 100

dpi = 1200

1200 dpi ÷ 100 lpi = 12 dots per halftone dot

Halftone cell size = 12 x 12

Number of shades of gray = 12 x 12 = 144

Appendix D

File Format Guide

FILE FORMATS

Contents vs. Containers

A good way to start to sort out the myriad and continually increasing number of file formats is to separate in your mind the difference between file contents (pixels and vectors) and file containers (formats). There are basically two kinds of file contents or building blocks: pixels and vectors. All graphic files contain one or the other, or sometimes both, of these basic contents. The file formats are the containers into which these pixel and/or vector contents are stored.

Different file formats are used for various purposes. When we change the use for which a graphic file is intended, we often change the file format. For instance, the two preferred file formats used in PostScript printing are TIFF and EPS. If we change these graphic files for use on the Web, these same images may be resaved as GIF, JPEG, PNG, or SWF format.

File Formats: Use-Specific

Pixel and/or vector-based images can be saved in many different file formats. As discussed above, it is useful to think of a file format as a container into which image components, pixels and/or vectors, are stored. The file format we choose for an image should be determined by how the image will be used. For example, if we are to use our images for printing to a PostScript printer, then a pixel-based TIFF or EPS would be most appropriate. If, however, our images will be used for placement on a Web page, then a GIF, JPEG, PNG, or SWF file format would be most appropriate. Some file formats such as PCX, PICT, and WMF tend to be more platform-specific and less flexible than TIFFs, and are therefore less desirable for use as a standard file format. For print, I recommend that you initially save your images in the TIFF format. The TIFF format is a flexible, pixel-based file format which is compatible with use on Mac, Windows, and UNIX systems for print. If you reuse and/or re-create your images for other purposes, you may change the file format of an image. Below is a review of file formats, color spaces, resolutions, and use.

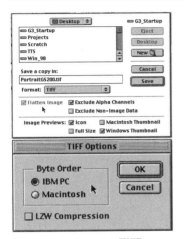

Figure D.1 Creating TIFFs
Using the Save As dialog box allows you to flatten and remove alpha channels on-the-fly as you save your image. I generally save my TIFFs in IBM PC format, without compression, to enhance cross-platform compatibility, and to reduce printing problems.

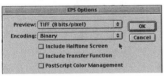

Figure D.2 Creating EPSs
EPS files require previews to be viewed in a page layout document. Choose either Mac or PC (TIFF) header. Most printing companies prefer binary encoding, although you should use ASCII encoding if you are working on a Windows network and are having problems transferring/printing binary files. Uncheck Include Halftone Screen, Include Transfer Function, and PostScript Color Management, unless you are informed otherwise.

File formats

TIFF: TIFF (Tagged Information File Format) (Fig D.1) is a general, pixel-based format that is used in PostScript printing, for grayscale and CMYK, at 200–300ppi for desktop through commercial printing. The TIFF file format is a good one for going cross-platform with pixel-based images. TIFFs can be saved in either Mac or PC format. I generally save mine in PC format as a Mac can read either one. As with all print file formats, I recommend no compression when saving images to TIFF.

EPS: Pixel-based EPS (Encapsulated PostScript) is an alternative to the TIFF format. Some RIPs, workflows, and applications prefer this format for printing pixel-based images. Pixel-based EPSs are typically used in grayscale and CMYK images at 200–300ppi for desktop and commercial printing. EPS files are basically sealed and therefore require that a screen preview be saved along with pixel image data. Other image-use information such as line screen, transfer function, and color management data can be saved along with the actual image information in an EPS. Only save this additional data if you are instructed to by your printing company.

EPS: Vector-based EPS (Encapsulated PostScript) (Fig D.2) is the preferred format for vector-based images which will be printed on PostScript printers. Vector-based EPS files are, like pixel-based EPS files, sealed and therefore require that a screen preview be saved along with the vector image data. This type of image file format is used for grayscale, spot color, and CMYK for desktop and commercial printing. Pixel-based TIFFs can be converted into vector-based EPSs through applications like Adobe Streamline.

DCS: DCS (Desktop Color Separations) (Fig D.3) is a special version of the EPS format. DCS is used for graphic images which will be separated during the printing process and can contain both process and spot color information. DCS files are pre-separated, which usually makes for faster RIPing. There are two versions of DCS: DCS 1.0, which supports four-color process separations, and DCS 2.0, which supports four-color process and spot color separations. DCS files can be constructed as single or multiple files with or without separate low-resolution composite screen preview images.

JPEG: JPEG (Joint Photographic Expert Group) (Fig D.4) is a pixel-based format commonly used on the Web for viewing and image transfer. This type of image file format is used mainly for grayscale and 24-bit RGB images. JPEG can also be used in CMYK format for storage and printing of high-resolution files, but a JPEG image should be converted into a CMYK, TIFF, or EPS file prior to printing.

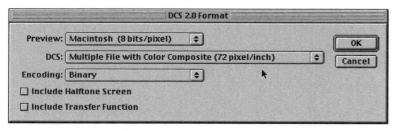

Figure D.3 Creating DCSs
Like regular EPSs, DCSs are used in printing. And like regular EPSs, DCS files require previews for them to be viewed in a page layout application. Choose either Mac or PC (TIFF) header.

When saving your image as a DCS file, you will have several DCS options that will determine the number of files and the type of composite file which will be created. Ask your printing company for specific instructions as to whether they use DCS files and how they prefer to have them set up.

As with other EPS graphic files, most printing companies prefer binary encoding, although you should use ASCII encoding if you are working on a Windows network and are having problems transferring/printing binary files. Keep the Include Halftone Screen, Include Transfer Function, and PostScript Color Management options unchecked, unless you are specifically informed otherwise.

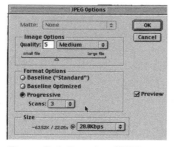

Figure D.4 Creating JPEGs
JPEGs are used mostly for Web images and storage. The image quality can be controlled through the amount of compression.

GIF: GIF (Graphic Interchange Format) (Fig D.5) is a common, pixel-based image format used on the Web. GIF format supports 8-bit (or lower) grayscale and index color images, typically at 72ppi.

PNG: PNG (Portable Network Graphic) (Fig D.6) is a pixel-based format commonly used on the Web for viewing and image transfer. This type of image file format is used mainly for grayscale and 24-bit RGB images.

SWF: SWF (ShockWave Format) is a vector-based format commonly used on the Web for animation graphics. This type of image file format can be used for grayscale, 8-, or 24-bit RGB images. SWF can also be used for printing high-resolution files, but should be converted into a spot or CMYK color space, TIFF, or EPS prior to printing.

PDF graphics: Any graphic which you have created for print can be converted on-the-fly for use in a PDF file. Configure the Job Options in Distiller (Settings – Job Options). Set the image resolution to match the final output device: e.g., 72ppi for Web viewing, 125ppi for 600-dpi laser, 200ppi for printing at 150 lpi, and 300ppi for printing at 200 lpi. I recommend turning off compression of your contone image to assure the highest possible printing quality.

STN: The STiNG file format (Fig D.7) is a resolution-independent file format for photographic images. Pixel-based contone images can be converted into .stn format with a program named GenuineFractals. The resolution-independent file format allows for changing the size and resolution of contone photographic images while maintaining high image quality. This is a particularly useful format for multi-purposing images.

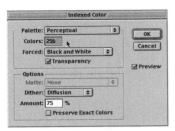

Figure D.5 Creating GIFs
GIFs are used for Web images, and support 8 bits or less information. Image quality and load speed can be controlled through color and dithering choices.

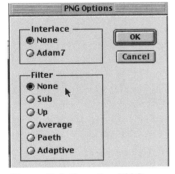

Figure D.6 Creating PNGs
PNGs are used in Web images, and support 8 or 24 bits. Image quality and load speed can be controlled through color and dithering choices.

File Naming

For the most flexible use, it is a good idea to place a proper three character, lowercase format identification extension or suffix at the end of your file names. Examples include: .tif for TIFF files, .eps for EPS files, .gif for GIF files, and .jpg for JPEG files. This three-character extension is not only important for the visual recognition of the file format, but is necessary for some computers to recognize the file format. Windows computers require the three-character extension, and Macs do not. Regardless, it is useful to have that three-character extension as it helps to quickly and easily identify the file format of a graphic file at a glance. Photoshop provides you with the ability to automatically add this extension. I recommend using this capability.

If you are sharing your images with others on other platforms and/or across the Internet, it is good practice to get in the habit of limiting your file names to eight (8) characters. If you do not, the other platforms and/or Internet will do the limiting for you, indiscriminately.

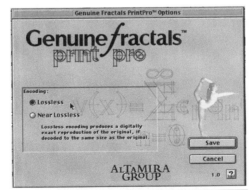

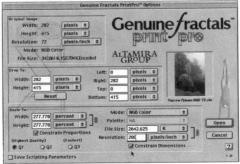

Figure D.7 Creating STN Files
GenuineFractals and saving an image in the STN file format are used to re-create and store an image as a resolution-independent graphic file. The resolution independence allows for higher quality scaling and resolution adjustments of contone images. Images can be saved as Lossless (highest quality) or Near Lossless (slightly lower quality, but smaller file size) images.
When an STN file image is opened, it can be cropped, scaled, resolution-adjusted, and even mode-converted.

Appendix E

Resources

BOOKS

Beyond The Mac Is Not A Typewriter, Robin Williams, Peachpit Press, 1996,
ISBN: 1-201-88598-0

CREF Computer Ready Electronic Files 2, Scitex Graphic Arts Users Association,
Brentwood, TN

Design For Non-Designers, Robin Williams,
Santa Fe, NM, http://www.zumacafe.com

Getting it Printed, 3rd Edition, Mark Beach and Eric Kenly, North Light Books, 1999,
ISBN: 0-89134-858-1

GRACOL General Requirements For Applications In Commercial Offset Lithography V. 2.0,
Graphic Arts Communication Association, 1998

How to Make Sure What You See is What You Get,
Peter Fink

One-Minute Designer, Revised Edition,
Roger C. Parker, MIS: Press, 1997, ISBN: 1-55828-593-8

Photoshop In Black And White, 2nd Edition,
Jim Rich and Sandy Bozek, Peachpit Press, 1995, ISBN: 1-56609-189-6

Pocket Guide to Color Reproduction, Miles Southworth and Donna Southworth, Graphic
Arts Publishing, 1994, ISBN: 0-933600-09-7

Pocket Guide To Digital Prepress, Frank Romano, Delmar Publishers, 1996,
ISBN: 0-8273-7198-5

Pocket Guide To Digital Printing, Frank Cost, Delmar Publishers, 1997,
ISBN: 0-8273-7592-1

Pocket Pal: A Graphics Arts Production Handbook, International Paper, 1963-1997,
Memphis, TN

PostScript: A Visual Approach, Ross Smith, Peachpit Press, ISBN: 0-938-151-12-6

Real World Photoshop, David Blatner and Bruce Fraser, Peachpit Press, (Various Editions)

Real World Scanning and Halftones, David Blatner and Steve Roth, Peachpit Press, 1995

The Art & Technology of Typography, Agfa Corp, 1988, Wilmington, MA

The Color Resource Complete Color Glossary, Miles Southworth, Thad McIlroy, and Donna
Southworth, The Color Resource, 1992, ISBN: 1-879847-01-9

The Color Scanning Success Handbook, Michael Kieran, Desktop Publishing Associates,
1997, ISBN: 1-896097-01-4

The Complete Guide To Trapping, 2nd Edition,
Brian Lawler, Hayden Books, 1995, ISBN: 1-56830-098-0

The Mac (PC) Is Not A Typewriter, Robin Williams, Peachpit Press, 1990,
ISBN: 0-938151-31-2

The Photoshop WOW Book,(series) Linnea Dayton and Jack Davis, Peachpit Press, (various versions)

Thinking In PostScript, Glenn C. Reid, Addison–Wesley, 1990, ISBN: 0-201-52372-8

Understanding Desktop Color, 2nd Edition, Michael Kieran, Desktop Publishing Associates, 1994, ISBN: 1-56609-164-0

PERIODICALS

Design Tools Monthly, Boulder, CO, 303.543.8300 (my favorite)

Step by Step Electronic Design, Dynamic Graphics, Peoria, IL,

Dynamic Graphics, The Idea Guide to Quick Desktop Success, Dynamic Graphics, Peoria, ILL

DTP Journal, Journal of the NADP (National Association of Desktop Publishers), Phone: 508.887.7900

Adobe Magazine, Adobe Systems, Mountain View, CA, www.adobe.com

Graphic Arts Monthly, Graphic Arts Communication Association, Alexandria, VA

GATF: Graphic Arts Technical Foundation, Various technical publications, Pittsburgh, PA

HOW: The Bottomline Design Magazine, Cincinnati, OH

Publish, Integrated Media, San Francisco, CA

Seybold Reports, Media, PA, Phone: 800.325.3830, www.seyboldreport.com

WEB RESOURCES

Viacom's Information Super Library: http://www.mcp.com – General, broad topics, electronic publishing information

Apple Computer: http://www.Apple.com – Apple computer information

Microsoft: http://www.microsoft.com – Microsoft information

Adobe Plug-in Source Catalog: http://www.imageclub.com/aps/ – Plug-in resources for

Adobe products

Extensis Phototools: http://www.extensis.com– Extension technologies for many products

Macromedia: http://www.macromedia.com: – Freehand and super Web-based product information and Help

Netscape Color: http://www.connect.hawaii.com/hc/webmasters/ – Web color information and resources

Pantone: http://www.pantone.com/whatsnew.html – Pantone-specific and general color information

Shareware: http://shareware.com – Wild and wooly world of shareware; bring your virus protection

Design Tools Creaticity: http://www.creaticity.com – Wonderful update and problem-solving information for a wide variety of DTP issues

Amazon Books: http://www.amazon.com/exec/obidos/subst/home/home.html/002-0754583-8019430 _ Online book reviews and ordering

Adobe Publications: http://www.adobe.com/publications/adobemag – Access to old versions of Adobe Magazine and other Adobe educational information

Apple Education Site: http://www.education.apple.com – Access Apple's extensive education library

Apple Information/Support: http://info.apple.com – Apple troubleshooting infomation

Digital Media: http://www.digitalmedia.net – Excellent multimedia training

TazTally Seminars: http://www.tazseminars.com – Seminar training topics and schedules

Quark Updates: http://www.quark.com/files/update_select.html – Get Quark updates

For PDF files and Acrobat technology in general, consult these sites:

• *PDF for Prepress:* www.prepress.ch/pdf_wp.pdf

• *PDF Bug List on Seybold Web site:* www.seyboldseminars.com, Includes a list of bugs and fixes and has an up-to-date list of PDF extensions

• *PDF-devoted sites:* www.pdfzone.com

• *Adobe PDF:* www.Adobe.com

• *UMAX Scanners:* www.UMAX.com

SPECIAL CALIBRATION TARGET OFFER

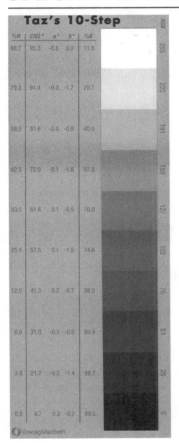

Improve the quality of your scanned images by calibrating your scanner. As discussed in Chapters 6 and 7, calibration of your scanner is one of the key variables to improving the quality and consistency of your scanned grayscale and color images.

Get your copy of Taz's calibration target specifically designed by Taz for use with desktop scanners.

Order your target today at a special book purchaser's discount price.

Calibration Target

Taz has created a special 10-step calibration target, made specifically for desktop scanners. It includes easy-to-read RGB and percent grayscale target values right on the target...No data sheets to lose!

Target list price $25.00

Your price $19.95!

This target is the one used with the step-by-step procedure provided in Chapters 6 and 7 of this book.

Calibration Kit

This custom developed by Taz kit includes one of Taz's 10-step calibration targets as well as a complete step-by-step calibration procedure. Taz includes descriptions for using your calibration target with both your scanner and with Photoshop.

Calibration Kit list price $35.00

Your price $29.95!

Phone Orders: 941-433-0622
Fax Orders: 941-267-8389
Web Orders: www.tazseminars.com
Mail Orders: Taz Tally Seminars
3616 Heritage Lane
Ft. Myers, FL 33908
__Calibration Target $19.95 ea._____
__Advanced Kit $29.95 ea.   _____
  Shipping & Handling $3.00
            Total _____

Ship To: Name_____
Company_____
Address_____
City_____State____Zip_____
Phone_____Fax_____
Email_____
Payment Method: ❑ Check ❑ Money Order
Credit Card: ❑ MC ❑ Visa
Card #_____
Expiration date_____

Titles

Order Form

BOOKS–	Qty	Price
Avoiding the Output Blues (updated version) by Dr. Taz Tally	___	$39.95
Avoiding the Output Blues (original version) by Dr. Taz Tally	___	$25.00

VIDEOS -

Preparing Files for Print I	___	$39.95
Preparing Files for Print II	___	$39.95
Print Set for	___	$74.95
Photoshop Techniques I	___	$39.95
Photoshop Techniques II	___	$39.95
Photoshop Set for	___	$74.95
Taming Your Scanner I	___	$39.95
Taming Your Scanner II	___	$39.95
Scanning Set for	___	$74.95
Keyboard Shortcuts	___	$39.95

Calibration Tools -

Taz's Calibration Target	___	$25.00
Taz's Calibration Kit	___	$35.00

INTERACTIVE CDs -

Scanning & Photoshop (M/W)	___	$79.95
Pagemaker (M/W)	___	$79.95
Quark (M)	___	$79.95
Illustrator (M/W)	___	$79.95
Acrobat (Mac)	___	$79.95
FlightCheck (M/W)	___	$79.95
Font Management. (M)	___	$79.95

Indicate Mac (M) or Windows (W) _____
Call for other available titles

*Shipping & Handling	$ _____
TOTAL	$ _____

*Shipping & Handling charges are $5.00 for the first item and $3.00 for each additional item. (A video set counts as one item.)

Phone Orders:
Please call:
941-433-0622

Fax Orders:
Fax completed forms to:
941-267-8389

Web Orders:
Reach us at
www.tazseminars.com

Mail Orders:
Mail to:
Taz Tally Seminars
3616 Heritage Lane
Ft. Myers, FL 33908
Ship to:

Name_____

Organization_____

Address_____

City_____ State____ Zip____

Phone_____

Fax_____

Email_____

Payment Method

❏ Check   ❏ Money Order

❏ Credit Card: ❏ MC ❏ Visa

Card #_____

Expiration

Date_____

Name on Card_____

Signature _____

The Taz!

Catch Taz in action at one of his informative seminars, offered in many cities across the U.S. and Canada. Taz is famous for his entertaining and interactive style and his ability to take complex topics and explain them in a clear and easy to understand manner. Plus, he is really funny!

Come see Taz, and you are guaranteed to have a great time and learn a lot.

The Topics

Taz offers a wide variety of seminar topics including: scanning, Photoshop, prepress, font management, Web graphics, and more! Check out his current offerings and locations on his web site **www.tazseminar.com.**

Host a Taz Tally Seminar!

Taz works with local businesses, such as printing companies, service bureaus and other graphic arts-oriented businesses and organizations, to produce his seminars. Taz's seminars are great educational experiences and serve as terrific marketing and networking opportunities. If you want your company or organization to be viewed as a technology leader, work with Taz to produce one of your own local Taz Tally Seminars. Taz Tally Seminars are fun, informative, and great positioning tools for your organization. To speak with Taz or his partner Jaz to discuss hosting a Taz Tally Seminar, contact him at **941-433-0622** or toss Taz an Email at **TTallyphd@aol.com**

What folks say about TTS!

"The best seminar I have ever attended."

"Taz is awesome!"

"I learned more in two days with Taz than I have learned in two years of college classes."

"Hosting a TTS was a great benefit for us. We generated tons of leads, made lots of contacts, elevated the visibility of our company, learned a lot and had a blast to boot!"

.TAZ TALLY TRAINING & CONSULTING

Taz is available for custom training and consulting

A sample of Taz's training and consulting topics:

- Scanning
- Photoshop
- Color correction
- DTP fundamentals
- Preflighting
- Work flow
- Font management
- QuarkXPress
- InDesign
- Streamline
- DTP training for sales and customer service staff
- DTP system management
- DTP project management

Taz Tally, Ph.D.
Taz Tally Seminars
3616 Heritage Ln.
Ft. Myers, FL 33908
Phone: 941-433-0622
Fax: 941-267-8389
e-mail: Ttallyphd@aol.com
www.tazseminars.com

OTHER PRENTICE HALL BOOKS BY TAZ

Current:

Avoiding Series
- *Avoiding the Output Blues*
- *Avoiding the Scanning Blues*

Soon to be released:

Avoiding Series
- *Avoiding the Color Management Blues*
- *Avoiding the Font Blues*

Visual Desktop Companion Series
- *InDesign Visual Desktop Companion*
- *Flash Visual Desktop Companion*
- *Acrobat/PDF Visual Desktop Companion*

Look for more books by Taz Tally and Tim Moore in the *Avoiding* and the *Visual Desktop Companion Series*

COMPANION WEB SITE RESOURCE LIST:

Visit our companion Web site to see:

- Images used in this book:
    - Low-Key Image
    - Grayscale of Still life
    - Apple Letters Image
    - Completed Projects
- Demo scanning software
- Demo of Streamline
- Access to other educational materials
- Ordering capabilities
- Links to other scanning and electronic publishing resources
- Link skills testing site
- Subscription service
- Images from Alaska
- Calibration chart information
- Additional calibration information

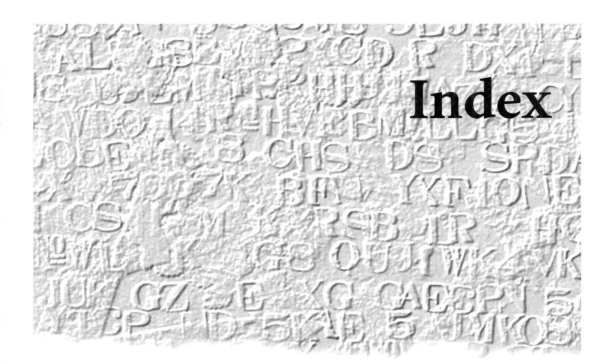

Index

Index list

Taz Tally

Dr. Taz Tally is the founder of Taz Tally Seminars, an electronic publishing, consulting and training company. Taz is the author of *Avoiding the Output Blues* a text book on electronic publishing fundamentals and PostScript file preparation, as well as *Avoiding the Scanning Blues* a comprehensive guide to desktop scanning, which was chosen as a featured selection of the DoubleDay book club. In addition Taz has created instructional CDs on Font management and Microsoft Publisher, and the UMAX MagicScan Manual, which is distributed worldwide. He has also produced several videos on scanning, prepress, Photoshop, and keyboard shortcuts, and was the co-developer and instructor for the video training series *DeskTop to Print*. Taz is a frequent presenter at seminars and trade shows throughout the U.S. and is best known for his entertaining,

content-rich seminars and his ability to present complex materials in a simple, easy-to-understand fashion. Taz invented a 10-step scanner calibration card and is the creator of and series editor for the Visual Desktop Companion series. Taz is currently working on books on Photoshop, InDesign, Acrobat, Flash, Color Management.

When Taz is not touring the country by plane or motor home presenting his seminars, he splits time between houses in Homer, Alaska and Ft. Myers, FL with his fabulous partner, Jaz. In their "spare time" Taz and Jaz generally head off to the outdoors. They can be found hiking or mountain biking in Alaska, skiing the powder snow in Utah, or diving with the whales in the waters off Hawaii.

Jaz & Taz

Taz is available for custom training and consulting.
Contact Taz & Jaz at Taz Tally Seminars
3616 Heritage Lane, Ft. Myers, FL 33908
941-433-0622 - Office, 941-267-8389 - Fax
ttallyphd@aol.com, jazkatz@aol.com
www.tazseminars.com

Color Plates

▼ Color Figures 7.4-C, 7.5-C, and 7.6-C,

Seen here are the color versions of Figures 7.4, 7.5, and 7.6 found on pages 130 and 131 in the manual. The "C" designation refers to the color version.

▼ Figure 7.4-C Original Color Photo
Numbered areas are referenced in the text.

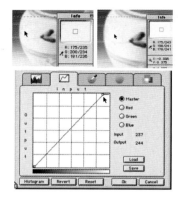

▼ Figure 7.6-C Highlight Adjustment

Here we are raising the highlight value using the curve on the Master Channel. This will raise all three (RGB) values simultaneously. Adjust the position of the highlight end of the curve until all the right side RGB values of the Info tool ~242 (right).

Before Correction   **After Correction**

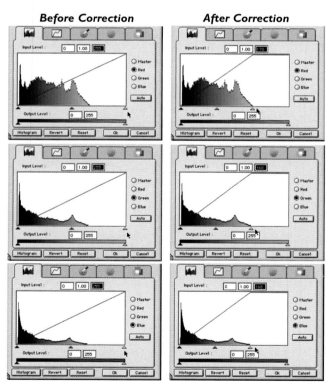

▼ Figure 7.5-C Setting Tone Compression
Setting highlight and shadow points should be performed on individual channels, as shown above, rather than on the Master Channel. As a starting point, set the highlight and shadow points visually by placing the highlight and shadow pointers at the beginning and the end of the image data in the histogram. These highlight and shadow points can be fine-tuned using the Info palette either here in the histogram or later with the Curves tool.

Color Figures 7.7-C, and 7.8-C

Seen here are the color versions of Figures 7.7 and 7.8 found on pages 131 and 132 in the manual. The "C" designation refers to the color version.

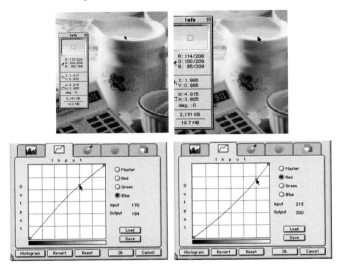

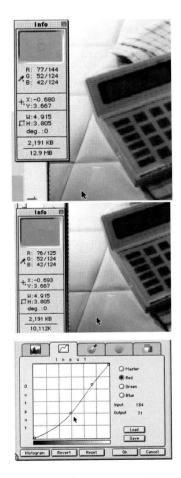

▼ Figure 7.7-C Neutralization of Quartertone

Here we are raising the highlight value using the curve on the Master Channel. This will raise all three (RGB) values simultaneously. Adjust the position of the highlight end of the curve until the right side RGB values of the Info tool ~242.

▼ Figure 7.8-C Neutralization of Midtone

Here we are measuring and adjusting a neutral area in the midtone region of the image. In the top, uncorrected image, the histogram shows a high red value of 144 compared with the 124 for the green and blue values. To correct this excess of red, we activate the red curve and lower the curve in the midtone until the red value ~124. The second, corrected image shows all three R,G, and B values = 124.

Color Figure ▼ Figure 7.9 and 7.11-C

Seen here are the color versions of Figures 7.9 and 7.11 found on pages 133 and 134 in the manual. The "C" designation refers to the color version.

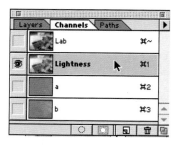

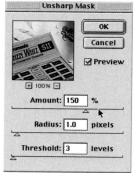

▼ Figure 7.11-C Lab Application of Unsharp Mask

By converting your image to Lab mode and applying unsharp mask (USM) to the "L" channel only, you avoid the risk of having color shifts occur along high-contrast edges in your color images. The Threshold for the unsharp mask is set here at 3. This is lower than the 4–6 we would have for a portrait image because there are fewer areas that need protection. Note the greater control in this Photoshop Unsharp mask dialog box compared with the scanner Unsharp mask dialog box. I often apply USM in Photoshop rather than my desktop scanning program for three reasons: 1) Photoshop's USM controls are often superior, 2) I can confine my USM to just the "L" channel, and 3) If I am performing image edits, I like to perform my USM mask after image editing is complete.

Figure 7.9-C Raw and Final Images

The top image was the image created with a raw scan, without corrections. The bottom image is the result of the tone compression, color correction, and unsharp mask performed Chapter 7. Note how the top image has a distinct red color cast, and is darker, lower contrast, and appears to be out of focus when compared with the lower, adjusted image. Compare your final image with the results seen here.

Note: If the top image does not appear to visually have a color cast when viewed on your monitor, then your monitor may be out of calibration. In either case, the numbers measured with and shown in the Info tool will show higher red values. Remember that an accurate printed version of your RGB scan will depend upon a correct RGB-to-CMYK conversion.

Unsharp mask note: The final image was sharpened by applying unsharp mask to the "L" channel after the image mode was converted to Lab.

Practice Images

PRINTED PRACTICE IMAGES

Use the three line art images below on this page as your practice line art images. Use the printed/halftoned version of the photograph below in the descreening exercise in Chapter 9. These are the same images used in the step-by-step sections of the manual. Use the grayscale and color photographs found in the image pocket attached to the inside of the back cover of this book as your practice images for scanning grayscale and color images. Use the order form Appendix E "Resources" section of this book to obtain the grayscale target for calibrating your scanner.

**Simple, Low-Detail
Line Art Image**

**Intermediate-Detail
Line Art Image**

Color Line Art Image

High-Detail Line Art Image

PRINTED PRACTICE IMAGES CONTINUED

*Low Edge Quality
Line Art Image*

*Printed/Halftoned
(AM Screened)
Grayscale Image*

*Printed (AM Screened)
Color Image*